BOOK-K

TEACH YOURSELF BOOKS

BOOK-KEEPING

A. G. Piper

Department of Accounting and Finance
University of Birmingham

TEACH YOURSELF BOOKS

Hodder and Stoughton

This book is based on the earlier work of Professor Donald Cousins, which in successive editions has benefited from substantial contributions by E. C. Turner and A. G. Piper. Now extensively revised and expanded by A. G. Piper, and completely reset, it constitutes a new book.

First published 1984
Fourth impression 1987

British Library Cataloguing in Publication Data

Piper, A. G.
Book-keeping—(Teach yourself books)
1. Bookkeeping
I. Title
657′.2 HF5635

ISBN 0 340 35579 4

Printed and bound in Great Britain for
Hodder and Stoughton Educational,
a division of Hodder and Stoughton Ltd,
Mill Road, Dunton Green, Sevenoaks, Kent,
by Richard Clay Ltd, Bungay, Suffolk
Photoset by Rowland Phototypesetting Ltd,
Bury St Edmunds, Suffolk.

Contents

Introduction

This book is based on the earlier work of Professor Donald Cousins as revised in successive editions, which included substantial contributions by E. C. Turner. The present revision is so extensive as to constitute a new book, but the style which has proved so successful in the past has been retained where appropriate, and the guidance provided by those authors is gratefully acknowledged.

The aim of the book is to provide a concise introductory text which is both readable and interesting, and clearly relevant to the routine recording of business transactions while covering the main syllabus requirements of elementary examinations in book-keeping – particularly those of the Royal Society of Arts and the London Chamber of Commerce and Industry.

Readers should remember that there is a difference between book-keeping and accountancy. Book-keeping is concerned with the initial recording of financial transactions – whether by quill pen or the keyboard of a visual display unit – and its subsequent processing to produce financial statements. These records provide an important part, but not all, of the material which is used and interpreted by the accountant and the manager.

Book-keeping is neither dull nor mysterious: indeed, its 'rules' are logical and straightforward, and readily mastered by practice. Thus the text includes many worked examples and carefully graded questions, while at the end of the book there are three complete examination papers with fully worked solutions.

A. G. Piper

1

What is Book-keeping?

Question What is book-keeping?

Answer The process of correctly recording in Books of Account transactions in money, or money's worth.

Question What are Books of Account?

Answer The **Ledger** is the only Book of Account, so called because all the transactions, after being first recorded in subsidiary books, are afterwards grouped or summarised in **Accounts** in the Ledger.

Question What is the difference between 'money' and 'money's worth' transactions?

Answer If £120 is paid in cash as wages to a workman, this is a transaction in *money*; if I buy goods on credit from Smith value £100, it is a transaction in *money's worth*.

Question Why should goods be bought on 'credit'?

Answer Almost all business dealings are conducted on a credit basis, that is, the supplier of goods, like Smith, is content to accept payment at some future date; the only exception is in the case of 'ready money' transactions in the retail trade, like those of a private individual, who buys goods over the counter.

Question How does the necessity for recording these transactions arise?

Answer Even in the smallest business the proprietor or manager will want to have accurate and up-to-date information about how much he has bought and sold, how much money he has received and paid away in respect of his purchases and sales, and so on. In respect of their cash receipts and payments, even private individuals often find it convenient to have the same information.

You can imagine that with a very large business, chaos would quickly result without this information.

Question So book-keeping really involves analysing in some way or another these various transactions?

Answer You should rather say, recording these transactions so as to permit analysis in a systematic fashion, and in some way that can be applied to all businesses of whatever kind, and that is intelligible not only now but at any future time.

Question Do you mean by this 'the Double Entry System of Book-keeping'?

Answer Yes.

Question What is its real meaning?

Answer That just as every transaction involves at least two parties, so the record of the transaction should be made in the light of its twofold aspect.

Question So it does not mean recording the same transaction twice?

Answer No, not at all. Let me put it in this way. If I have bought goods value £100 from Smith on credit, the first part of the twofold aspect is that my business has received goods for the disposal of which my storekeeper, or some other person, is accountable; the second part of the twofold aspect is that Smith, my supplier, has become my creditor, and has a claim on me for £100.

Question Would it be the same if you had bought the goods and paid for them at once, instead of getting credit?

Answer Yes, that would be a cash purchase. But instead of Smith, my banker or cashier would be my creditor, having paid money away for me. They then would have the claim on me for £100.

Question I do not quite see how your cashier or your banker could be your creditor. The cashier would be a servant, dependent on a weekly or monthly salary.

Answer What you say about the position of the cashier is true, but in the first place, when you began business, you would entrust a sufficient sum of money to these people for which you would at the outset consider them as accountable or indebted to you. They would be your debtors. So if later they paid money away for you, such payments reduce their indebtedness which after all is just the same thing as saying they are your creditors to that extent, the position of the creditor being the reverse of that of debtor.

Question What is the real advantage of the Double Entry System?

Answer For the reason that every transaction can be looked at from its twofold aspect, the record made is complete instead of being partial only.

The practical advantage is that you put the whole of the facts on record. These are:

(*a*) Your storekeeper is answerable for £100 worth of goods.
(*b*) Somebody, Smith or your banker, has a claim on you for £100.

Obviously, to know these facts is of first importance in any business.

Question Well, does this hold good with other than just buying transactions? Would the same state of affairs exist with the selling of goods?

Answer In exactly the same way. The first aspect in the selling transaction is that your storekeeper has issued £100 worth of goods as an ordinary sale. The second is that the person who has received them has become your debtor, i.e. he is indebted to you, on the assumption that you, in this case, are giving him credit, because *you* are the supplier.

Question Does the Double Entry System stop at this?

Answer No. It goes much further. Because of this twofold aspect I have been talking about, it enables you to compare the proceeds of the sales you have made with the cost to you of the goods you have bought, and so obtain your profit or loss on trading.

Similarly, as it shows the claims other people have on you (your creditors), and the claims you have on other people (your debtors) you can tell very quickly what is the position of affairs of your business at any particular date so far as these people are concerned.

Question Is the latter point important?

Answer Yes. If the creditors of the business exceed in amount its debtors, any stock in its warehouse which it hopes to sell, and the ready money it has available, it may be insolvent, that is to say, it cannot pay its debts as they become due.

Question When we began talking, you said the Ledger was the only Book of Account, and that all transactions were first recorded in what you called 'subsidiary books'.

What are these Subsidiary Books, and why are they kept in addition to the Ledger?

Answer The Subsidiary Books are termed *Journals* or *Day Books* because, very much like a journal or diary, they are entered up daily.

They are designed to relieve the various accounts in the Ledger of a great amount of detail which, while indispensable to the business, can better be given in a subsidiary book than in the Ledger itself.

If you take, for example, the purchasing side of a business, a very great amount of detail may have to be recorded as to the supplier, the quantity, quality and price per unit of the goods, total amount payable and so on.

But, so far as the Double Entry or twofold aspect of all the buying transactions is concerned, they are all in the first place purchases or goods for which the storekeeper is responsible. In the second place, credit must be given to all the various suppliers from whom the purchases have been made. Thus there will be one account in the Ledger for incoming goods, or purchases, and other accounts, also in the Ledger, for the individual suppliers.

Question So the Journals or Day Books do not form part of the Double Entry System at all?

Answer That is so. These Subsidiary Books are outside the Double Entry System altogether. Their function is to provide, in the first instance, the material from which the Ledger Accounts are entered up subsequently.

That is why they are so often referred to as books of **prime** or **first entry**. With very few exceptions indeed, it is a well-recognised rule in book-keeping that no transaction shall be recorded in a Ledger Account that has not first been made the subject of record in a subsidiary book, or Book of First Entry.

2

The Business Transaction, Purchases and Sales

The business transaction

We are familiar in our daily life with buying articles we want and paying cash for them. But unless we are in business the idea of selling goods is not so familiar, nor is the process of receiving payment for what we have sold. And yet every business is concerned with buying and selling goods or services, usually on a credit basis, so that at some later date it pays for what it has bought and is in turn paid for what it has sold.

These are clearly recurrent transactions in particular goods which the business merchants or manufactures.

Merchanted goods are those which it resells in the same condition as when purchased. *Manufactured goods* are the finished article which, with the assistance of employees, are worked up from the raw material.

Thus from the purely trading standpoint a kind of trade cycle can be recognised. Goods are bought first of all in sufficient quantity to meet customers' requirements, either as the finished article or as raw material. They are what is called the **Stock** or Stock in Trade of the business.

When the goods are sold in the finished state to customers at selling price, and on credit terms, these customers become the **debtors** of the business; that is, they are indebted to it, and when they in turn make payment the **Cash in Hand** or **Cash at Bank** of the business is replenished.

From these increased cash resources, moneys once again become available for the business to buy more goods, and so the cycle repeats itself.

We should remember that not only is this the case, but that at any given time a business will necessarily possess:

(*a*) Stock in Trade;
(*b*) claims on customers, which may shortly be described as Debtors, or Book Debts;
(*c*) Cash in Hand and/or Cash at Bank.

These forms of property, property of very different kinds, represent the trading resources of the business, and in total form part of its **Capital**.

It is very important to understand correctly the meaning of Capital in the book-keeping sense.

Supposing we bought goods from Jones, value £100, for payment a month after they had been delivered, Jones would be our creditor, and during that month we might sell the goods at a profit and so obtain the cash to pay him when the time came.

That would be an ideal case, because then the business apparently need have no cash resources *of its own*; it could rely on Jones, and other suppliers, to finance its operations. The capital invested in the business, represented by the stock of goods value £100 supplied by Jones, would be in effect *Jones's* Capital, and not the proprietor's Capital at all.

In practice we find, however, that such an ideal state of affairs can seldom, if ever, arise.

First of all, we may not be able to sell all the goods we purchased from Jones in the credit period of one month.

Secondly, we shall in all probability be obliged to extend credit to our customers, just as Jones did to us.

Thirdly, we shall be obliged to possess certain (cash) resources to pay our staff and workpeople week by week, and

Fourthly, if ours is a new business, Jones or any other supplier may be unwilling to supply us with goods on credit until they have experience of what may be called our 'credit-worthiness'.

There is also to be remembered that an important part of every business's resources is a factory, or warehouse, or office, or the right to occupy these, for which a rent is paid. Such property does not, and cannot form part of the trading resources, because it would clearly never occur to us to sell our business premises in which all the work was carried on.

Enough has been said for us to realise that a certain minimum amount of property, or of Capital, must be possessed by the business from the time it was commenced, and we can realise also how varied are the forms which this Capital may take.

Our task will always be rendered easier if we think of Capital as the resources or the property of a business. Indeed, the term *Capital* has no meaning to the business man unless it is represented by property of some kind or another, property to which he refers as the business **Assets**.

While we are going to examine Capital more fully at a later stage, let us now remember that there are such forms of property as **Fixed Assets**, such as the factory or warehouse mentioned above, and other forms which we call **Current Assets**, which correspond to our trading assets, such as stock in trade, claims on customers and money in the bank.

The distinction between these two kinds of property is of the utmost importance, because our Fixed Assets have been bought to be retained, while our Current Assets, as we have seen, are an essential result of the business's everyday transactions. Indeed, they enter into and form part of these transactions.

There are just two more points, and the first is for us to grasp the businessman's definition of Capital as representing not merely the Assets, but

The Excess of the Assets over the Liabilities of a Business

An example will help to make this clear:

Example 2.1

Brown begins business on 1 January 19x1, with £10000 in cash. He leases for five years factory premises at a cost of £6000, and obtains goods on credit from Smith costing £2000.

The total assets of his business are:

Factory lease	£6000	
Stock of goods, cost	2000	
Cash in bank	4000	
		£12000

but this is not the amount of Brown's Capital invested in the business because £2000 of these assets have been supplied on credit by Smith, for which the business is liable to him. What is owing to Smith is, therefore, a liability of the business and because we define Capital above as corresponding to 'the excess of the Assets over the Liabilities of a business', Brown's Capital = Total Assets £12000, *less* Liabilities £2000 = £10000, or put in another way, Brown's Capital of £10000 is represented by

Fixed assets		£6000
Current assets	£6000	
Less Liabilities	2000	
		4000
		£10000

We are justified in deducting the liability to Smith from the total of the *Current* Assets, since it is out of them that we intend to pay him.

The other point which we ought now to be in a position to appreciate is that

Capital is a Liability of the Business to its proprietor

At first sight this appears to be rather different from what we should expect.

We have seen that from its commencement the business must be provided with a certain minimum amount of property, or Capital, and for the sake of convenience we defined Capital in the first place as the equivalent of property, or Assets, and more fully in the second place as representing 'the excess of the Assets over the Liabilities of a business'.

Let us now see if we can reconcile what appears to be a contradiction in terms.

If the proprietor, instead of investing a part of his Capital in setting up the business, had lent £10000 to a friend in consideration of the payment of interest at 12% per annum, the loan would clearly be an investment yielding an annual income of £1200, and the amount of the loan, looked at from the standpoint of the borrower, would as clearly be a liability.

The borrower's financial position could be stated thus:

Liability £10000, represented by **Cash** £10000.

In exactly the same way, when the proprietor invests Capital in a business, he is just as truly entitled to regard it as an investment, answerable to him for interest, or in this case **Profit**, period by period.

From the standpoint of the business, looked at as distinct from its proprietorship, there is a **Liability** to account for the amount of the proprietor's Capital put at its disposal for the purpose of profit earning.

At any time, therefore, the business should be able to prepare a statement of its position, and of how it has dealt with such Capital, that is to say, by what kinds of property that Capital is represented.

The financial position of the business would similarly be:

Liability to proprietor £10000, represented by, in the first instance, **Cash** £10000.

The only difference between the examples is that, in the first case, the borrower would sooner or later have to repay the loan, while in the second the repayment of the proprietor's Capital would involve shutting down the business.

For this reason, in the latter case, the Capital invested is usually regarded as a *permanent* or *fixed liability*, or indeed, as it is in law, a postponed or deferred liability.

The Purchase and Sales Journals in the book-keeping system

Most of us are familiar with the practice of making a daily note of matters in which we are interested. For this purpose we use our diary, as a kind of daily record, entering in it brief but sufficient details of what has taken place.

Such entries may be made by the private individual, and they form very often a useful reference for the future.

In the early stages of business development it is not difficult for us to imagine the proprietor of the business making a similar record of his transactions with people who had become his suppliers and customers, narrating what he had bought, and from whom; what he had sold, and to whom. Just as a diary is a daily record, so also is a **Journal**. It is written up as soon as possible after the transaction has taken place. It is essentially a *primary* record, and hence we derive the meaning of the term 'Journal' in book-keeping as a book of **first entry**. No matter what subsequent use we make of the particulars recorded in it, the desirability of a primary record is obvious.

To the extent that the transactions of the business are recurrent, even in the smallest undertaking we should expect to see a record of:

(*a*) purchases:
(*b*) sales;
(*c*) payments to suppliers;
(*d*) receipts from customers.

As soon as the transactions entered into became more numerous, some kind of analysis of the Journal would be imperative if the proprietor at any time wished to know:

(*a*) how much he had purchased;
(*b*) how much he had sold;
(*c*) what was the total of his cash payments, and of
(*d*) his cash receipts.

With numerous daily transactions, putting on record the fact that £100 worth of goods had been purchased on credit from Jones, and £100 worth of goods had been sold on credit to Smith, the Journal entries might take the following form:

(*a*) Warehouseman chargeable with incoming goods **at cost** £100. Jones to be credited with £100.
(*b*) Smith chargeable with goods £100. Warehouseman to be credited with issue of goods at selling price £100.

If, however, we took matters a step further, and used the symbols **Dr.** (debtor) instead of 'chargeable with' and **Cr.** (creditor) instead of 'to be credited', the entries could easily be stated in the following way:

(*a*)	Warehouseman	Dr. £100.00
	Jones	Cr. 100.00
and		
(*b*)	Smith	Dr. £100.00
	Warehouseman	Cr. 100.00

This would be a much simpler and more concise way of putting the transaction on record, but the repetition of the recurrent entries over a period of time would make detailed analysis always essential to arrive at, for example:

(*a*) our total purchases, and
(*b*) our total sales for that period,

quite apart from the need for similar analysis as regards cash paid and cash received.

For that reason, the first form of Journal was modified to accord with these requirements of the proprietor, and in one section of it were recorded **purchases**, in another **sales** and in yet another **cash**, either in total, or as in many cases today:

(*a*) **Cash received**, and
(*b*) **Cash paid**.

To the first of these subsections of the Journal was given the title:
Purchase Journal,
to the second: **Sales Journal**,
and to the third: **Cash Book** or **Cash Journal**,

with the result that in them we now find:

(*a*) our total purchases;
(*b*) our total sales; and
(*c*) our purely cash transactions, in as great a detail as we desire, or the requirements of the business demand.

If it be said that certain transactions take place which do not permit of entry in the above three subdivisions of the Journal, the answer is that the early form of Journal is still retained for such (comparatively infrequent) transactions, and is dealt with in Chapter 7.

Supposing we begin with the **Purchase Journal**, or **Day Book**:

Example 2.2

Enter the following purchases in the Purchase Day Book of H. Yates, a cycle dealer, total the Day Book, but do not post the entries to the Ledger.

19x1
Feb. 2 Received invoice from the Speedy Cycle Co. Ltd, for:
2 Gent's Roadsters, model A625 at £125, less 20% trade discount.
2 Ladies' Roadsters, model A725 at £110, less 20% trade discount.
2 crates at £5.00 each.
15 The Drake Cycle Co. Ltd, invoiced:
3 Gent's Special Club models B21 at £140, less 15% trade discount.
3 Ladies' Special Club models B20 at £120, less 15% trade discount.
2 crates at £6.00 each.
27 Received invoice from the Victoria Manufacturing Co. Ltd:
2 Racing models A16 at £170, less 15% trade discount.
1 crate at £5.00.

In these three purchase transactions, we notice:

(*a*) That the goods purchased are exclusively for resale, i.e. they are goods in which Mr Yates is dealing.

(*b*) That a deduction is made on account of **trade discount**.

This is a usual allowance made by a supplier to a retailer with whom he has regular dealings, and may represent:

1 A margin of profit for the retailer, who sells the goods at the advertised list price.
2 An inducement to the retailer to continue to trade with the supplier.

Prior to entry in the last four columns of the Day Book, it is seen that the trade discount has been deducted in the 'details' column, and we must always be careful to follow this procedure.

All that concerns Mr Yates is the **net cost** to him of the cycles he has bought.

(*c*) That the suppliers have in each case included in their invoice price the cost of crates. These clearly do not refer to the cost of the goods dealt in, and are therefore entered in a separate column. Moreover, it is usual for the suppliers to issue **credit notes** as and when the crates are later returned to them in good condition. There may in consequence be a recovery of all or the greater part of the total purchase cost under this heading.

H. YATES

Purchase Day Book

February 19x1

Date	Supplier	Description	Details	Goods Total	Gent's Models	Ladies' Models	Crates and Packing
19x1			£	£	£	£	£
Feb. 2	Speedy Cycle Co. Ltd	2 Gent's Roadsters, Model A625, at £125.00	250.00				
		2 Ladies' Roadsters, Model A725, at £110.00	220.00				
			470.00				
		Less 20% Trade discount	94.00				
			376.00				
		2 Crates at £5.00	10.00				
				386.00	200.00	176.00	10.00
15	Drake Cycle Co. Ltd	3 Gent's Special Club models, B21, at £140.00	420.00				
		3 Ladies' Special Club models, B20, at £120.00	360.00				
			780.00				
		Less 15% Trade discount	117.00				
			663.00				
		2 Crates at £6.00	12.00				
				675.00	357.00	306.00	12.00
27	Victoria Manufacturing Co. Ltd	2 Racing models, A16, at £170.00	340.00				
		Less 15% Trade discount	51.00				
			289.00				
		1 Crate at £5.00	5.00				
				294.00	289.00	—	5.00
				£1 355.00	£846.00	£482.00	£27.00

The solution to the example, as shown, enables Mr Yates to see at a glance:

(*a*) from whom he has purchased;
(*b*) what has been purchased;
(*c*) the total cost of the purchases, suitably analysed, including
(*d*) the cost of crates, packing, etc.

What about VAT? More about VAT is provided at the end of Chapter 3 and at this stage it is only necessary to say that an extra column would be required in the Purchase and Sales Day Books. This is illustrated in the next example, where VAT at the rate of 15% is assumed in respect of all sales and purchases.

Example 2.3

From the following particulars compile the Purchase Day Book, Sales Day Book and Returns Books of D. Morris.

Full details must be shown in the Day Books. No posting to the Ledger is required.

Mar. 10 Sold to W. Humphrey, Lincoln, 200 metres floral cotton cloth at £2 per metre; 100 metres of best blue cotton cloth at £2.40 per metre. Whole invoice less 10% trade discount.

12 Received invoice from R. Ridgwell, Bolton, for 50 sheets at £3.50 each; 40 tee-shirts £2.80 each.

15 Sent a debit note to W. Hunt for £12, being an overcharge on cotton supplied on February 5.

18 Sent an invoice to S. Boham, Coventry, for 100 metres of linen at £5.00 per metre, less 5% trade discount; 300 metres of floral cotton at £2 per metre; trimmings £15.

20 Bought goods from B. Davis, Ely, 500 metres of floral cotton at £1.00 per metre; 400 tee-shirts at £2 each; sundry remnants £15.

22 W. Humphrey, Lincoln, returned 50 metres of the floral cotton supplied on March 10, as being of inferior quality.

23 Received a debit note from A. Jenkinson, Wolverhampton for 20 metres of linen returned at £7 per metre less 20% trade discount.

24 Sent an invoice to T. Butterworth, Norwich, for 300 metres of linen at £7.00 per metre less 5% trade discount; 150 metres of best blue cotton at £2.40 per metre less 10% trade discount; assorted buttons £10.

27 Received a credit note from V. Luxton, for 30 metres of white cotton returned at £1.00 per metre.

29 Bought from General Supplies Ltd, London, showcases and fittings £1000 net.

Note: Great care must be exercised in setting out the Day Books. It may be a useful exercise for students to prepare their own day books, and then compare them with the entries which follow rather than merely reading the entries.

Before beginning to record these transactions in the Purchase and Sales Journals, it is essential for us to realise that they are being stated from the point of view of the business of which D. Morris is the proprietor.

Indeed, we may first proceed to classify each of them as being:

(*a*) A purchase transaction.
(*b*) A sales transaction.
(*c*) The return of goods to a **supplier**, or the obtaining of an allowance *from* him.
(*d*) The return of goods by a **customer**, or the granting of an allowance *to* him.

In the two latter cases the result will be, as we shall expect, that the amount of the original purchases and sales will be reduced accordingly, but *instead of altering* the entries in the Purchase and Sales Journals, we shall make use of **Purchase Returns Journals** and **Sales Returns Journals** (see page 18).

D. MORRIS — Fo. 1

Purchase Day Book

March 19x1

Date	*Supplier*	*Description*	*Invoice No.*	*Details*	*Total*	*VAT*	*Cotton*	*Linen*	*Sheets*	*Tee-shirts*	*Sundries*	*Special Items*
19x1				£	£	£	£	£	£	£	£	£
Mar. 12	R. Ridgwell, Bolton	50 sheets at £3.50 each		175.00					175.00			
		40 tee-shirts at £2.80 each		112.00						112.00		
				287.00								
		VAT 15%		43.05		43.05						
			1		330.05							
20	B. Davis, Ely	500 metres floral cotton at £1.00 per metre		500.00			500.00					
		400 tee-shirts at £2.00 each		800.00						800.00		
		Remnants		15.00							15.00	
				1315.00								
		VAT 15%		197.25		197.25						
			2		1512.25							
29	General Supplies Ltd, London	Showcases and fittings		1000.00								1000.00
		VAT 15%		150.00		150.00						
			3		1150.00							
					£2992.30	£390.30	£500.00		£175.00	£912.00	£15.00	£1000.00

D. MORRIS

Sales Day Book

Fo. 2

March 19x1

Date	Customer	Description	Invoice No.	Details	Total	VAT	Cotton	Linen	Sheets	Tee-shirts	Sundries
19x1				£	£	£	£	£	£	£	£
Mar. 10	W. Humphrey, Lincoln	200m Floral cotton @ £2 per m		400.00							
		100m best Blue Cotton @ £2.40 per m		240.00							
				640.00							
		Less 10% Trade discount		64.00							
				576.00			576.00				
		Add VAT 15%		86.40		86.40					
			4		662.40						
18	S. Boham, Coventry	100m Linen @ £5 per m		500.00							
		Less 5% Trade discount		25.00							
				475.00				475.00			
		300m Floral cotton @ £2 per m		600.00			600.00				
		Trimmings		15.00							15.00
				1090.00							
		Add VAT 15%		163.50		163.50					
			5		1253.50						
23	T. Butterworth, Norwich	300m Linen @ £7 per m		2100.00							
		Less 5% Trade discount		105.00							
				1995.00				1995.00			
		150m best Blue cotton @ £2.40 per m		360.00							
		Less 10% Trade discount		36.00							
				324.00			324.00				
		Assorted buttons		10.00							10.00
				2329.00							
		Add VAT		349.35		349.35					
			6		2678.35						
					£4594.25	£599.25	£1500.00	£2470.00			£25.00

D. MORRIS

Purchases Returns and Allowances Book

Fo. 1

March 19x1

Date	Supplier	Description	Debit Note No.	Details	Total	VAT	Cotton	Linen	Sheets	Tee-shirts	Special Items
				£	£	£	£	£	£	£	£
19x1 Mar. 15	W. Hunt	Overcharge goods supplied Feb. 5		12.00			12.00				
		Add VAT at 15%		1.80		1.80					
			7		13.80						
27	V. Luxton	30 metres White cotton returned at £1.00 per metre (Their credit note)		30.00			30.00				
		Add VAT at 15%		4.50		4.50					
			8		34.50						
					£48.30	£6.30	£42.00				

D. MORRIS

Sales Returns and Allowances Book

Fo. 2

March 19x1

Date	Supplier	Description	Credit Note No.	Details	Total	VAT	Cotton	Linen	Sheets	Tee-shirts	Special Items
19x1				£	£	£	£	£	£	£	£
Mar. 22	W. Humphrey	50 metres floral cotton, invoice Mar. 10, inferior									
		at £2.00 per metre		100.00							
		Less 10% Trade discount		10.00							
				90.00			90.00				
		Add VAT at 15%		13.50		13.50					
			9		103.50						
23	A. Jenkinson, Wolverhampton	20 metres Linen at £7.00 per metre		140.00							
		Less 20% Trade discount		28.00							
		(Their debit note)		112.00				112.00			
		Add VAT at 15%		16.80		16.80					
			10		128.80						
					£232.30	£30.30	£90.00	£112.00			

Let us now summarise the points arising in this and the second example.

In the first place, the *analysis columns* which follow the total column, enable us to dissect as fully as we may wish the details of our purchases and sales.

Secondly, we see that an *Invoice No.* column is provided. In this is entered the reference number *given by the business* to its suppliers' invoices, as well as to its own invoices to customers. If for any reason the original purchase invoice or copy sales invoice has to be consulted, it can quickly be referred to on the purchase or sales invoice files.

Thirdly, Returns and Allowances Books, whether for purchases or sales, are ruled in almost exactly the same way as the Purchase and Sales Journals themselves, the difference being that the heading 'Invoice No.' is replaced by 'Debit Note No.' and 'Credit Note No.' respectively, thus facilitating reference to these documents.

Fourthly, it is apparent that a check can be placed on the arithmetical accuracy of the book-keeping work by agreeing periodically, say at the end of each month, the 'cross' cast or 'cross addition' of the Analysis Columns with the cast or addition of the Total Column in each of the subsidiary books.

Finally, in the third example we have an instance of the purchase by the business of capital goods, or Fixed Assets, in the shape of the showcases and fittings.

As these have been bought for retention and not for resale, it is essential to provide an additional analysis column, in this case headed 'Special Items'. Alternative headings might be 'Capital Items', or 'Capital Additions'.

The provision of this column enables us to see at a glance the total value of such special or capital purchases during the period.

As VAT (Value Added Tax) was applicable to these transactions we required an additional analysis column in which to record the VAT. On the purchase from R. Ridgwell, which totalled £287.00, there would be VAT; at 15% this is £43.05 and would be added to the invoice to give a new total of £330.05. Similarly with the invoice from B. Davis, VAT of £197.25 is added, giving a new total of £1512.25, and with that from General Supplies VAT is £150, making a total of £1150. These will be recorded in the Purchase Day

Book and the VAT analysed into the extra column that has been added.

Exactly the same procedure takes place with the Sales. The VAT must be added to each invoice. This will increase each one by 15%, e.g. invoice no. 4 to W. Humphrey for £576.00 will now have £86.40 added and the new invoice total will be £662.40; and similarly for the other sales, and purchases and sales returns.

Questions

1 Explain briefly the theory of 'Double Entry', and of 'Debit and Credit'.

2 What do you understand by the term Double Entry, as applied to a system of account keeping? Give examples to illustrate.

3 'Book-keeping by Double Entry means recording the same transaction twice.' Criticise this assertion briefly.

4 State the advantages to be derived from keeping a set of books on the Double Entry System and contrast this method with any other system you know of.

5 In arranging the work of the counting house of a manufacturing company, enumerate your recommendations for dealing with inward invoices and give the ruling of the book in which you suggest they should be entered.

6 Explain fully the functions of the Purchase Analysis Journal. Give a specimen ruling thereof and insert six entries therein, showing totals, and explain how these should be dealt with.

7 Goods purchased by a business may comprise either goods for resale at a profit, or goods for retention and use. Give two examples of each, and explain how such purchases are recorded in the books of account.

8 'The books of prime entry are developments from the ordinary Journal.' Comment on this statement, and give draft rulings for a Purchase Day-Book and a Sales Day-Book in a business having three main departments.

9 Explain clearly the nature of the following documents: invoice, debit note, statement.

10 What is the columnar method of recording credit purchases and sales? Illustrate your answer by examples.

11 P.Q. & Co., Merchants, have three departments, A, B and C. It is desired to keep separate trading accounts for each. With this end in view, give the ruling of the Sales Day Book, making therein six specimen entries, and explain how the book would function.

12 A trader wishes to ascertain separately the gross profit earned by each of the two departments which comprise his business.

Show how the columnar system of book-keeping would allow him to do this without opening any additional books or accounts. Give any necessary rulings and explain how the system works.

13 What are the Returns Inwards and Outwards? Where should these items be entered in the books of a trader? What effect has each upon the profits of a business?

14 On 1 February, B. Grey owed A. White £16 for goods supplied.

On 13 February he bought from White on credit three shirts at £8 each, six pairs of socks for £7 and a pair of jeans for £17. The following day he sent a cheque for £20 on account, and on 20 February he bought a dressing gown for £14.

Set out in full the invoice made out by White relating to the purchases on 13 February, and the statement at the end of the month.

15 XY is a manufacturer of electrical appliances. Give the ruling for a Purchase Book which you would recommend he should keep, entering therein the undermentioned items, representing invoices received, and explain how the book would function in the system of Double Entry book-keeping.

Feb. 2 AB, £250 for goods.
4 PQ, £120 for repairs to machinery.
5 CD, £70 for advertising.
6 AB, £575 for goods.
8 X City Council, £1240 for general rates.
P.O. telephones, £84.
12 GH, £100 for goods.
14 Y Railway Company, £30 for carriage.
15 AB, £2250 for new plant.

16 On 1 February 19x1, you supplied to T. Thomas, 20 doz. grey pullovers at £7 each, less a trade discount of 7½%. Thomas returned 4 doz. pullovers as not up to sample and you agreed to credit him with their value.

Enter the items in the Returns Book concerned and draw up the credit note to Thomas. How would you deal with this transaction in the Ledger?

17 On 1 January 19x1, R. Rich sold G. Jones goods to the amount of £50.25; on 13 February Jones paid Rich £25 on account; on 27 February Rich sold Jones £48.5 of goods; on 3 March Jones returned to Rich £7.75 goods (not being up to sample); on 13 March Jones paid Rich £24 and was allowed £1.25 discount to clear the January account. On 31 March Rich sent a quarterly statement to Jones. Set out the statement so sent in proper form.

18 Enter the following transactions of Milner & Co. Ltd in the appropriate books of prime entry; rule off at 28 February 19x1, and post as necessary to the Impersonal and Private Ledgers.

Note: Special care should be taken in drafting the form of the books of prime entry.

19x1

Feb. 4 Bought of T. Lloyd, Lincoln, 500 metres of baize at £2.35 per metre, 2000 metres of satin at £5.60 per metre, less 10% trade discount in each case.

10 Sold to T. Williams, York, 400 metres curtain material at £6.50 per metre, and sundry fittings £8. Box charged £10.

11 Bought showcase and counter for showroom from Universal Supplies, Ltd, London, £750.00.

12 Returned to T. Lloyd, Lincoln, 200 metres of satin as invoiced on 4 February.

Feb. 18 Bought of J. Grey, Taunton, 300 metres linen at £7.25 per metre, less 5% trade discount and 250 metres baize at £2.35 per metre net.

20 Received debit note from T. Williams, York, for box invoiced on 10 February.

24 Sold to D. Wilson, Coventry, 300 metres baize at £4.00 per metre net, and 600 metres satin at £7.00 per metre less 10% trade discount.

3

Purchase and Sales Transactions and the Ledger Accounts

Question As I see it, the Purchase and Sales Day Books are written up from the original purchase invoices, and the copies of the sales invoices to customers?

Answer Yes, that is so, but it is of the utmost importance that every purchase invoice, whether for goods or services, shall be certified by the responsible officials of the business as to its correctness before being entered in the Purchase Journal. With regard to sales invoices, these may be issued on the basis of the warehouseman's record of deliveries.

Question The final column in the first example's Purchase Journal was headed 'Crates and Packing', but there was no similar column in the second one. Why is this?

Answer Suppliers may or may not charge for crates and packing material. If they do so, a record must clearly be made of the expense. Under this head, it is, however, a cost which we should record separately because it may be recoverable if and when such items as crates are returned to the suppliers; otherwise the cost must be borne by the business.

Question With both the Purchase and the Sales Journals there is then no one particular form of ruling?

Answer No. There cannot be. The system of book-keeping must be such as will give the information in each particular case in the form in which it is required, or can be of the greatest use. For this reason care must be exercised in the choice of the analysis columns.

These may represent the principal materials dealt in, or the departments responsible for their production and sale, and so on.

Question If goods are bought and sold on credit, I should have thought it was also very important to know:

(*a*) How much the business has purchased *from any one supplier*, and
(*b*) How much it has sold *to any one customer*.

But as there are numerous transactions with different suppliers and customers, how could this be done from the Journals alone?

Answer By means of the Ledger, or principal book of account, we are able to discover very quickly not only what has been purchased from or sold to any particular person, but *how that person stands in relation to the business at any particular time*, that is, whether he is its creditor or debtor. Put in another way, we want to know how much we have sold to each customer period by period because if possible we hope to increase our sales to him, and we also want to know how much that customer owes us for goods delivered, since his payments to us provide the monies out of which we have to pay our suppliers.

Question So the Ledger Account records not only the trading aspect of our transactions, but also the *cash aspect*?

Answer Yes. Both aspects must be recorded as affecting suppliers and customers, but at the moment we are only concerned with the *trading aspect.*

The Ledger

Personal Accounts

We have spoken of Ledger Accounts as playing an essential part in summarising the transactions of the business so far as they concern those with whom it deals.

It is now necessary to describe the Ledger Account rather more precisely, and to consider its other functions.

Its usual form is as follows:

JONES

Dr.					Cr.
Date	*Details*	*Amount*	*Date*	*Details*	*Amount*
		£			£

In the form, we notice:

(*a*) **Name of Account**. This may be the name of the person, in this case Jones, who is either a supplier or a customer of the business. It may represent, on the other hand, the impersonal subject-matter with which the account deals. For the moment, we will take it to be the former only.

(*b*) The vertical double line in the centre divides the account into two equal parts. That on the left we term the **Debit** or debtor side, denoted by the symbol **Dr.**, and that on the right the **Credit**, or creditor side, with the symbol **Cr**. *On both sides* of the account, it will be observed, there are three columns, headed respectively: Date, Details, and Amount.

In the ordinary way, a separate page, or folio of the Ledger, is used for each account opened, and the Ledger itself may be a bound book; a loose-leaf book; in the form of cards, with a separate card for each account; or a series of files in a computer-based system.

If we assume that Jones is a supplier of goods to the business, the structure of the account enables us to put to his credit, i.e. on the right-hand, or *credit* side, the value of the goods supplied by him. The right-hand side may also be regarded generally as that on which we enter benefits received *by the business*. The supply of goods on credit is clearly such a benefit and Jones may be said to have performed, to this extent, a 'credit-worthy' action.

Furthermore, his account is said to be 'in credit', in that he is a *creditor* of the business. Let us suppose Jones has supplied goods to the value of £10. This being an ordinary purchase transaction, the first record will be made in the Purchase Journal, as we have seen. It will ultimately be put (or 'posted' as we must accustom ourselves to saying) to the credit of Jones's account, as follows:

JONES

Dr. Cr.

Date	*Details*	*P.R.J. Fo.*	*Amount*	*Date*	*Details*	*P.J. Fo.*	*Amount*
				19x1			£
				Jan. 1	Goods	2	10.00

At this point we must remember:

(*a*) It is not necessary but in appropriate circumstances it might be helpful to repeat here the full description of the goods. By inserting a column for the Purchase Journal (P.J. Fo.) we can readily turn back to the initial entry in the Purchase Journal and, if we wish, to the original document, on which it was based, i.e. the supplier's invoice.

(*b*) The purpose of our Ledger Account with Jones is to summarise or assemble within it *all our transactions* with him; otherwise it would be impossible to determine the position of the business in relation to him.

Because we are now thinking of Jones as a *supplier*, it is logical to assume, in the first instance, that any items on the left-hand or *debit* side will be in respect of payments made to him; off-setting the amounts standing to his credit.

If, however, the business has had occasion to return goods to him owing to unsatisfactory quality, or error in price, and a *credit note* is received signifying his acceptance of them, this also is a matter which must be recorded on the *debit* side. The effect of the return of the goods is *to reduce the liability of the business* to Jones as its creditor. In this case, the initial entry will have been made in the **Purchase Returns** or **Allowances Book**, and from that we shall post to the *debit* of Jones's Ledger Account, as under:

JONES

Dr. Cr.

Date	*Details*	*P.R.J. Fo.*	*Amount*	*Date*	*Details*	*P.J. Fo.*	*Amount*
19x1			£	19x1			£
Jan. 6	Returns or allowances	3	1.50	Jan. 1	Goods	2	10.00

Should Jones, on the other hand, be a *customer* of the business a Ledger Account will be opened in identical form, but if goods to the value of £10 are *sold* to him, his account will be debited, that is the entry will be made on the *left-hand* side:

JONES

Dr.							Cr.
Date	*Details*	*S.J. Fo.*	*Amount*	*Date*	*Details*	*S.R.J. Fo.*	*Amount*
19x1			£				
Jan. 1	Goods	2	10.00				

He now appears as a *debtor* to the business, as indeed he is, the details of the original sale being found on Folio 2 of the **Sales Journal**.

The business in this case has performed the 'credit-worthy' action, and as such is entitled to regard Jones as *chargeable* with it. He is *indebted* to the business, and therefore the entry appears on the debit side.

Finally, should goods be returned by him, or the business make him any kind of allowance, the amount, as posted from the **Sales Returns and Allowances Book**, will be put to his credit.

The result will be, as we should expect:

(*a*) To offset to that extent his original indebtedness of £10.
(*b*) To indicate that the business, having delivered defective goods, or made an overcharge, now proceeds to gives Jones the necessary *credit*.

The Ledger Account would then appear:

JONES

Dr.							Cr.
Date	*Details*	*S.J. Fo.*	*Amount*	*Date*	*Details*	*S.R.J. Fo.*	*Amount*
19x1			£	19x1			£
Jan. 1	Goods	2	10.00	Jan. 6	Returns or allowances	3	1.50

When the *cash* as well as the *trading aspect* of these transactions has been dealt with, we shall be in a position to determine, at any time and irrespective of the number of items, the *balance of indebtedness* due either *to* or *by* the business.

So far as we have been ealing with persons *external* to the business, the *personal* aspect f the sales and purchase transactions has now been recorded.

By that we mean *the effect upon the persons* with whom the transactions have been entered into, resulting in their becoming, until the question of *payment* arises, the creditors or debtors of the business.

If we have carefully followed the construction of the Ledger Account as shown, it is apparent that the entries are postings from the various books of first entry – from the Journals. That is to say, the Journals provide the basis for the writing up of all Ledger Accounts.

We may even lay it down as a rule with very few exceptions that: *No entry shall be made in a Ledger Account, unless it has first appeared in the Journal.*

We should remember that the Journal will not necessarily be a bound book. It may consist of tabulation prepared by a computer or a file of invoices.

Impersonal Accounts

It was stated on page 26 that the name of the account might be that of the person with whom the business dealt, or of the impersonal subject-matter referred to in it.

The former we may now term a **Personal Account**, and the latter an **Impersonal**, or **Nominal** Account.

Jones's account, whether he be a supplier or a customer, is a *Personal Account.* His position, as someone external to the business, has been looked at from the personal aspect.

There is, however, another aspect to be considered, and that is *the effect upon the business* as an impersonal unit, of the transactions with Jones and any other suppliers and customers.

When in the first place we regarded him as a *supplier* his account was credited with £10, but at the same time we must remember that the business then came into possession of £10 worth of *goods*. It is therefore natural to regard the stores or warehouse as *chargeable* in this amount. As a department of the business it may further be regarded *impersonally*, and the necessary charge made to it in an *impersonal account*, headed 'Warehouse', or 'Goods purchased' or, more usually, **Purchases**.

Thus the heading refers to the *subject-matter* of the account and not to the name of the warehouseman, or storekeeper, which is immaterial because he represents the *business*. If at first sight it seems strange that the charge to the warehouse for goods purchased should call for record in such an account, we may find an explanation in the following:

(*a*) The essence of the double-entry system is to record the dual aspect of each transaction *within the Ledger*, or book of account.

In the event of no 'Warehouse' or 'Purchases' Account being opened we should have recorded in the Ledger *one aspect of the transaction only* – the personal aspect.

(*b*) The business, or its proprietor, desires to know, period by period, how much has been *purchased* of the various kinds of goods dealt in.

The opening of the Ledger Account for 'purchases' permits the periodic totals of the Purchase Journal to be posted to it on the chargeable, or *debit* side.

Sometimes it is contended, and with truth, that the total cost of purchases, suitably analysed, can be seen at a glance in the Purchase Journal.

This, however, is no reason for eliminating the Ledger Account for 'purchases', because, as stated above, we desire to complete the *double entry within the Ledger*, and also obtain, *in the summarised form which the Ledger Account gives*, the total charge to the warehouse for goods received by it month by month during the trading year.

As in practice the various subdivisions of the Journal are ruled off at monthly intervals, a note of the monthly totals in summarised form is clearly very helpful.

The following illustrates in another way what has been described above:

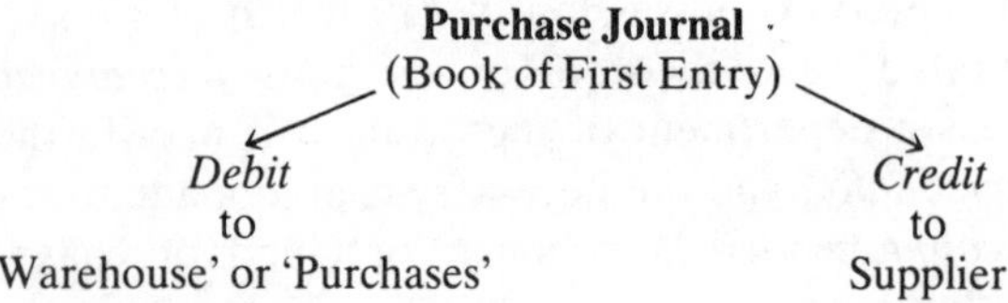

or, in account form, assuming the total purchases for the month were £1410:

Impersonal Ledger Account

PURCHASES

Dr. Cr.

Date	*Details*	*P.J. Fo.*	*Amount*	*Date*	*Details*	*Fo.*	*Amount*
19x1			£				
Jan. 31	Total purchases for month	2	1410.00				

We may also add that, from the point of view of the business, the charge or *debit* to the 'Purchases' Account may be made by taking the *total* only of the appropriate column in the Purchase Journal.

This is in striking contrast to the necessity for giving *credit* to each separate supplier in *his own personal account*. We cannot avoid this latter step because we must know at any time *how the business stands in relation to each supplier*.

Purchase returns and allowances

It was seen on page 28 that Jones, as a supplier, was charged or *debited* with the goods returned to him, or the allowance claimed from him. As the result in either case is to *reduce the initial debit* to 'Purchases' Account, the double entry will be completed by *crediting* that account, as follows:

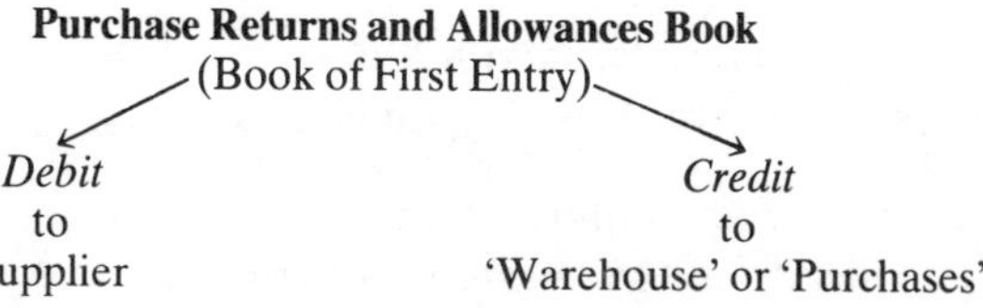

or, in account form, assuming total purchase returns for the month were £71.50:

Impersonal Ledger Account

PURCHASES

Dr. Cr.

Date	*Details*	*P.J. Fo.*	*Amount*	*Date*	*Details*	*P.R.J. Fo.*	*Amount*
19x1			£	19x1			£
Jan. 31	Total purchases for month	2	1410.00	Jan. 31	Total returns and allowances for month	3	71.50

Purchases of a capital nature

In Example 2.3 we saw that the purchase by D. Morris of showcases and fittings was recorded, together with his other purchases, in the Purchase Journal kept by him.

The personal aspect of this transaction is a credit to the suppliers in the Ledger Account opened in their name, i.e. a *personal account*.

But, as with the receipt of goods by the warehouse on behalf of the business, we have similarly to put on record somewhere the purchase of these capital goods, or *fixed assets*.

There can be no question of charging them to the warehouse, since they are not goods in which the business is dealing.

But, nevertheless, an account must be opened for them in the Ledger, having regard to the necessity for completing the double entry *in the Ledger*, and so we may decide to open an account under the general heading of 'Fixtures and Fittings'.

In this case the business has acquired property for the use or value of which it is liable to account to its proprietor, even though such property is not intended for resale, and it is right that it should be charged or, as we say, *debited* with the purchase cost of £1000.

The question now arises: in which *section* of the Ledger shall the account be opened?

What we have already done is to describe:

(*a*) **Personal Accounts**, as with Jones,
(*b*) **Impersonal Accounts**, e.g. Purchases,

the latter being the counterpart, in summarised form, of the former, so far as concerns *the effect upon the business*.

It is customary, in practice, having regard to the existence of these two types of account, to utilise *two entirely separate Ledgers*, known respectively as the **Personal Ledger** and the **Impersonal Ledger**.

As in the ordinary trading business of even quite moderate size the number of customers may be very large, we often find that the personal Ledger is divided into two parts. The first part we call the **Sales Ledger**, as it is restricted to accounts with customers, and the latter the **Purchase Ledger**, as in it all the suppliers' accounts are opened.

By contrast, the accounts in the Impersonal Ledger will not be very numerous, and in the main they relate to those matters which affect the business in its *ordinary trading activities*, such as purchases, sales, wages, etc.

We could, of course, from the standpoint of the effect upon the business, open the 'Fixtures and Fittings' Account in the Impersonal Ledger, and in that account record all dealings in that particular class of property.

But because the fixtures and fittings have no direct relation to the day-to-day trading activities, *a further section of the Ledger* is provided for the accounts of this and similar types of fixed asset.

This further section is termed the **Private Ledger**, and represents the third and final division of the Ledger as a book of account.

Once again, we post the *total* of the 'special items' or 'capital items' column in the Purchase Journal, so that the Fixtures and Fittings Account appears as follows:

FIXTURES AND FITTINGS

Dr. Cr.

Date	*Details*	*P.J. Fo.*	*Amount*	*Date*	*Details*	*Fo.*	*Amount*
19x1			£				
Mar. 31	Showcases and fittings	1	1000.00				

or in diagram form:

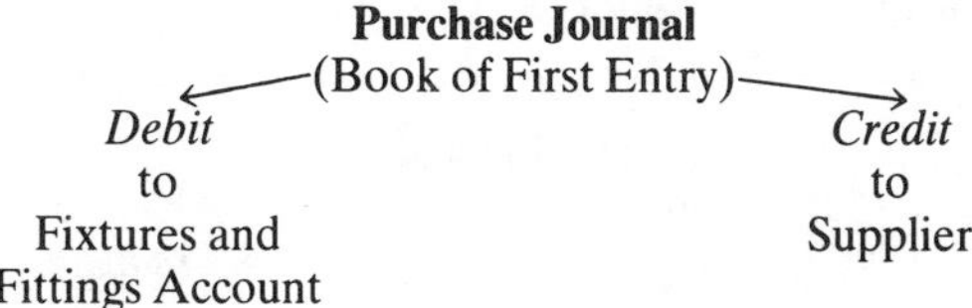

Sales

Much of what we have said in regard to the completion of the double entry under the heading of purchases will apply in the case of sales, although in the *reverse direction*.

We are still dealing with the *impersonal aspect, or the effect upon the business* of the delivery of goods from the warehouse to the customer.

What we must realise is that if goods are sold to Brown, for example, in his capacity as a *customer*, the warehouse having delivered the goods, is entitled to take credit to itself, as representing the business, for the goods that have passed out of its possession.

From the *personal aspect*, the customer Brown must, of course, be charged or *debited* with what he has received at *selling price*.

Impersonally the business is thus entitled to credit in an impersonal account, which may be headed: 'Warehouse', or 'Goods sold', or more usually, Sales.

Our reasons for so doing are:

(*a*) As in the case of purchases, the double entry must be completed *within the Ledgers*.
(*b*) The business, or its proprietor, desires to know, period by period, how much has been sold of the various kinds of goods dealt in.

Therefore, if we open an account in the Impersonal Ledger, headed 'Sales', the periodic totals of the Sales Journal will be posted to it on the *credit* side, and, as with purchases, the Sales Journal will usually be ruled off at monthly intervals.

At any time, therefore, we may obtain a comparison of the *cost of purchases*, with the *proceeds of sales*, by examining these two accounts in the Impersonal Ledger.

Stated in another way, we have:

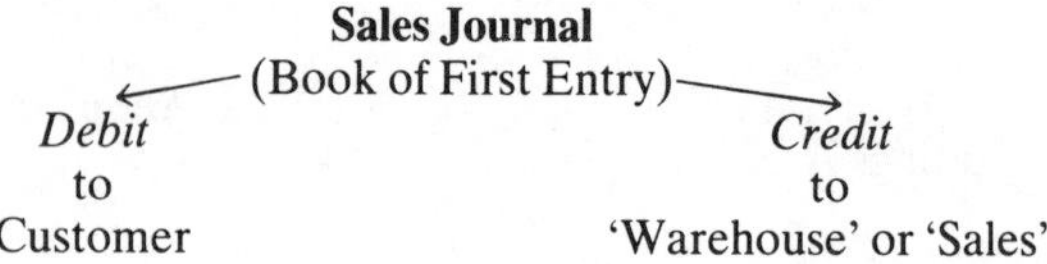

or, in account form, assuming the sales value for the month to be £2000.00:

SALES

Dr. Cr.

Date	*Details*	*Fo.*	*Amount*	*Date*	*Details*	*S.J. Fo.*	*Amount*
				19x1			£
				Jan. 31	Total sales for month	4	2000.00

It will be noted from the 'Details' column in the account, that we need concern ourselves only with the *total sales* as shown in the Sales Journal.

This is because, irrespective of the *kind* of goods sold, they may all be regarded as *sales*, and dealt with in the Ledger as one item.

In recording the *personal aspect,* however, a separate debit to each customer in his own *personal account* is essential if we are to know precisely:

(*a*) How much has been sold to him.
(*b*) The amount of his indebtedness to the business at any particular time.

Sales returns and allowances

Should Brown, to whom £20 worth of goods have been sold, return any part of the goods, or make a claim on the business for an allowance in respect of the invoice price to him, the effect upon the business will be to reduce the initial *credit* to 'Sales' Account. In other words, the latter account will be *debited*:

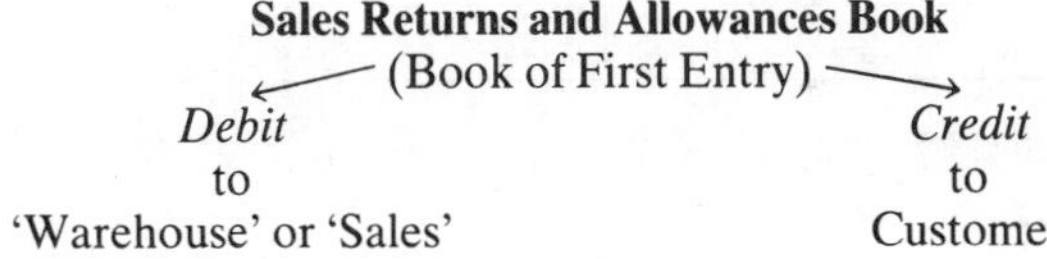

or, in account form, assuming the total amount of the sales returns and allowances for the month to be £50:

Impersonal Ledger Account

SALES

Dr. Cr.

Date	*Details*	*S.R.J. Fo.*	*Amount*	*Date*	*Details*	*S.J. Fo.*	*Amount*
19x1			£	19x1			£
Jan. 31	Total returns and allowances for month	5	50.00	Jan. 31	Total sales for month	4	2000.00

Sales of a capital nature

These are far less frequently encountered than purchases of this class of goods.

It is possible to record such sales by inserting a 'special items' column in the Sales Journal, but in practice use is almost always made of the earliest form of Journal, or the ordinary Debtor and Creditor Journal (without analysis columns) as illustrated in Chapter 7.

Examples that may be cited are the sale of a motor lorry, traveller's motor-car or machine tool.

The Journal entry in such a case provides the basic narrative of the transaction for entry in the Ledgers, these being the personal (Sales) Ledger so far as the person to whom they are sold is concerned, and the account of the particular asset in the Private Ledger so far as concerns the effect on the business.

For the sake of completeness we may take the following example.

Example 3.1

On 1 January 19x1, D. Morris had in his factory machinery of a book value of £5000. On 15 January a stitching machine was sold to a dealer, realising £150.

Private Ledger Account

MACHINERY

Dr. Cr.

Date	*Details*	*Fo.*	*Amount*	*Date*	*Details*	*Fo.*	*Amount*
19x1			£	19x1			£
Jan. 1	Balance		5000.00	Jan. 15	A. Dealer, Stitching machine		150.00

An important point in connection with this transaction would be the loss or profit on sale, i.e. the proceeds of sale of £150 would have to be compared with that proportion of the commencing balance of £5000 which represented the actual machine sold.

Once again, we may state the transaction in diagram form:

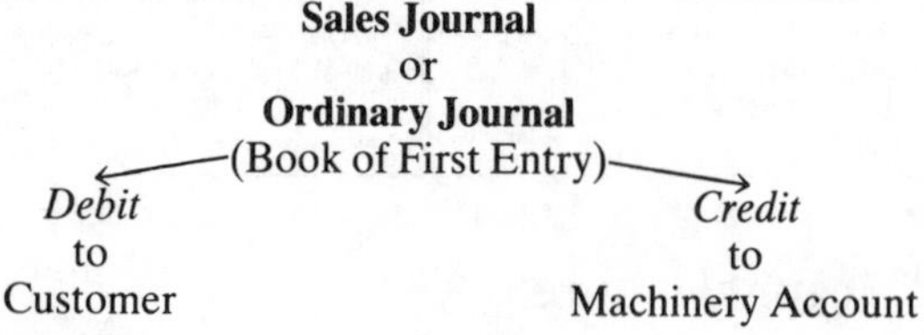

Impersonal and Private Ledgers

While the Personal Ledger is restricted to the accounts of suppliers and customers in its purchase and sales sections respectively, the following examples are typical of the accounts appearing in the Impersonal Ledger and the Private Ledger:

Impersonal Ledger (also called the *Nominal Ledger*)	**Private Ledger**
Purchases	Capital (of Proprietor)
Sales	Factory, warehouse or office premises
Purchase returns	Machinery
Sales returns	Tools
Wages	Fixtures and fittings
Carriage	Motor vehicles
Salaries	Patents
Cash discounts allowed	Trade marks
Cash discounts received	Stock
Bad debts	Bills of exchange (payable and receivable)
Travelling expenses	Investments
Packing expenses	Loans
Repairs	
Interest paid	*and so on.*
Interest received	
Rent	
Rates	
Commission	

It might be added that in a general way, of the items appearing above, those under the heading 'Impersonal Ledger' relate to accounts in which we find details of the *profit and loss*, or *revenue position* of the business.

Those, on the other hand, under the heading of 'Private Ledger' relate to the *assets and liabilities* of the business.

Ledger Accounts

Now that we have become acquainted with the general application of Double Entry principles to the recording of Purchases and Sales transactions *within the Ledgers*, let us carry Example 2.3 (p. 14) a stage further, and imagine we have been instructed to *post to the Ledger Accounts* from the various books of Prime Entry which we have already written up.

1 Purchases

In the Purchase Day Book of D. Morris we see it is necessary to give **credit** to each one of the three suppliers whose names appear therein. Such credit will clearly be given in the Personal (Purchase) Ledger, and the three accounts required will be opened as follows:

D. MORRIS

Purchase Ledger

R. RIDGWELL, BOLTON

Dr.							Cr.
Date	*Details*	*Fo.*	*Amount*	*Date*	*Details*	*P.J. Fo.*	*Amount*
				19x1			£
				Mar. 12	Goods & VAT	1	330.05

B. DAVIS, ELY

Dr.							Cr.
Date	*Details*	*Fo.*	*Amount*	*Date*	*Details*	*P.J. Fo.*	*Amount*
				19x1			£
				Mar. 20	Goods & VAT	1	1512.25

GENERAL SUPPLIES LTD, LONDON

Dr.							Cr.
Date	*Details*	*Fo.*	*Amount*	*Date*	*Details*	*P.J. Fo.*	*Amount*
				19x1			£
				Mar. 29	Goods & VAT	1	1150.00

In each case the entries appear on the *credit side* since, until payment is made to them, the suppliers are creditors of the business.

The use of the words 'Goods and VAT' in the 'Details' column is all that is necessary, as full particulars of the goods can quickly be found on Folio 1 of the Purchase Journal itself.

We must now consider the *impersonal aspect*, which is the charge to the warehouse for 'Goods Purchased' or 'Purchases'. It is necessary, too, for us to remember that by this is meant 'goods purchased for resale', so that we must in any event exclude the item of Showcases and Fittings.

Our Impersonal Ledger Account for Purchases will then be:

PURCHASES

Dr. Cr.

Date	*Details*	*P.J. Fo.*	*Amount*	*Date*	*Details*	*Fo.*	*Amount*
19x1			£				
Mar. 31	Total for month:						
	Cotton		500.00				
	Sheets		175.00				
	Tee-shirts		912.00				
	Sundries		15.00				
		1	1602.00				

But it is scarcely likely that we shall rest content with the *form* of this account, because month by month new totals will appear in it, and the subsequent addition of the 'Amount' column will be somewhat complicated.

For this reason, it may be preferred to open a separate Purchases Account *for each class of goods*, or to enter them in one account, but in *columnar* form.

Let us assume the former method is selected. We shall then have:

Impersonal Ledger

PURCHASES – COTTON

Dr. Cr.

Date	*Details*	*P.J. Fo.*	*Amount*	*Date*	*Details*	*Fo.*	*Amount*
19x1			£				
Mar. 31	Total for month	1	500.00				

PURCHASES – SHEETS

Dr. Cr.

Date	*Details*	*P.J. Fo.*	*Amount*	*Date*	*Details*	*Fo.*	*Amount*
19x1			£				
Mar. 31	Total for month	1	175.00				

PURCHASES – TEE-SHIRTS

Dr. Cr.

Date	*Details*	*P.J. Fo.*	*Amount*	*Date*	*Details*	*Fo.*	*Amount*
19x1			£				
Mar. 31	Total for month	1	912.00				

PURCHASES – SUNDRIES

Dr. Cr.

Date	Details	P.J. Fo.	Amount	Date	Details	Fo.	Amount
19x1			£				
Mar. 31	Total for month	1	15.00				

In regard to the showcases and fittings purchased, an account in the private Ledger will be opened, as below:

FIXTURES AND FITTINGS

Dr. Cr.

Date	Details	P.J. Fo.	Amount	Date	Details	Fo.	Amount
19x1			£				
Mar. 31	Total for month	1	1000.00				

It must be noted that the charge to the business for *purchases* and *fixtures and fittings* is made on the *debit* side, the amount in each case being the *total* of the appropriate analysis column in the Purchase Journal.

We thus see that:

(*a*) The Purchase Journal as a Book of Prime Entry provides a basis for the Double Entry.

(*b*) The dual aspect of the transactions has been recorded *within the Ledgers*.

(*c*) Arithmetical agreement has been obtained, in that the sum of the *credit* entries or postings in the Purchase Ledger is equal to the sum of the *debit* postings in the Impersonal and Private Ledgers.

(*d*) While the postings to the Impersonal and Private Ledger Accounts are made on 31 March and in *total* only, those to the Personal Ledger are made as soon as possible after the initial record in the Journal. It is essential to have our Ledger Account with each supplier 'up to date'.

2 Purchase Returns and Allowances

In the Purchase Returns Book we see there are two entries relating, in the first case, to an overcharge, and in the second, to the return of goods by the business to one of its suppliers.

In recording the *personal aspect* we must therefore remember that the suppliers' accounts in the Purchase Ledger will be *debited*, resulting in a reduction of any amounts hitherto standing to their *credit*.

This is a logical step to take because, had the overcharge not been detected, we should have *debited* Hunt with a payment *greater* than was actually due to him. The issue of a Debit Note now clearly reduces the amount of any subsequent payment to him by the business.

Further, the *receipt of a Credit Note* from Luxton enables the business to debit him with the cost of the goods returned for which, when purchased, it had originally given him credit.

The Purchase Ledger Accounts of the two suppliers will then appear as follows:

Purchase Ledger

W. HUNT

Dr. Cr.

Date	*Details*	*P.R.J. Fo.*	*Amoun*	*Date*	*Details*	*P.J. Fo.*	*Amount*
19x1			£				
Mar. 15	Overcharge	1	13.80				

V. LUXTON

Dr. Cr.

Date	*Details*	*P.R.J. Fo.*	*Amoun*	*Date*	*Details*	*P.J. Fo.*	*Amount*
19x1			£				
Mar. 27	Returns	1	34.50				

As this is the only information we have concerning these suppliers the result is that they are shown as *debtors* to the business to this extent, it being assumed that they have received payment in full in some previous period.

In practice, however, it is almost certain that in the first case at least, payment would not be made until the overcharge in question had been corrected.

With regard to the *impersonal* aspect, we can now appreciate that the warehouse will be *credited*. The reason for giving it credit now, is that it was originally charged or *debited* with the goods purchased at the invoice or cost price to the business. The credit thus given to it puts on record the fact that its responsibility is lessened by the amount, in total, of £42.00.

The Purchase Returns, or Returns Outwards Accounts, will then be credited on 31 March with the **total of** the appropriate analysis columns in the Purchase Returns Journal as below:

PURCHASE RETURNS – COTTON

Dr. Cr.

Date	Details	Fo.	Amount	Date	Details	P.R.J. Fo.	Amount
				19x1			£
				Mar. 31	Total for month	1	42.00

You will have noticed that the suppliers of goods were credited with the total of 'Goods and VAT' and the purchases accounts debited with the cost of goods only from the analysis columns. To complete the double-entry and record the position of the business in respect of VAT the appropriate entries must be made in the VAT account in the Nominal (impersonal) Ledger, using the monthly totals from the analysis columns in the books of prime entry.

When the Nominal Ledger account is written up, the balance will be the amount that is due to be paid to the Customs and Excise. Occasionally more may have been paid with purchases than has been charged on sales and a claim can be made for repayment.

Nominal Ledger Account

VAT

Dr. Cr.

Date	Details	Fo.	Amount	Date	Details	Fo.	Amount
19x1			£	19x1			£
Mar. 31	Total for purchases during month	1	390.30	Mar. 31	Total for sales during month	2	599.25
	Total for sales returns and allowances for month	2	30.30		Total for purchase returns and allowances for for month	1	6.30

These figures show that VAT of £599.25 has been charged to customers and will be collected from them, less £30.30 in respect of returns and allowances, i.e. 568.95

We have been charged, and will pay to the suppliers £390.30 less £6.30 i.e. 384.00

so the remaining balance of 184.95

is due to the Customs and Excise. VAT is not a charge on the business: the business charges the customer and accounts for the total charge to the Customs and Excise after the appropriate allowance is made for the VAT that has been paid to suppliers.

Once more, it is seen that:

(*a*) The Double Entry is completed within the Ledgers, Personal and Impersonal.
(*b*) Arithmetical agreement is maintained, the sum of the *debit* items being equal to the sum of the *credits*, and
(*c*) While the postings to the accounts of Hunt and Luxton are made on the dates of the transactions with them, those to the Purchase Returns Accounts are made in total on 31 March.

3 Sales

The Sales Journal gives us full particulars of the sales to the three customers for whom we shall open separate accounts in the Sales Ledger.

To record the personal aspect, we must show that they are debtors to the business, and therefore their accounts will be in *debit*, taking the following form:

W. HUMPHREY, LINCOLN

Dr. Cr.

Date	*Details*	*S.J. Fo.*	*Amount*	*Date*	*Details*	*Fo.*	*Amount*
19x1			£				
Mar. 10	Goods	2	662.40				

S. BOHAM, COVENTRY

Dr. Cr.

Date	*Details*	*S.J. Fo.*	*Amount*	*Date*	*Details*	*Fo.*	*Amount*
19x1			£				
Mar. 18	Goods	2	1253.50				

T. BUTTERWORTH, NORWICH

Dr. Cr.

Date	*Details*	*S.J. Fo.*	*Amount*	*Date*	*Details*	*Fo.*	*Amount*
19x1			£				
Mar. 24	Goods	2	2678.35				

We should now be able to understand the meaning of what has been done in our book-keeping work. If in the case of *personal* accounts, like those set out above, the entries appear on the debit side, or there is an excess in value of debit entries over credit entries, the person whose name appears at the head of the account is always a debtor to the business. He is chargeable to the extent of paying the business for the goods it has sold to him.

If a similar state of affairs is found to exist in an *impersonal* account, such as 'Purchases', it indicates that the official of the business under whose control the goods have come is chargeable to account for them until the time of their ultimate sale.

But as we are here dealing with *sales*, it is necessary to give *credit* to the warehouse which has parted with goods on the instructions of the Sales Department, and has therefore reduced its responsibility to account in the proper way.

Thus, an account will be opened in the Impersonal Ledger for 'Goods Sold' or 'Sales', as follows:

SALES

Dr. Cr.

Date	*Details*	*Fo.*	*Amount*	*Date*	*Details*	*S.J. Fo.*	*Amount*
				19x1			£
				Mar. 31	Total for month:		
					Cotton	2	1500.00
					Linen		2470.00
					Sundries		25.00
							3995.00

As explained on page 39, in connection with the analysis of purchases, we shall, however, almost certainly prefer to open separate Sales Accounts for the various kinds of goods to correspond with the columns in the Sales Journal.

The result will then be:

SALES – COTTON

Dr. Cr.

Date	*Details*	*Fo.*	*Amount*	*Date*	*Details*	*S.J. Fo.*	*Amount*
				19x1			£
				Mar. 31	Total for month	2	1500.00

SALES – LINEN

Dr.							Cr.
Date	*Details*	*Fo.*	*Amount*	*Date*	*Details*	*S.J. Fo.*	*Amount*
				19x1			£
				Mar. 31	Total for month	2	2470.00

SALES – SUNDRIES

Dr.							Cr.
Date	*Details*	*Fo.*	*Amount*	*Date*	*Details*	*S.J. Fo.*	*Amount*
				19x1			£
				Mar. 31	Total for month	2	25.00

By means of these analysed Impersonal Accounts it is now possible for the proprietor of the business to compare, month by month, the **purchase cost** with the **proceeds of sale** of the various articles in which he is dealing.

Obviously, in the long run sales should exceed purchases but from month to month there will be changes in the level of stocks owned by the business and the direct comparison of purchases and sales may be inappropriate.

4 Sales Returns and Allowances

As with Purchases, we find in this book two entries which must be posted to the Ledger, involving the completion of the *personal aspect* at once and as a separate posting to the account of each customer, and of the *impersonal aspect* at the end of the month, and in total only.

We find, however, this difference from Purchases: The goods returned by Humphrey are part of those sold to him during the month under review; while both items come under the head of 'Returns', there being no question of an overcharge.

Let us try to visualise what these two entries mean. If we are in any doubt, it may be simpler to deal first with the Impersonal aspect.

The warehouse has received the goods, increasing its stock, for which it is accountable. It is, therefore, logical that we should charge or *debit* it with the *total* value of the returned goods.

At the same time, the customers have performed a 'credit-worthy' action, to this extent offsetting the original charge or debit made to them individually. It is equally reasonable, therefore, to *credit* them with the returned goods. This credit, in the case of Humphrey, will cause his account to appear as follows:

W. HUMPHREY, LINCOLN

Dr.							Cr.
Date	*Details*	*S.J. Fo.*	*Amount*	*Date*	*Details*	*S.R.J. Fo.*	*Amount*
19x1			£	19x1			£
Mar. 10	Goods	2	662.40	Mar. 22	Returns	2	103.50

and from it we can see that his original indebtedness is now reduced, *which is in line with the facts*.

As regards Jenkinson, he too will receive *credit*, as follows:

A. JENKINSON, WOLVERHAMPTON

Dr.							Cr.
Date	*Details*	*Fo.*	*Amount*	*Date*	*Details*	*S.R.J. Fo.*	*Amount*
				19x1			£
				Mar. 23	Returns	2	128.80

But, since we know nothing of his original indebtedness to the business, the position is that he appears as a creditor for the amount shown above. Payment may either be made to him in settlement, or more probably, the credit will be taken into account by him when he next pays for any further goods supplied.

Finally, to complete the double entry, we shall post the totals of the appropriate columns in the Sales Returns Journals to the Debit of the Impersonal Ledger Accounts for 'Sales Returns – Cotton' and 'Sales Returns – Linen', just as we did with Purchases.

In both cases, the warehouse has received goods, either from a supplier, or from a customer.

SALES RETURNS – COTTON

Dr.							Cr.
Date	*Details*	*S.R.J. Fo.*	*Amount*	*Date*	*Details*	*Fo.*	*Amount*
19x1			£				
Mar. 31	Total for month	2	90.00				

SALES RETURNS – LINEN

Dr.							Cr.
Date	*Details*	*S.R.J. Fo.*	*Amount*	*Date*	*Details*	*Fo.*	*Amount*
19x1			£				
Mar. 31	Total for month	2	112.00				

Summary

With each of the Journals we have been careful to regard them as providing the basis for the completion of the double entry *within the Ledgers*. They have, therefore, served their purpose in enabling us to look at each one of the *purchasing* and *selling transactions* from their *dual aspect*, or the Personal and Impersonal aspect.

Irrespective of the *number* of these transactions during any particular period, we are now in a position to tabulate the information contained in the Ledger Accounts in the form of the *balances* thereon. These balances will be obtained by a scrutiny of each account, so that the amount of one item or of the total items on the debit side will be termed a *debit balance*, and one on the credit side a *credit balance*. Where entries appear on both debit and credit sides, the excess of the one side over the other will also be termed the balance, according to its nature, but this we shall appreciate more readily after dealing with Cash Receipts and Cash Payments.

W. HUMPHREY, LINCOLN

Dr.							Cr.
Date	*Details*	*S.J. Fo.*	*Amount*	*Date*	*Details*	*S.R.J. Fo.*	*Amount*
19x1			£	19x1			£
Mar. 10	Goods	2	662.40	Mar. 22	Returns	2	103.50
				31	Balance	c/d	558.90
			662.40				662.40
31	Balance	b/d	558.90				

In the meantime, we will extract and state the balances as they now appear in the various Ledger Accounts:

Page	*Ledger*	*Name of Account*	*Dr.*	*Cr.*
			£	£
38	Purchase	R. Ridgwell		330.05
		B. Davis		1512.25
		General Supplies Ltd		1150.00
41		W. Hunt	13.80	
		V. Luxton	34.50	
47	Sales	W. Humphrey	558.90	
43		S. Boham	1253.50	
		T. Butterworth	2678.35	
46		A. Jenkinson		128.80
39	Impersonal	Purchases – Cotton	500.00	
		Sheets	175.00	
		Tee-shirts	912.00	
40		Sundries	15.00	
42		Purchase returns – Cotton		42.00
44		Sales – Cotton		1500.00
45		Linen		2470.00
		Sundries		25.00
46		Sales returns – Cotton	90.00	
47		Linen	112.00	
42		VAT		184.95
40	Private	Fixtures and fittings	1000.00	
			£7343.05	£7343.05

* Note that the Ledger account on page 43 with only the sale recorded has been subsequently updated to reflect the 'returns and allowances'.

It should be mentioned that in the average business by far the greater number of accounts will be found in the Personal Ledgers, and especially in that section of those Ledgers containing the accounts of customers, or Sales Ledger. So large may this become as a result of the business enlarging its sales connection that its division on an alphabetical or territorial basis may be essential if the Accounting Department is to do its work with speed and efficiency.

Control accounts

Reference was made earlier (p. 4) to 'one account in the ledger for incoming goods or purchases and other accounts for the individual suppliers'. If these suppliers become numerous it may be simpler to have one account, called a **Creditors Control Account**, for recording the totals of the transactions, and subsequently analysing these totals to the individual suppliers. Similarly there would be an account for the customers, for which the control account would be called the **Debtors Control Account**.

The illustration on page 39 showed first an account for total purchases which was subsequently replaced by separate accounts for different types of purchases. Use of the total purchases account provides one illustration of a control account – in this case a control account for purchases. The more usual control account is for the personal accounts, and it is preferable to have at least two, one for debtors and the other for creditors.

If a Creditors Control Account had been used, the entries made in it for the transactions in the recent example would have been

Creditors Control Account

Dr.							Cr.
Date	*Details*	*P.J. Fo.*	*Amount*	*Date*	*Details*	*P.R.J. Fo.*	*Amount*
19x1			£	19x1			£
Mar. 31	Purchases returns and allowances for the month	1	48.30	Mar. 31	Goods supplied for the month, and VAT thereon	1	2992.30

and separate subsidiary records would be kept to show the position of each individual supplier. The net balance on the creditors control account (£2992.30 minus £48.30, i.e. £2944.00) should equal the sum of the balances on the individual suppliers accounts.

					£
	R. Ridgwell			Cr.	330.05
	B. Davis			Cr.	1512.25
	General Supplies Ltd			Cr.	1150.00
					2992.30
minus	W. Hunt	Dr.	13.80		
	V. Luxton	Dr.	34.50		
					48.30
					£2944.00

With opening balances and more entries, as is usual in practice, the benefits from the use of the control account became more apparent.

Value Added Tax

Question What is VAT?

Answer Many countries have introduced a tax calculated as a percentage of the sales of the business. In Britain this is known as the Value Added Tax (VAT) and the appropriate percentage (currently 15%, originally 10%) on the value of sales has to be accounted for to the Customs and Excise. As allowance is given for VAT paid on purchases, a business in effect pays over the VAT on the value added by the business and recovers it from the customer. The balance of VAT charged to customers over the VAT suffered on purchases must be handed over to the Commissioners of Customs and Excise. On the other hand, if the tax suffered by him exceeds that which he has charged, repayment is due. Only registered traders are affected by this tax. Any trader may register. He is not obliged to register unless his turnover exceeds £18700 per annum. A person not registered cannot charge VAT nor can he recover VAT suffered on his purchases.

Question What extra records does the business have to keep?

Answer The business with proper records will require very little extra; another column in the Purchase and Sales Day Books and an additional nominal ledger account is all that is necessary. The example in this chapter illustrated the book-keeping requirements.

Question This seems to be a simple procedure. Why do some businessmen complain about the complexity of VAT?

Answer The book-keeping is straightforward. The difficulties arise because certain goods and services are exempt, others are zero rated.

Question Where should a trader go for advice?

Answer The local officer of the Customs and Excise or his accounting advisor should be consulted for the precise details applicable to a particular enterprise.

Exemption

Exemption for a transaction means that no liability to account for tax to the tax authorities arises when the transaction is performed.

Equally, the trader undertaking the exempt transaction is given no credit by the tax authorities for any tax invoiced to him by his suppliers, or paid at importation, in respect of the goods and services he uses for his exempt business. The operation of the credit mechanism throughout a chain of transactions is thereby interrupted.

Zero rating

Zero rating a transaction means that it is brought within the scope of the tax, but the rate applied to output is zero. If the person carrying out the transaction is a taxable person he is accountable in the usual way; but the result is that his outputs carry no tax because a zero rate is applied to them, while he is allowed credit for or repayment of tax on his inputs. Exports are relieved from tax by means of this technique.

Questions

1 Name the different Ledgers employed in the ordinary trading concern, and mention the classes of account you would expect to find in each.

2 Explain carefully:
(*a*) Nominal Accounts.
(*b*) Real Accounts.
(*c*) Personal Accounts.

3 On which side of the following Ledger Accounts would you expect to find the balance? Give reasons for your answer in each case:
(*a*) Bad Debts Account.
(*b*) Plant and Machinery Account.
(*c*) Sales Account.
(*d*) Discount Account.
(*e*) Returns Outwards Account.

4 W. Green has the following transactions with J. Black:

19x1			£
July	10	Goods sold to W. Green	422.00
	15	Goods returned by W. Green	20.00
Oct.	10	Cheque received from W. Green	392.00
	10	Discount deducted	10.00
	11	W. Green charged with discount deducted in error	10.00

You are required to show how each of the foregoing items would be recorded in the books of J. Black.

5 Brown and Smith are two merchants. At 1 January 19x2, Smith owes Brown £146.40 and during the month of January the following transactions took place between them:

19x2			£
Jan.	5	Brown purchased goods from Smith	126.21
	12	Smith sends goods to Brown	50.09
	15	Brown pays cash to Smith	95.00
		Smith allows discount	5.00
	20	Smith allows Brown's claim for damaged goods	10.00
	24	Smith sells to Brown goods	131.33
	30	Brown borrows from Smith for temporary accommodation	50.00

You are required:
(*a*) To give the account of Brown in the Ledger of Smith, and
(*b*) To bring down the balance at the end of January 19x2, and
(*c*) To state which party is indebted to the other.

6 From the following particulars, draw up the Capital Account of J. Owen as it would appear in his books for the year 19x3. Balance it off as on 31 December 19x3, and bring down the balance:

	£
Capital as 1 January 19x3	4416.25
Profit for the year 19x3 was	3314.27
On 15 October J. Owen paid in additional capital	1500.00
During the year J. Owen drew out of the business for private expenses	2250.00
On 31 December 19x3, interest on capital was allowed	522.00

7 (*a*) Make entries to record the following:

19x5
Jan. 5 Purchase of goods from B. & Co., £300
Feb. 5 Payment by cheque to B. & Co., *less* 5% cash discount.

(*b*) On 20 February 19x5, it was discovered that bank charges under date of 31 December 19x4, amounting to £5.25, had not been recorded. Adjust.

(*c*) On 31 December 19x4, the balance on Motor Vans Account was £12000, representing an Élite lorry. A new Élite lorry was purchased for cash on 31 March 19x5, for £25000, and £7500 was allowed in part exchange for the old lorry, the cash passing being £17500. Make the appropriate entries to record and dispose of the matter. (Assume no VAT.)

8 In what Ledger or other accounts, and upon which side of such accounts, would you expect to find the following:
(*a*) £500 paid for new machinery.
(*b*) £170 received from J. Robinson in full settlement of his account of £172.60.

(*c*) £600 received from an Insurance Company in settlement of a claim for damages to premises by fire.
(*d*) £750 received for the sale of old motor van.
(*e*) £250 paid to J. Fitter in full settlement of an account due to him three months hence of £260.75.

9 The following sales have been made by Sevenoaks Trading during the month of July 19x1. The values represent the value of the goods, before adding VAT at 15%.

19x1			
July	1	to High Rise	£120
	5	to Brown & Co.	£70
	10	to Carter Brothers	£240
	12	to Singh & Co.	£160
	31	to Jones Ltd	£190

You are required to enter these transactions in the Sales Day Book, Sales Ledger and Nominal Ledger.

10 The credit sales and purchases for the month of October 19x1 for Teachers & Co. are shown below exclusive of VAT.

19x1			
Oct.	1	Bought from Kent Traders	£170
	3	Bought from Canterbury Ltd	£360
	5	Sold to Davenport & Co.	£250
	10	Sold to East Ltd	£120
	12	Bought from Canterbury Ltd	£420
	31	Sold to Davenport & Co.	£460

You are required to enter these transactions in the appropriate records of the company assuming that Teachers & Co. are (*a*) not registered for VAT; (*b*) registered for VAT.

11 The following transactions relate to November 19x1.

19x1			£
Nov.	1	Sales Ledger balances	3276
	30	Totals for the month:	
		Sales Day Book	4347
		Sales returns and allowances	265
		Cheques received from customers	1984
		Discounts allowed	29
	30	Total of individual Sales Ledger balances	5345

You are required to write up the Sales Ledger control account.

4

Cash Transactions

Question From what you have been saying about the accounts in the various Ledgers, am I correct in thinking that all they show at the moment are balances in respect of Trading Transactions?

Answer Yes, in respect of Purchases and Sales on Credit Terms. What we now have to do is to consider the Receipt and Payment of *Cash* by the business, usually at the end of the period of credit allowed to or by it.

Question You said at an earlier stage that some portion of the Capital with which the business was begun must necessarily be in the form of Cash. That would be in order to pay its running expenses?

Answer Not only such expenses as Wages and Salaries, but also to pay suppliers who might at the outset be unwilling to give credit to a new business.

Question Would it be right to describe such Cash as the **Working Capital** employed?

Answer It forms a part, but by no means the whole, of the Working Capital, as we shall see later. A better definition would be that it is a **Liquid Asset**, and its subsequent use for the purposes of the business may result in its becoming a **Current Asset**, as when goods are bought for stock, or a **Fixed Asset**, when Plant, Fittings, etc., are purchased.

Question In the case of goods in which the business dealt, you said these were entrusted to the warehouse manager, who was responsible for their receipt and issue. Is the cashier similarly responsible for the Cash Assets?

Answer No, only for what is termed **Cash in Hand**; this, however, is negligible in amount as compared with the moneys lying in the Bank Account of the business, or **Cash at Bank**. Between the two, there is this difference; the *Cashier*, as a servant of the business, will always be, on balance, accountable to it for cash held by him. The *Bank*, on the other hand, may sometimes be the creditor of the business, as where moneys are advanced on loan or by way of overdraft.

Many business transactions take place by the use of cash in the form of coin and notes. Others, including most large transactions, use cheques. There are clearly differences between cash and cheques but there are also similarities in the book-keeping entries when purchases or sales are settled. Instead of using separate cash-received and cheques-received books and ledger accounts, one is used for all receipts (and payments) except when a cash fund is used for small payments under the control of a particular person.

Office procedure on receipt of cash

On the opening of each day's incoming mail, all remittances from customers will be passed on to the cashier. They will usually be accompanied by the statements of accounts which the business has issued at monthly intervals to its customers.

The cashier will:

(*a*) Compare the amount remitted with the total of the statement and, at the same time, check the *Cash Discount* which the customer may have deducted.

(*b*) **Cash Discount** is the inducement offered by the business to its customers to pay within the recognised period of credit. As such it is an expense to the business, which must always be taken into account with the accompanying remittance. If the terms upon which business is done are '2½% monthly account', and the customer's debt is £100, then *if he pays on or before the end of the month following delivery of the goods to him,* he need remit £97.50 only. On the other hand, if he pays after the expiry of the credit period, the discount will not ordinarily be allowed.

To the extent that Cash Discount refers to the customers of the business, it is termed **Discount Allowed**, and it differs from *Trade Discount*, which we discussed on page 12, in that it always relates to the cash or financial aspect of each transaction. Looked at in another way, it assists the business in collecting what is due to it from its customers.

The cashier will also:

(*c*) So far as cheques are received, cross these, if they are uncrossed, or if already crossed, insert the name of the bankers of the business who are, of course, the collecting bankers.

(*d*) Enter the remittances in detail in either a rough cash diary or Journal, as a preliminary to entry in the Cash Book proper, or enter them at once in the Cash Book. Whichever alternative is adopted, such initial entry is a **Prime** or **First** entry, and therefore corresponds to the record of Purchases or Sales in the Purchase and Sales Journals.

(*e*) List the remittances on the counterfoil of the bank paying-in book, so that the total thereof is in agreement with the total of the entries for the particular business day appearing in the Cash Book of the business. Thus, the amount actually banked will agree with the business records.

(*f*) Make out, in the name of each customer, formal receipts, which may be attached to the statements of account and then issued to the customers for retention by them. (In some businesses it is no longer usual to issue receipts for cheque payments.)

The Cash Book or Cash Journal will then be available for the ledger clerks, whose duty it will be to post the amount of each remittance *to the credit of the Ledger Account of the customer from whom it was received*.

Book-keeping entries: Cash receipts

We can best approach these by considering the cashier as being very much in the same position as the warehouseman, with the difference that he is responsible for **cash** instead of **goods**.

If, therefore, we apply the same reasoning to his responsibility as a servant of the business we shall charge him with *all incoming cash*.

It is logical to do this, so that he may at any time be accountable for its safe custody and disposal.

Using a term with which we have now become familiar, the cashier will be *debited* with all moneys received and, as was indicated above, each of the customers will be *credited*, the latter having performed a 'credit-worthy' action in paying to the business what is due by them.

We may, therefore, if we so desire, as is often done in practice, commence our records by opening a **Cash Received Journal**, or **Cash Received Book**, in which all moneys received from customers, whether in the form of cheques, notes, coin, etc., will be entered. Bearing in mind the fact that in many cases Cash Discount has been allowed to the customers, it will be helpful to show the amount of the discount *by the side of* the item to which it relates, as follows:

Cash Received Journal

Date	*Customer*	*Total*	*Discount*	*Cash*
19x1		£	£	£
Feb. 20	G. Green	100.00	2.50	97.50

From this it is apparent that G. Green has now settled his debt of £100, and in collecting its due from him, the business has been obliged to incur an expense of £2.50 which, clearly, must reduce the figure of profit it expects to make.

Like the Purchase and Sales Journals, the Cash Book will probably be ruled off and totalled at the end of each month, with the result that, as with our Purchase and Sales transactions, we shall find it desirable:

(*a*) To give *credit* to *each customer* immediately on receipt of his separate remittance.

(*b*) To *debit* or charge the *cashier* in total with the cash receipts, irrespective of the individual details making up the total.

The Cash Received Journal enables us to do this, and at the same time to comply with *double entry principles*, as the following diagram shows:

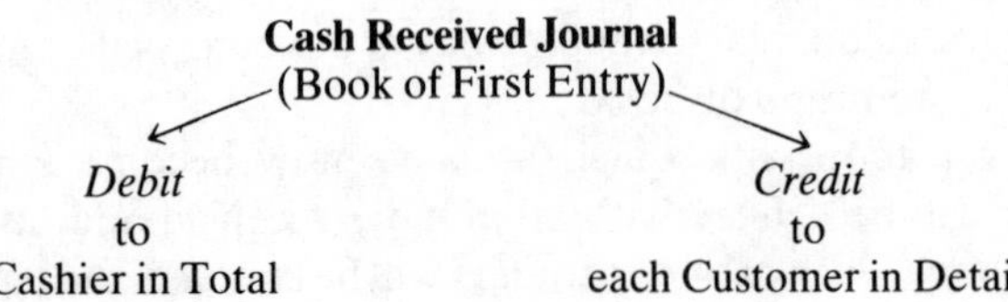

or in account form:

Fo. 1

Cash Received Journal

Date	*Customer*	*Total*	*Discount*	*Cash*
19x1		£	£	£
Feb. 20	G. Green	100.00	2.50	97.50
22	B. Brown	50.00	—	50.00
		£150.00	£2.50	£147.50

Sales Ledger

G. GREEN

Dr. / Cr.

Date	*Details*	*Fo.*	*Amount*	*Date*	*Details*	*C.R.J. Fo.*	*Amount*
				19x1			£
				Feb. 20	Cash	1	97.50
					Discount	1	2.50
							£100.00

B. BROWN

Dr. / Cr.

Date	*Details*	*Fo.*	*Amount*	*Date*	*Details*	*C.R.J. Fo.*	*Amount*
				19x1			£
				Feb. 22	Cash	1	50.00

Private Ledger

CASH

Dr. / Cr.

Date	*Details*	*C.R.J. Fo.*	*Amount*	*Date*	*Details*	*Fo.*	*Amount*
19x1			£				
Feb. 28	Total cash	1	147.50				

In the above, we note firstly that the *Cash Account* appears in the *Private Ledger*. This is as we should expect because the Private Ledger is concerned with Assets and Liabilities, and Cash Received is manifestly an Asset.

Secondly, we note that, while our aim is to complete the Double Entry *within the Ledgers*, the sum of the two credit balances on the accounts of Green and Brown is £150, whereas we have a debit balance on Cash Account of £147.50 only.

That is to say, so far as *discount allowed* is concerned, we have given credit to G. Green personally *in the Ledger* for that amount, but we have not impersonally noted its effect upon the business. The business must be charged with that amount as an expense or loss resulting from its dealings with Green, and it is therefore necessary to open in the Impersonal Ledger an account for discount allowed.

DISCOUNT ALLOWED

Dr. Cr.

Date	*Details*	*C.R.J. Fo.*	*Amount*	*Date*	*Details*	*Fo.*	*Amount*
19x1			£				
Feb. 28	Total discount	1	2.50				

Arising from this we see that:

(*a*) The double entry is completed within the Ledgers.

(*b*) A Debit Balance in an Impersonal Ledger Account, e.g. Discount, is a business *expense*, and a debit balance on a Private Ledger Account is for our present purpose an Asset of the business.

(*c*) Any Debit Balances formerly appearing on the accounts of Green and Brown in the Sales Ledger will have been extinguished by the posting to their credit of the cash now received.

Office procedure on payment of cash

Periodically, say at monthly intervals, the business will pay its *suppliers* for what has been purchased from them. At the end of each month a statement of account may have been received from them setting out the balance in their favour. This will be compared with the total standing to their credit in the various Purchase Ledger Accounts. Care will be taken to deduct, if omitted in the statement, the value of any goods returned to them by the business, and similarly a deduction will be made for Cash Discount, discount which in this instance we may rightly term **discount received**, or **receivable**, considering it, that is, from the standpoint of the business.

Thus on or before the end of the month following delivery of the goods a list will be prepared for all *accounts payable*, setting out:

(*a*) The folio of the supplier's account in the Purchase Ledger,
(*b*) The name of the supplier,
(*c*) The total amount due,
(*d*) The amount of the discount, and
(*e*) The sum now payable.

This list, together with the Statement of Account received from the suppliers, will be submitted to the proprietor, or to some responsible official of the business, by whom the cheques issued in settlement will be signed.

Book-keeping entries: Cash payments

When the warehouseman issued goods to customers, it was seen at an earlier stage that he would be given credit for their value at *selling price*, the credit being given in 'Goods Sold' or *Sales* Account.

With the *payment* of cash, we have likewise to give *credit* to the cashier, which is only logical, having charged or *debited* him with cash *received*.

We shall, at the same time, *debit* the cash payment to each of the suppliers, thus offsetting the amounts for which they appear as *creditors*, and indicating that the liability of the business to them is now discharged.

For this purpose, a *Cash Paid Journal*, or *Cash Paid Book*, may be opened, as a Book of First Entry, ruled with columns for discount and the actual cash paid.

Cash Paid Journal

Date	*Supplier*	*Total*	*Discount*	*Cash*
19x1		£	£	£
Feb. 23	L. Lindsay	30.00	0.75	29.25

The record shown above indicates that a liability to L. Lindsay of £30 has been satisfied by a cash payment of £29.25 and that a **profit** of £0.75 has been earned.

The Cash Paid Journal enables us to:

(*a*) Charge or *debit each supplier* immediately on payment of money to him.
(*b*) *Credit the cashier* in total with the total cash payments, irrespective of the individual details.

This may be put in another way:

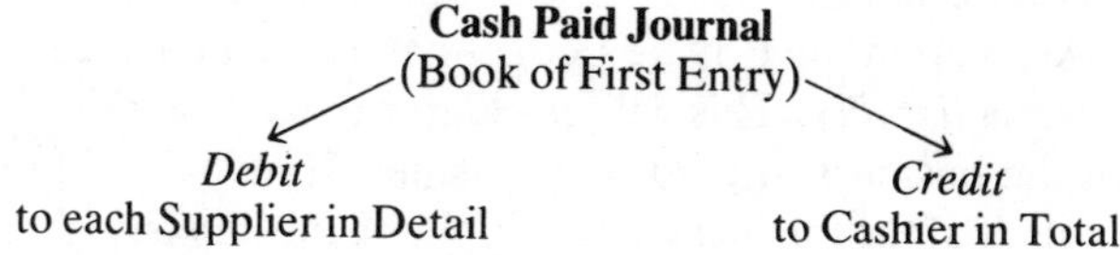

or in account form:

Cash Paid Journal

Fo. 2

Date	*Supplier*	*Total*	*Discount*	*Cash*
19x1		£	£	£
Feb. 23	L. Lindsay	30.00	0.75	29.25
26	M. Morris	60.00	1.50	58.50
		£90.00	£2.25	£87.75

Purchase Ledger

L. LINDSAY

Dr. Cr.

Date	*Details*	*C.P.J. Fo.*	*Amount*	*Date*	*Details*	*Fo.*	*Amount*
19x1			£				
Feb. 23	Cash	2	29.25				
	Discount	2	0.75				
			£30.00				

M. MORRIS

Dr. Cr.

Date	*Details*	*C.P.J. Fo.*	*Amount*	*Date*	*Details*	*Fo.*	*Amount*
19x1			£				
Feb. 26	Cash	2	58.50				
	Discount	2	1.50				
			£60.00				

Private Ledger

CASH

Dr.							Cr.
Date	*Details*	*Fo.*	*Amount*	*Date*	*Details*	*C.P.J. Fo.*	*Amount*
				19x1			£
				Feb. 28	Total cash	2	87.75

As the counterpart of cash received, but in the reverse direction, the Cash Account in the Private Ledger has a credit balance, which here denotes a *liability*. This will be clearer to us if we think of the banker of the business instead of its cashier. If he has paid money away on behalf of the business to its suppliers, the banker will have a claim upon it to that extent, and this claim is, of course, a liability of the business.

So far as the balances on the Ledger Accounts are concerned, the sum of the *debits* in the Purchase Ledger is seen to be £90, while the *credit* on Cash Account is £87.75.

The impersonal aspect of discount received, or discount earned, is that a profit of £2.25 has been made for which credit may be taken. We may therefore open, again in the Impersonal Ledger, the following account:

DISCOUNT RECEIVED

Dr.							Cr.
Date	*Details*	*Fo.*	*Amount*	*Date*	*Details*	*C.P.J. Fo.*	*Amount*
				19x1			£
				Feb. 28	Total discount	2	2.25

Once more, the double entry is completed *within the Ledgers*, and we see that a credit balance on an Impersonal Ledger Account is a business *profit*, a similar balance on a Private Ledger Account being a *liability* of the business.

Goods and cash compared

1 When *goods* are bought, Purchases Account is debited and the individual suppliers credited; when goods are sold, the individual customers are debited, and Sales Account is credited.

In the Impersonal Ledger there are thus two accounts in respect of the trading transactions, purchases and sales.

But in our *cash* dealings, recorded in total in the Private Ledger, we have *only one cash account*, debited as regards cash received and credited with cash paid.

2 Goods purchased will be valued at *cost price* per unit, but goods sold at *selling price*. Moreover, in a manufacturing business at least, goods purchased may largely consist of raw materials, while goods sold will be the finished product – an essentially different article. With cash, however, whether it be cash received or cash paid, the value per unit is the same in a country having a stable currency.

For these reasons, we are able to **merge** our cash received and our cash paid **in one account** only, or by using the figures given above:

CASH

Dr. Cr.

Date	*Details*	*C.R.J. Fo.*	*Amount*	*Date*	*Details*	*C.P.J. Fo.*	*Amount*
19x1			£	19x1			£
Feb. 28	Total cash	1	147.50	Feb. 28	Total cash	2	87.25

It is clear that the excess of the debit side, or £60.25, represents an *asset* of the business, while if the larger amount appeared on the credit side, it would be a *liability*.

From this we may draw three conclusions:

(*a*) That instead of having two Books of First Entry, a Cash Received Journal and a Cash Paid Journal, *one book* will suffice, and we may call it the Cash Journal, or as is more usual the **Cash Book**.

(*b*) That if such is the case the Ledger Account for cash can be dispensed with, and because it contains all our cash receipts and payments, *the Cash Book is not only a Book of Prime Entry, but is also a Ledger Account*, in that,

(*c*) Whether the cashier or the banker is entrusted with the cash resources, *the position of the business in relation to either* can quickly be seen from a perusal of the Cash Book.

Proceeding on the basis that incoming cash remittances are banked intact on the day of receipt, and all payments are made by cheque, writing up the Cash Book daily as Book of First Entry is equivalent to writing up the Ledger Account with the bank.

If, however, a minimum amount of cash must be retained by the business in order to pay petty expenses, and if, also, wages and salaries have to be paid in cash and not by cheque, it is necessary to provide *additional columns* in the Cash Book to record purely cash, as distinct from banking transactions.

We may now take an example to make this clear:

Example 4.1

From the following particulars, draw up the three-column Cash Book of V. Treat. No posting to the Ledger is required and no money is to be paid into the bank unless and until instructions are given.

19x1

Jan. 1 Commenced business with cash in hand £210 and a balance at the bank of £175.

2 Paid into bank out of office cash £150.

3 Cash sales £336.

4 Drew cheque £70 for private use; paid Wages by cash £260.

5 Paid Rent by cheque £220.

6 Paid into bank additional capital £1000.

8 Received a cheque from Light Bros. £240 in settlement of their account of £250.

9 Paid Brown & Sons cheque for £480, receiving discount £20.

Jan. 10 Received a cheque from Bilton Ltd, value £140, in settlement of their account £145.

11 Drew cheque £120 for cash for office use.

12 Paid into bank the two cheques received from Light Bros. and Bilton Ltd, respectively.

13 Paid Jennens Ltd, cheque £190, having deducted discount 5% from their account.

16 Light Bros. cheque was returned by the bank marked R/D.

18 Paid wages by cash £230.

31 Bank charges for the month £15.

Balance off the Cash Book and bring down the balances as on 31 January 19x1.

V. TREAT

Cash Book

Dr. Date		Fo.	Discount	Cash	Bank	Cr. Date		Fo.	Discount	Cash	Bank
19x1						19x1					
Jan. 1	Capital A/c			210.00	175.00	Jan. 2	Bank			150.00	
2	Cash				150.00	4	Drawings				70.00
3	Cash Sales			336.00		4	Wages			260.00	
6	Capital A/c				1000.00	5	Rent				220.00
8	Light Bros.		10.00	240.00		9	Brown and Sons		20.00		480.00
10	Bilton Ltd		5.00	140.00		11	Cash				120.00
11	Bank			120.00		12	Bank, cheques from Light Bros. and Bilton Ltd			380.00	
12	Cash, cheques per contra				380.00	13	Jennens Ltd		10.00		190.00
16	Light Bros. discount charged		(10.00)*			16	Light Bros. cheque returned				240.00
						18	Wages			230.00	
						31	Interest and bank charges				15.00
						31	Balances c/d			26.00	370.00
			£5.00	£1046.00	£1705.00				£30.00	£1046.00	£1705.00
19x1											
Feb. 1	Balances b/d			26.00	370.00						

* When Light Bros.' cheque is returned the discount previously allowed to him must be *deducted* from discounts allowed and *debited* to his account.

If we look more closely at this example, we shall see that provision is made in the columns headed 'Cash' and 'Bank' respectively for a statement at any time of the position of the business as regards:

(*a*) its cashier, and
(*b*) its banker.

At the beginning of the month the proprietor introduced as Cash Capital £385, divided as shown, and the description of the item 'Capital A/c' indicates that that is the Account in the Ledger which is to be credited.

In addition, during the month, as we should expect, cheques are drawn on the Bank Account in order to replenish the moneys in the hands of the cashier. It should not be difficult for us to realise what happens in this case. Firstly, the bank pays out money, and thereby reduces its accountability to the proprietor of the business. For this it must be **credited**, but, simultaneously, the accountability of the **cashier** is increased, and so, on the left hand, or debit side of the Cash Book we enter the amount of £120 in the **cash** column.

Secondly, in our wording of the items in the Cash Book, we must be careful to choose words which will indicate at once *where the corresponding (debit or credit) entry is to be found*. For example, on 2 January, when money is paid *from cash* into the bank, we say on the *credit side*, 'Bank,' indicating that the bank column is to be charged with the amount.

Thirdly, when a cheque received from a customer is returned by the bank marked R/D (refer to drawer, or Light Bros.) we must bring the Cash Book into line with the bank's own view of the position, and having *charged* the bank with £240 on 12 January now give them credit on 16 January. We thus cancel the original charge to the bank and, *to complete the double entry within the Ledgers*, post the amount to the *debit* of Light Bros.' Account, thereby reviving the original debt due from them. Their position is thus what it was before the worthless cheque was received.

Fourthly, we see that columns are provided in which to record cash discount *allowed* and *received*. When the cheque from Light Bros. was first received on 8 January, £10 was allowed to them as discount, the *total* due by them being £250. But as their cheque is returned on 16 January it is not enough merely to credit the bank with the amount of the *cheque*; we must in addition write back to

Light Bros. the discount which was, of course, only allowed by the business in the belief that the cheque was good. It is this third column for discount which led to the use of the phrase 'three-column cash book'.

And lastly, credit is given to the bank for charges made by them for the month. They will, *in their own books*, have debited the business with this sum, and in order that the two sets of records shall be in agreement, this entry must be made.

In the result, and on 31 January, balances can be inserted on the *credit side* of the Cash Book (representing the amount by which the debit side exceeds the credit side) and *brought down* on 1 February, as the *opening balances* for the new period. The balances, it will be noted, are in both cases *debit balances*, indicating the existence of an Asset in the form of:

(*a*) Cash in hand £26.00, and
(*b*) Cash or Balance at bank £370.00.

Before we pass from this example let us look at the Discount Allowed and Discount Received Accounts in the Impersonal Ledger.

DISCOUNT ALLOWED

Dr. Cr.

Date	*Details*	*Fo.*	*Amount*	*Date*	*Details*	*Fo.*	*Amount*
19x1			£				
Jan. 31	Total for month		5.00				

DISCOUNT RECEIVED

Dr. Cr.

Date	*Details*	*Fo.*	*Amount*	*Date*	*Details*	*Fo.*	*Amount*
				19x1			£
				Jan. 31	Total for month		30.00

To deal with the former, we notice that while both the cheques received from *and* the discount allowed to Light Bros. and Bilton Ltd appear on the *debit* side of the Cash Book, these customers will each receive *credit* for the **total** in their respective Ledger Accounts. But only the amount of the *actual money* they pay is debited in the cash and bank columns. Accordingly, to complete the double entry, we must have in the Impersonal Ledger an account for *discounts* *allowed*, in which the further debit required will be shown, *and correspondingly for discounts received.*

Let us take one other example:

Example 4.2

John Smith, a merchant, does not pay all cash received into his bank. He desires to record all cash received and paid and all his bank transactions in one Cash Book. His transactions during the first few days of January 19x2 were as below:

19x2			£
Jan.	1	Cash in hand	150
		Bank overdraft	72
		Received cash from A.B. (after allowing him discount £10)	150
	2	Paid into bank	245
	3	Drew cheque for C.D. (after deducting discount £3)	27
	4	Received cheque from E.F. (after allowing him discount £30) and paid it into bank	270
	5	Drew from bank in cash	20
		Paid wages (on presentation of an open cheque at bank)	80
	7	E.F.'s cheque returned by bank, dishonoured.	
	8	Received cash from G.H. (after allowing discount £2)	48
	9	Paid into bank	25
	10	Paid cash to J.K. (after deducting discount £4)	36

You are required (*a*) to record these transactions in a suitable form of Cash Book; (*b*) to rule off and balance the book; (*c*) to state clearly how the discounts are dealt with in the Ledger. (Prepare your own record and then compare it with the printed solution.)

JOHN SMITH

Cash Book

Dr. | January 19x2 Cr.

Date	*Receipts*	*Discount*	*Cash*	*Bank*	*Date*	*Payments*	*Discount*	*Cash*	*Bank*
19x2					19x2				
Jan. 1	Balance b/d		150.00		Jan. 1	Balance b/d			72.00
1	A.B.	10.00	150.00		2	Bank		245.00	
2	Cash			245.00	3	C.D.	3.00		27.00
4	E.F.	30.00		270.00	5	Cash			20.00
5	Bank		20.00		5	Wages			80.00
7	E.F. discount not allowed	(30.00)*			7	E.F. cheque returned			270.00
8	G.H.	2.00	48.00		9	Bank		25.00	
9	Cash			25.00	10	J.K.	4.00	36.00	
					11	Balances c/d		62.00	71.00
		£12.00	£368.00	£540.00			£7.00	£368.00	£540.00
19x2									
Jan. 12	Balance b/d	↓ Debited to 'Discount Allowed' Account	62.00	71.00			↓ Credited to 'Discount Received' Account		

* When E.F.'s cheque is returned, the discount previously allowed to him, £30, must be recharged to him. It is therefore *deducted* in the discounts allowed column and *debited* to E.F.'s account.

Cash Book postings to Ledger Accounts

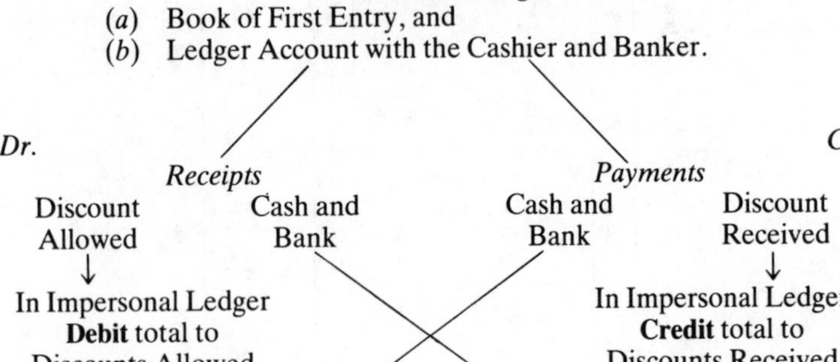

(*a*) In Purchase Ledger **debit** to individual suppliers total of cash and discount.
(*b*) In Impersonal Ledger **debit** to Wages, Cash Purchases or other Expense Accounts.
(*c*) In Private Ledger **debit** to Asset Accounts (if purchased) or Liability Accounts if paid off or reduced.

(*a*) In Sales Ledger **credit** to individual customers total of cash and discount.
(*b*) In Impersonal Ledger **credit** to Bank Interest Received, Cash Sales, or other Income Accounts.
(*c*) In Private Ledger **credit** to Asset Accounts (if sold) or Liability Accounts if, e.g. money borrowed, or new capital introduced.

Questions

1 Say what benefits a trader will derive from his having an account at a bank, and explain how he would open the account.

2 Define trade discount and cash discount. State clearly how these are treated in books of account.

3 What is a cheque? What is the effect of crossing it? How many parties are there to a cheque?

4 A trader receives an account from X.Y., his landlord, for £75 in respect of one month's rent, which he pays on the date of receipt.

Explain the different ways which might be adopted to record this item in books kept on the Double Entry System.

Note. These questions relate to the recording of cash and do not require the consideration of VAT related entries.

5 From the following particulars write up A. Bondman's Cash Book for the week commencing 5 July 19x1 and balance the Cash Book as at 10 July 19x1:

July 5 Cash in hand £15.50, and in bank £176.
5 Paid by cheque to F. Abbott his account of £47, less 5% cash discount.
6 Paid in cash, postage stamps £2.75.
7 Purchased goods for cheque £10.50.
Received cheque from R. Beal in payment of his account of £40, less 2½% cash discount, and paid the cheque into bank.
8 Purchased for cheque office desk £30.
10 Paid wages in cash £120.
Cash sales for week £150.75.
Withdrew from bank for office purposes £20.
Withdrew from bank for self £15.

Post the items in your Cash Book to the Ledger.

6 Leslie Morris commences business on 1 January 19x1. Record in a suitable ruled Cash Book the following transactions for the first week of January 19x1 and bring down the balances on 7 January:

19x1				£
Jan.	1	L. Morris paid into bank on account of Capital		700.00
	2	Received and paid into bank direct the following:		
		Jones (after allowing discount £5)		45.00
		Wilson (after allowing discount £0.50)		12.50
		Graham (after allowing discount £0.75)		15.00
	2	Draw cheque for office cash		40.00
	4	Wilson's cheque returned by bank unpaid.		
	5	Drew cheque for		330.00
		Covering Wages	£200.00	
		Salaries	130.00	
	5	Bought goods for cash		25.00
	6	Received the following (in notes):		
		Peters, covering goods	£250.00	
		Rent receivable	10.00	
		Sanders (after allowing discount £1)	60.00	
				320.00
	6	Paid cash into bank		300.00
	7	Paid by cheque:		
		Lister (after deducting discount £0.50)		19.50
		White (after deducting discount £1.50)		58.50

How would you deal with the totals of the columns Discounts Allowed, and Discounts Received, when the Cash Book is ruled off on 7 January 19x1.

7 On 20 June 19x1, H. Rivers received from S. Wells an invoice for £514. Of this amount £510 represented the cost of goods purchased and £4 the carriage thereon.

On 30 June 19x1, H. Rivers returned to S. Wells goods to the value of £60.

After the invoice had been entered in the books, it was discovered that a trade discount of 20% had not been deducted from the cost or from the item relating to goods returned and an adjusting entry was made to correct these mistakes.

The account was paid by cheque on 31 July 19x1, less 2½% discount.

You are required to show the entries in the respective books of account of H. Rivers to record the foregoing transactions.

8 From the following particulars write up the Cash Book of Thomas Mixture for the month of January 19x2, and bring down the balances at the end of the month. It is not Mr. Mixture's rule to bank all cash and make all payments by cheque.

19x2			£
Jan.	1	Cash in hand	18.00
	1	Balance overdrawn at bank	36.75
	2	Received cash sales	242.50
	4	Banked cash	115.00
	4	Paid Jackson & Co. by cheque	14.25
	5	Received Jones' cheque (direct to bank)	14.50
	6	Paid salaries in cash	134.75
	7	Bought goods for cash (paid from office cash)	11.00
	8	Drew office cash from bank	16.00
	9	Received cash sales	225.00
	13	Paid salaries in cash	133.50
	16	Received Smith's cheque direct to bank	56.75
	20	Paid Brown by cheque	16.00
	20	Received from Jones in coin and notes	55.50
	20	Paid salaries in cash	134.75
	23	Drew office cash from bank	135.00
	26	Received Jones' cheque (direct to bank)	17.50
	27	Paid salaries in cash	134.75
	27	Paid office cash into bank	20.00
	28	Jones' cheque returned by bank unpaid	17.50

9 The Cash Book of Thomas Jones for the first week of January 19x1 is as follows:

19x1		Discount £	Bank £	19x1		Discount £	Bank £
Jan. 1	Balance		752.00	Jan. 3	Wages		159.00
2	Sundry customers:			5	Sundry suppliers:		
	L. Smith	1.00	39.00		G. Green	3.00	57.00
	V. Latham	4.00	76.00		T. Robson	2.00	78.00
4	Rents receivable		117.00	5	V. Latham cheque returned		76.00
6	Plant A/c (machine tool sold)		26.00	6	Cash purchases		18.00
		£5.00	£1010.00			£5.00	£388.00

You are required:

(*a*) To indicate to which Ledger each entry in the above Cash Book would be posted.

(*b*) To make the Cash postings in such Ledger Accounts, including the Discount Account.

10 From the following particulars you are required to write up the three-column Cash Book of K. Walker. No posting to the Ledger is required:

19x1

Mar. 1 Cash in hand £246.50.
1 Overdrawn at bank £93.60.
2 Paid into bank £30.00.
3 Paid wages by cash £141.50.
4 Received cheque from R. Francis value £35.75 in settlement of an amount owing £37.00.
4 Cash sales £153.60.
4 Received a cheque from M. Scott £23.75, and allowed him discount £0.75.
5 Paid S. Marsh by cheque the balance of his account £34.00, less 5% discount.
5 Cash purchases £33.00.
6 Paid cheques from R. Francis and M. Scott into the bank.
8 K. Walker paid into the bank additional capital £240.00.
9 Drew cheque £36.00 for office use.
10 Paid L. Hopecraft cheque £18.80, being allowed discount £0.80.
10 Paid wages by cash £90.60.
10 M. Scott's cheque was returned by the bank marked R/D.
11 Drew cheque £15.00 for private use.
11 Bought plant and machinery £370.00 and paid the amount by cheque.
12 Paid sundry small expenses by cash £16.40.
31 Bank charges £7.20.

Balance the Cash Book as on 31 March and bring down the balances.

5

The Bank Reconciliation

It is the practice of banks to render periodically to their customers, whether they are business houses or private individuals, a statement of their position in relation to the bank. This statement is a copy of the customer's account in the bank's Ledger, and usually will be rendered from the bank's standpoint. That is to say, moneys paid in, or *lodgments* by the customer will be put to his credit, and moneys withdrawn by cheque will be debited to him. Thus, at any time, there will be a balance either in favour of or against the customer.

Before the use of book-keeping machines and computers became general, *Bank Pass Books* were issued to all new customers, the items in which were written up by the bank for the customer to compare with the bank columns in his own Cash Book. He could thus satisfy himself that:

(*a*) The bank had given him credit for all moneys which he had debited to it in his Cash Book.
(*b*) Similarly, when the bank *debited him* with paid cheques, he could see that the name of the payee and the amount for which the cheque had been drawn were also in agreement with the *credit* side of his Cash Book.

At intervals it was, of course, necessary for the Pass Book to be returned to the bank in order to be written up to date.

In many cases today, however, the bank's statement is rendered in the form of *loose sheets*, which the customer can insert in a suitable cover or binder, so that he has a continuous record of the bank's version of the position between them.

We have seen elsewhere that it is the custom for suppliers of goods to the business to render statements of account which are valuable corroborative evidence of the accuracy of the Purchase Ledger Accounts.

This being the case, the importance of a similar statement as regards cash itself – the most liquid asset of the business – can readily be appreciated, more particularly if the bank is the *creditor* of the business, as on loan or overdraft account to which a limit has been set.

The occasions on which a bank makes a mistake in writing up the Pass Book or loose sheets are rare indeed, but we do not infrequently find that at times mistakes are made by the cashier in the Cash Book, and also in *omitting to record* some particular receipt or payment.

Many banks, to prevent lack of agreement between their own records and the Cash Books of their customers, print at the bottom of each Pass Book sheet:

> 'The items and balance shown on this statement should be verified and the bank notified promptly of any discrepancy.'

In ordinary business practice, it is the custom to rule off and balance the Cash Book at monthly intervals, bringing down the ascertained balance to the beginning of the new period. To the extent that it refers to the bank columns in the Cash Book, this balance represents:

either (*a*) Cash at bank (Dr.)
or (*b*) Bank overdraft (Cr.)

and as such will certainly be required for the information of the proprietor of the business, or of the Board of Directors in a Limited Company.

It will, therefore, be the cashier's duty to prepare at the end of each month what is termed a **bank reconciliation**, or **bank agreement**, attesting the accuracy and completeness of his Cash Book records. Some authorities suggest that the person responsible for preparing, or reviewing, this reconciliation should *not* be the cashier, but someone independent, who is not involved with the actual handling of cash or cheques.

In the affairs of a private individual, this reconciliation may be easily and quickly prepared; it may be the work of a few minutes only, but with a business house, where lodgments are being made daily throughout the month, and the number of cheques drawn by the business is very large, the labour involved may be much greater.

We must now consider the nature of the work to be done, bearing in mind that the **Pass Book** shows the position of the business *in the light of the information in the bank's possession*.

Supposing the reconciliation is to be prepared on 31 January, we may commence with the Pass Book balance at that date, using a sheet of cash-ruled paper which we can later file away for future reference. Our task is then to *reconcile* or *agree* this balance with the balance appearing in the Cash Book.

If, as is usually the case, there is a difference between the two balances, it may be due to:

(*a*) *Cheques drawn and issued by the business to its suppliers* and entered in the proper way on the credit side of the Cash Book, *but not yet presented* by the collecting banker for payment.

As the cheques so drawn have to be sent to suppliers, banked by them, and subsequently passed through the clearing, several days may elapse before they reach the paying bank. We must thus *deduct* from the Pass Book balance if favourable to the business, the amount of the unpresented cheques, or *add* if an overdraft exists. On the other hand, if we have begun by taking the Cash Book figure, we should add the amount to a debit balance, or deduct it from a credit balance.

(*b*) *Cheques paid in by the business* which on presentation to the paying bank are refused because of, e.g:

1 Lack of funds to meet them.
2 Countermand of instructions to pay by the Drawer.
3 Death of the Drawer.
4 Some irregularity on the face of the cheque, such as absence of Drawer's signature, inacceptable endorsement, etc.

In these cases, the collecting banker, having given credit when the cheque was lodged, will now *debit the account*, returning the unpaid cheque to the business. The latter will at once take up the matter with its own customer, and endeavour to obtain satisfaction.

In any event, as we saw on page 70, the cashier should credit the bank with the amount involved, i.e. enter it as though it were a payment on the credit side of the Cash Book. Should he have omitted to do this, for purposes of the reconciliation he must, if beginning with a favourable Pass Book balance, add the amount, or deduct it if unfavourable.

In beginning with the Cash Book, the reverse steps would of course be taken.

(*c*) 1 *Bank interest allowed.*

2 *Bank interest and commission charged.*

We have already explained these items as representing, so far as the business is concerned, either a *profit* or an *expense*.

The bank will enter them in its own account with the customer at half-yearly intervals, as on 30 June and 31 December, but does not usually give the customer a separate advice that it has done so. Accordingly, the latter may be altogether unaware of the items until he receives his Pass Book. The proper course is then to *debit* the Bank Column in the Cash Book with the interest allowed by the bank, or *credit* it with the interest and commission charged.

If this has not been done, we shall proceed as follows in preparing the Bank Reconciliation:

Interest Allowed

(*a*) *Commencing with the Pass Book balance.*
If 'in favour', deduct.
If overdrawn, add.

(*b*) *Commencing with Cash Book balance.*
If a debit balance, add.
If overdrawn, deduct.

The reverse, of course, applies with interest and commission charged, i.e.:

(*a*) *Commencing with Pass Book balance.*
If 'in favour', add.
If overdrawn, deduct.

(*b*) *Commencing with Cash Book balance.*
If a debit balance, deduct.
If overdrawn, add.

In making these adjustments, we must always remember the aim in view, which is *to link the Pass Book balance with the Cash Book balance*, or vice-versa. Whether we begin with the Pass Book or the

Cash Book does not affect the result, but the former may give the more reliable commencing figure, as it is so much less subject to the risk of error.

Example 5.1
The balance shown by the Bank Statement on 31 March 19x7, indicates an overdraft of £209.80, while, on the same date, the Bank Column in the Cash Book shows a credit balance of £419.00.

Comparing the two records, you find that two cheques drawn on 31 March, one for £204.00 and the other for £77.20, had not been presented for payment, while one of £72.00 paid into the bank on the same date had not yet been credited.

Prepare a Reconciliation Statement.

	£	£
Overdrawn per Pass Book		209.80
Add cheques drawn but unpresented:		
March 31	204.00	
,, 31	77.20	
		281.20
		491.00
Less cheque paid in but not yet credited by bank		72.00
Credit balance as per Cash Book		419.00

In this second illustration, we will begin instead with the balance according to the Cash Book.

Example 5.2
On 30 March 19x5, your Cash Book shows that you have in the bank the sum of £817.24.

On checking your Cash Book with the Bank Pass Book you find that cheques drawn by you amounting to £214.17 have not passed through the bank, that a cheque for £84.12 has not yet been credited to you, and that the bank has credited you with interest £22.07, and debited you with sundry charges £14.36. Draw up a reconciliation statement, showing adjustments between your Cash Book and Bank Pass Book.

	£
Balance in hand per Cash Book	817.24
Add cheques drawn but unpresented	214.17
	1031.41
Less cheque paid in but not credited	84.12
	947.29
Add interest credited by bank	22.07
	969.36
Less charges made by bank	14.36
Balance per Pass Book	£955.00

Here we see that only the balance per Cash Book is given, and that we have to calculate the Pass Book figure.

Our third illustration introduces some of the errors that may be made in the Cash Book:

Example 5.3

From the following particulars, prepare a reconciliation of the Bank Pass Book balance with the Cash Book balance.

	£
Balance per Pass Book in favour	60.00
Balance per Cash Book overdrawn	80.00
Unpresented cheques (cheques paid by the business, sent to the suppliers, but not yet paid by the bank)	144.00
Uncleared cheques inwards (cheques received from customers and paid into the bank, but not yet credited by the bank to the business account)	26.00

Further,

(*a*) A cheque for £20 paid to J. Jones has been entered in error in the Cash Column of the Cash Book.

(*b*) The debit side of the Cash Book (Bank Column) has been undercast by £50.

(*c*) The cashier has omitted to record bank commission of £8.

If we decide to begin with the Pass Book figure:

	£
Balance per Pass Book (in favour)	60.00
Adjust unpresented cheques	144.00
i.e. when presented there will be an **overdraft** of	84.00
Less uncleared cheques (Paid in but not credited by bank)	26.00
	58.00
Less cheque to J. Jones (As this has been paid by the bank and will appear in the Pass Book)	20.00
	38.00
Less Commission (Charged by the bank and appearing in the Pass Book)	8.00
	30.00
Add undercast in Bank Column of Cash Book	50.00
Overdrawn per Cash Book	£80.00

If we preferred, we could begin instead with the Cash Book:

	£
Overdrawn per Cash Book	80.00
Adjust unpresented cheques (Drawn and entered in Cash Book but not in Pass Book)	144.00
Favourable balance of	64.00
Less uncleared cheques (Paid in but not credited in Pass Book)	26.00
	38.00
Less cheque to J. Jones (Paid by bank and therefore appearing in Pass Book)	20.00
	18.00
Less commission charged by bank	8.00
	10.00
Add undercast in Bank Column of Cash Book	50.00
Balance per Pass Book (in favour)	£60.00

Having identified these errors, we must remember to make the appropriate entries in the books of original entry. The reconciliation confirms the correctness of the data but does not correct the original error. If these adjustments are not made, the balances per pass book and cash book will not agree next time a reconciliation is prepared.

Questions

1 Upon a cashier obtaining the Pass Book from the bank, he finds that the amount of the overdraft appearing therein differs from that shown by his Cash Book.

Give the possible explanations of this difference and, using your own figures, prepare a statement showing how the two amounts would be reconciled.

2 On 1 January 19x4, a trader obtained his Pass Book and on comparing it with his Cash Book discovered that all items agreed except the following:

(*a*) Cheques drawn and entered in the Cash Book, totalling £317.28, had not been presented at the bank.

(*b*) A country cheque for £17.50, lodged the previous day, did not appear in the Pass Book.

(*c*) The Pass Book showed an item of interest on overdraft amounting to £7.16 not entered in the Cash Book.

(*d*) The trader had, in December, discounted with the bank bills of exchange for £1200 and entered this amount in his Cash Book. The proceeds credited, as shown by the Pass Book, amounted to £1193.07.

The trader's Cash Book showed a balance, on 31 December 19x3, of £219.87 overdrawn.

State (*a*) what balance the Pass Book showed on the same day, and (*b*) what would be the balance of the trader's Cash Book after making the necessary additional entries.

3 On 30 June 19x6, a trader's Cash Book showed his bank balance to be £71.18 overdrawn.

On procuring his Pass Book from the bank he found that a country cheque for £19.50, lodged by him on 29 June had not yet been credited by the bank, four cheques drawn on 30 June, amounting in total to £181.34, had not yet been presented for payment, and the bank on 30 June had entered a charge of £10.27 for commission and interest.

Draw up a statement showing the balance as shown by the Pass Book.

4 From the following particulars prepare a statement showing how the differences between the Cash Book balance and the Pass Book balance is reconciled:

	£
Pass Book balance – 30 June 19x1	1401.62
Cash Book balance – 30 June 19x1	557.52

Cheques drawn prior to 30 June 19x1, but not presented until after that date:

	£
P.	29.20
Q.	801.17
R.	5.73
S.	132.32

	£
Country cheques paid into the bank on 30 June 19x1, not collected until 2 July 19x1	116.20
Bank charges and interest to 30 June 19x1, not entered in the Cash Book	8.12

5 On 30 November 19x2, the Cash Book of E. Simpson disclosed a debit balance of £212, and his Bank Pass Book at the same date a balance in his favour of £361.

Prepare a bank reconciliation at 30 November, taking into account that a cheque payable to E. Simpson in respect of a 4% dividend (less tax at 25%) on his holding of 1000 ordinary shares of £1 each in Greystones Foundry Ltd was entered in the Cash Book on 30 November, but not credited in the Pass Book until 1 December, and that cheques drawn by E. Simpson on 28 November, as follows, were not presented at the bank by the payees until 3 December.

	£
H. Simpson, salary	108.32
Corporation electric supply	35.68
Trade Supplies Ltd (a creditor)	35.00

6 On 31 December 19x9, John Smith found that his Bank Pass Book showed a balance in the bank of £88.62, whereas according to his Ledger his Bank Account was overdrawn by £57.69. On checking over the figures he discovered that the following cheques had not been presented:

	£
Wilkins & Co.	96.17
Turnbull & Snow	63.00
Samuel & Son	85.50

while a payment in of £90 on 31 December had not yet been credited by the bank, and the bank's charges for the half-year amounting to £8.36 had not been entered in his Ledger.

How would John Smith reconcile his Ledger with the Pass Book, and how would this affect his accounts?

7 A. Shiner's Cash Book for July 19x6 is as follows:

Dr.					Cr.
19x6		£	19x6		£
June 30	Balance	817.22	July 3	Lomas & Co.	151.23
July 4	J. Bell	15.75	8	Smith Ltd	32.00
9	Salt & Son	92.53	10	C. Jervis	1.84
18	Williams Ltd	31.22	20	Evans & Co.	10.91
29	E. Harris	81.17	27	P.M.G. Telephones	35.32
31	James & Co.	14.81	29	D. Greene	1.80
			30	J. Johnson	84.89
			31	Kenrick Ltd	25.72

His Bank Pass Book shows, for August 19x6, the following:

19x6		£	19x6		£
July 31	Balance	806.59	Aug. 3	Kenrick Ltd	25.72
Aug. 2	James & Co.	14.81	6	F. David	10.53
3	Saul & Co.	100.78	7	D. Greene	1.80
			7	J. Johnson	84.89

Prepare a Bank Agreement as at 31 July 19x6.

8 At 31 January 19x8, the Cash Book of Hugh Gibson showed a balance overdrawn of £117, while according to his Bank Pass Book at that date there was a balance in his favour of £72. A comparison of the two records revealed the following:

(*a*) A cheque for £25 sent to B. Murray had been entered in the cash column of the Cash Book.

(*b*) Bank charges of £17 at 31 December 19x7 were not entered at all in the Cash Book.

(*c*) The Bank had debited Gibson's Account with a cheque for £11 received from D. Carter, which had been returned dishonoured. The fact of dishonour was not shown in the Cash Book.

(*d*) The Bank Column on the Receipts side of the Cash Book was found to be undercast £10.

(*e*) Unpresented cheques amounted to £232.

You are required to prepare the Bank Reconciliation at 31 January 19x8, in proper form, setting out your adjustments clearly.

6

Petty Cash

We have seen that the general rule in cash transactions is to pay all cash received into the bank on the day of receipt, and to make all payments by cheque.

We have also seen that as regards wages and salaries payable by the business to its employees, some departure from this rule is inevitable, although in the first instance a cheque is issued to the Cashier in order that he may obtain the necessary notes and coin from the bank.

It is, however, necessary in all businesses, irrespective of their type or size, to make provision for the payment in notes or coin of a great variety of *small amounts* which may be regarded as sundry or incidental expenses. They are usually termed **Petty Cash payments**, and must receive our attention because:

(*a*) They recur at regular intervals.
(*b*) It is usually impracticable to issue a cheque in payment of any one of them.
(*c*) The person receiving payment may be an employee of the business.
(*d*) In total they may amount, period by period, to a not inconsiderable sum.

From the standpoint of the business it is most desirable to separate the records of Petty Cash payments from the main Cash Book records. It would clearly be inconvenient to have the latter cumbered with a large number of miscellaneous small payments and for this reason, *as a separate book of prime entry*, it is usual to keep a Petty Cash Book. The responsibility for the entries in this, and for the *Petty Cash balance* may be entrusted to the Cashier or, in the case of a large business, to one of his assistants.

Weekly or monthly, the latter may be handed a sum in cash thought sufficient to meet all demands for the selected period. He will then submit a list of all his payments to the Cashier and receive a sum to replenish his reduced cash balance.

It is often made a rule that the Petty Cashier shall take a receipt for each payment, and frequently specially printed forms bearing the name of the business are provided for this to be done. These receipt forms, when completed with the name of the recipient, and details of the amount and nature of the expense, are preserved by the Petty Cashier as independent evidence of payment.

To permit a suitable classification of expense items, the Petty Cash Book may be ruled with *analysis columns* into which the total paid can be extended. This facilitates the subsequent posting of the analysis columns to the Impersonal and other Ledger Accounts.

Example 6.1

On 1 March, £100 cash was handed to the Petty Cashier to pay Petty Cash expenses for the month, which were as follows:

			£
Mar.	1	Postage stamps	20.00
	3	Carriage	2.30
	4	Bus fare	0.30
	5	Shorthand note books	5.20
	6	Postage stamps	10.00
	8	Fare to London	12.55
	9	Sundry trade expenses	5.14
	11	Pencils	1.40
	14	Newspaper	0.50
	16	Envelopes	2.41
	18	Stationery	8.70
	31	Carriage	7.20

Rule a Petty Cash Book in analysis form, with five analysis columns, headed Postages and Telephone, Carriage, Travelling Expenses, Stationery and Sundry Trade Expenses respectively. Enter the foregoing items and close the books as on 31 March, showing clearly the balance of cash in hand.

Petty Cash Book

Dr. Cr.

Cash Received	*Date*	*Details*	*Receipt No.*	*Total*	*Postages and Telephone*	*Carriage*	*Travelling Expenses*	*Stationery*	*Sundry Trade Expenses*
£	19x3			£	£	£	£	£	£
100.00	Mar. 1	Per Cashier							
	1	Brown, Stamps	1	20.00	20.00				
	3	Collins, Carriage	2	2.30		2.30			
	4	Hunt, Fares	3	0.30			0.30		
	5	White, Notebooks	4	5.20				5.20	
	6	Brown, Stamps	5	10.00	10.00				
	8	Lyle, Rail fare, London	6	12.55			12.55		
	9	Sundry expenses	7	5.14					5.14
	11	White, Pencils	8	1.40				1.40	
	14	Hunt, Newspaper	9	0.50					0.50
	16	White, Envelopes	10	2.41				2.41	
	18	White, Stationery	11	8.70				8.70	
	31	British Rail, Carriage	12	7.20		7.20			
				75.70	30.00	9.50	12.85	17.71	5.64
	31	Balance	c/d	24.30					
£100.00				£100.00					
24.30	Apr. 1	Balance	b/d						

As regards the above, it should be noted that in certain cases, e.g. Rail Fares, the nature of the payment does not permit of a receipt being obtained from an outside source. For this reason, the employee receiving the money should be required to fill in a Voucher Form giving the required details, but wherever possible an independent receipt should always be filed with the firm's voucher.

Further, *like the main Cash Book*, the Petty Cash Book is not only a book of First Entry; it is also a Ledger Account with the Petty Cashier. In other words, he is debited with what he receives, and given credit for what he pays away on behalf of the business. The balance of £24.30 is therefore the sum for which he is accountable at the end of the month. Since credit is given to him personally for his payments, it remains to consider *their effect upon the business*. Impersonally, the business must be debited with the **totals** of the expenses set out in the analysis columns, for each one of which an account will be opened in the Impersonal Ledger. With Postages and Telephones we should have, for example:

POSTAGES AND TELEPHONES

Dr. Cr.

Date	*Details*	*P.C.B. Fo.*	*Amount*	*Date*	*Details*	*Fo.*	*Amount*
19x3			£				
Mar. 31	Petty Cash total	1	30.00				

Imprest system

As applied to Petty Cash, this means that a definite sum of money, say £100, is handed to the Petty Cashier and at the end of the week or month he is reimbursed the *amount expended*, e.g. £75.70 in the above example. His Petty Cash balance is thus restored to its original figure.

The merits of the system are that:

(*a*) At any time actual cash, or vouchers and receipts should be available for the imprest of £100.

(*b*) As the periodic reimbursements are the actual expenses paid, and not mere advances on account only, they are as such brought prominently to the notice of the Chief Cashier or other responsible official of the business.

Postage Book

It will be observed that in the last example an analysis column headed 'Postages' was provided in the Petty Cash Book.

This is a typical Petty Cash payment, recurring at regular intervals. The employee of the business having the custody of the stamp money may or may not be the Petty Cashier, but in any case it is desirable to have a record of the outgoing mail.

For this purpose it is customary to use a **Stamp Book** or **Postage Book**, of which the following is a suitable layout:

Date	*Cash Received*	*Name of Addressee*	*Town*	*Stamps used*
	£			£

The Postage Book may be properly described as a **Memorandum Book** whose purpose is to amplify and serve as a check upon the payments appearing in the 'Stamps' column. It does not form a part of the Double Entry System.

The Petty Cashier, when making each payment, should himself enter the *date* and *amount* in the first two columns, and it should be expected that the difference between the 'Cash Received' column and the 'Stamps Used' column represents either the value of the stamps in hand and unused or, alternatively, the balance of cash in hand available for their purchase.

It is desirable that when further advances are made for buying stamps, the Postage Book should be produced to the Petty Cashier and initialled by him after seeing that it is written up to date and verifying the balance shown.

Questions

1. Give a ruling for an analysed form of Petty Cash Book; insert specimen entries for a short period and show what postings are made.

   How would you deal with any exceptional payments not falling under one of the columnar headings provided for?

2. What is the Imprest System of dealing with Petty Cash?

   Rule a columnar Petty Cash Book illustrating the principle, and insert *three* entries therein.

7

The Debit and Credit Journal

Question You said on page 36 that the Journal in its earliest form was still used for certain purposes, and that it would be referred to at a later stage?

Answer Yes, and for the reason that while the majority of the transactions carried out relate to purchasing, selling and the receipt and payment of cash, there are nevertheless others which do not fall under these headings.

Question So that in the absence of a Book of Prime Entry, like this earliest form of the Journal, you cannot set out the dual aspect of these particular transactions prior to entry in the Ledger?

Answer As was stated earlier, it is desirable that *no entry shall be made in a Ledger Account unless it has first been recorded in a Book of Prime Entry*. Thus in certain cases the use of the Journal, or Debit and Credit Journal as it is sometimes termed, is essential. Moreover, while the information that can be given in the ordinary form of Ledger Account is limited, as much information as may be required including reference to documents, correspondence, etc., may be shown in the Journal proper. This we describe as the **Narration**.

Question Can you give me examples of such entries?

Answer It will help you to consider them as representing business transactions which are not capable of entry in the ordinary Purchase, Sales and Cash Journals. For example, if Brown, a customer, owes the business £20 which he cannot pay, a Bad Debt of £20 has arisen. Brown will be *credited* with £20 in his Personal Account in the Sales Ledger, and *Bad Debts* Account (an expense to the business) will be *debited* with that amount in the Impersonal

Ledger. Supposing also that Smith both buys goods from and sells goods to the business, in the Purchase Ledger there will be an account with him as a supplier, and in the Sales Ledger as a customer. If on balance he is indebted to the business he will only remit the difference in full settlement, therefore the balance on his Purchase Ledger Account must be transferred or posted to the credit of his Sales Ledger Account.

Question In effect, then, for these and other similar transactions the Debit and Credit Journal is the only book in which the prime or first entry can be made?

Answer Yes, but it is also appropriate, as we shall see shortly, for recording what are termed **opening** and **closing** entries. The former relate to the introduction into the business of Capital in one form or another; the latter refer either to the construction of the periodic *Profit and Loss Account* and the *Balance Sheet*, or to the realisation of the business property by sale or otherwise, and so on.

Question And in all these cases it is important to give adequate *narration*?

Answer If this were not done, the exact meaning of each Journal entry might be difficult to explain at some later date. Further, the making of the entry enables us conveniently to summarise the position for subsequent posting to the Ledger Accounts. Let us now proceed to work through some definite examples.

Example 7.1

Give the necessary Journal entries to record the following:

(*a*) Having deducted 5% cash discount when paying the account of Lakeside Ltd, a letter is received from them notifying us that only 2½% can be allowed.

The difference (£2.77) is being carried forward in their books.

(*b*) Goods to the value of £51.50 have been purchased from C. Ridley and goods value £30 sold to him. Both accounts are subject to a cash discount of 5%, and a cheque for the net balance is forwarded to him. Close the account.

			Dr.	Cr.
(*a*)				
19x8			£	£
Feb. 1	Discounts received	Dr.	2.77	
	To Lakeside Ltd			2.77
	Being discount not allowed as per their letter January 29, 19x8.			
(*b*)				
Feb. 4	Sundries	Dr.		
	C. Ridley (B.L. A/c)		28.50	
	Discounts allowed		1.50	
	To C. Ridley (S.L. A/c)			30.00
	Being transfer of Sales Ledger Balance and Discount Allowed to Bought Ledger on settlement.			

Should it happen, as in (*b*) above, that *either* the *debit* or *credit* aspect affects more than one Ledger Account, it is usual to prefix the word 'Sundries' to the entries, in this case to the debits.

C. Ridley's account in the Bought Ledger will then be as follows:

C. RIDLEY

Dr. Cr.

Date	*Details*	*J.O. Fo.*	*Amount*	*Date*	*Details*	*Fo.*	*Amount*
19x8			£	19x8			£
Feb. 4	Sundries	1	28.50	Feb. 1	Balance	b/d	51.50
	Sundries		1.50				
4	Bank	C.B.2	20.43				
	Discount	2	1.07				
			£51.50				£51.50

In posting from the Debit and Credit Journal to the Ledger Accounts, the word 'Sundries' again appears in the 'Details' Column. It is unnecessary, and would indeed be a waste of time, to repeat the whole of the information in the Ledger Account, when all that is required can be found on Fo. 1 of the Journal.

The two entries for the cheque £20.43, and discount £1.07, will, of course, be posted from the Cash Book in the ordinary way.

With both (*a*) and (*b*) we must observe that adequate narration is always an essential feature of Journal entries.

Example 7.2

A.B. purchased from C.D. a motor delivery van for cash £8980 in April 19x5, and in October he bought another for £11 210, giving the one bought in April in part payment, and paying the balance of £4360 in cash. Show these entries in A.B.'s books of entry, and post to the relevant Ledger Accounts.

Fo. 6

Purchase Journal

Date	*Supplier*	*Description*	*Inv. No.*	*Ledger Fo.*	*Total*	*Goods*	*Special Items*	
19x5					£	£	£	
Apr.	C.D.	Motor Van	1	2	8980.00		8980.00	Motors a/c PL8
Fo. 34								
19x5								
Oct.	C.D.	Motor Van	40	2	11210.00		11210.00	Motors a/c PL8

Fo. 10

Cash Book

Dr. Cr.

Date	*Details*	*Fo.*	*Amount*	*Date*	*Details*	*Fo.*	*Amount*
				19x5			£
				Apr.	C.D.	2	8980.00
Fo. 25 (the October entry)				Oct.	C.D.	2	4360.00

Fo. 19

Journal

			Fo.	Dr.	Cr.
19x5					
Oct.	Sundries	Dr.		£	£
	Motors A/C		P.L.8		8980.00
	C.D.		B.L.2	6850.00	
	Loss on Sale of Assets A/c		I.L.9	2130.00	
	Being Sale in part exchange of Ajax Van per C.D.'s invoice No. 40, October 29, 19x5.				

Fo. 2

Purchase Ledger

C.D.

Dr. Cr.

Date	*Details*	*Fo.*	*Amount*	*Date*	*Details*	*Fo.*	*Amount*
19x5			£	19x5			£
Apr.	Bank	C.B.10	8980.00	Apr.	Goods	P.J.6	8980.00
Oct.	Sundries	J.19	6850.00	Oct.	Goods	34	11210.00
	Bank	C.B.25	4360.00				
			£11210.00				£11210.00

Fo. 8

Private Ledger

MOTORS

Dr. Cr.

Date	*Details*	*Fo.*	*Amount*	*Date*	*Details*	*Fo.*	*Amount*
19x5			£	19x5			£
Apr.	Goods	P.J.6	8980.00	Oct.	Sundries	J. 19	8980.00
Oct.	Goods	34	11210.00				

In looking at this illustration, we see that the cost of the van purchased in April is extended in the Purchase Journal into the 'Special Items' column. It would be wrong to analyse it as *goods*, because it is apparently a *Capital* Asset. As such, it is debited to Motors A/C in the Private Ledger of A.B. When the second van is bought in October, exactly the same procedure is followed. At this point, however, a record has to be made of the disposal of the first van in part payment.

Having charged the business with two vans, we must, in effect, give it credit in *Motors Account* for:

(*a*) The part exchange value of £6850. As we paid £4360 for the new van which cost £11 210 the difference of £6850 is the value allowed on the old one.

(*b*) Loss on Sale of £2130. The old van cost £8980 and its part exchange value was £6850, the difference of £2130 represents a loss.

We may charge only the former to C.D. as we have done in his personal account. The latter is a special kind of expense remaining to be borne by the business and will be shown separately in the Impersonal Ledger:

Impersonal Ledger

Fo. 9

LOSS ON SALE OF ASSETS

Dr. Cr.

Date	*Details*	*Fo.*	*Amount*	*Date*	*Details*	*Fo.*	*Amount*
19x5			£				
Oct.	Sundries	J.19	2130.00				

It is desirable that we should notice from now on the utility for reference purposes of the Folio Column in each Ledger Account. The insertion of the folio numbers prefixed by the initial letter of the book of prime entry makes immediate reference a simple matter.

Example 7.3

Give Journal entries for the following transactions in the books of L. Denton:

Jan. 1 L. Denton commenced business with stock valued at £1493, cash at bank £2078, and fixtures value £655. £140 was owing to M. Robinson.

Mar. 10 Plant and machinery bought on credit from Langham Bros., value £523.

Apr. 1 K. Atkins, a debtor for £23, is known to be insolvent and the debt is written off as bad.

June 23 Goods valued £118.15 bought from Blake Bros. entered in the Purchase Day Book and posted in error to the debit of Blake Bros. Account in the Bought Ledger.

June 28 Cheque £15.17 posted to the debit of Jones Bros. instead of to the debit of Jones Ltd.

The entries on 1 January are an instance of the use of the Journal for *opening* the books of a business. It is also apparent that the amount of L. Denton's Capital at this date is £4086.

The Cash Book balance will be debited in the bank column of the Cash Book, and the £140 owing to M. Robinson credited to his personal account in the *Bought Ledger*. The other items will be posted to accounts in the *Private Ledger*.

The purchase of machinery on 10 March could quite well be shown in the 'special items' column of the Purchase Journal, and the present record is only an *alternative* to this.

Journal

			Fo.	Dr. £	Cr. £
Jan. 1	Sundries:	Dr.			
	To Sundries				
	Cash at bank			2078.00	
	Stock			1493.00	
	Fixtures			655.00	
	M. Robinson				140.00
	Capital				4086.00
	Being Assets and Liabilities introduced this day.				
Mar. 10	Plant and machinery	Dr.		523.00	
	To Langham Bros.				523.00
	Being purchase on credit of drilling machinery and lathe for tool shop.				
Apr. 1	Bad debts	Dr.		23.00	
	To K. Atkins				23.00
	Being amount written off per collector's report dated 1 April.				
June 23	To Blake Bros.				236.30
	Being goods purchased £118.15 posted in error to the debit of A/c and now adjusted.				
June 28	Jones Ltd	Dr.		15.17	
	To Jones Bros.				15.17
	Being cheque posted in error to debit of Jones Bros.				

The entry on 23 June is interesting as showing the correction of an error in *one Ledger Account*, that of Blake Bros.

Purchases Account in the Impersonal Ledger will have been

debited on 30 June with the total of the Purchase Day Book for the month, which includes the item of £118.15.

At the same time, because of the error, there is also a *debit* on a personal account in the Purchase Ledger of £118.15. Clearly Blake Bros. should have been credited originally with £118.15, and to adjust the position it will now be necessary to enter in the Journal a credit to them of double the amount, or £236.30. In so doing, we shall cancel the debit error and record their position as creditors for £118.15. Because the original error was two debits instead of a debit and a credit, the correcting entry must be a credit: either one credit of twice the amount of the error or two credits of the same amount, one cancelling the wrong entry and the other recording the correct entry.

The 28 June entry is simpler as a debit entry had been made, but to the wrong account. The credit to this account and debit to the proper one is straightforward.

The point cannot be too strongly emphasised that ability to make Journal entries successfully presupposes a thorough understanding of double entry principles. Transactions of the kind dealt with in the foregoing examples, while not so common as purchasing, selling and cash transactions, will inevitably arise in all businesses at some time or another, and call for initial record in the Debit and Credit Journal, in the manner illustrated.

Questions

1 Explain the uses of the Journal in the system of double entry book-keeping.

2 Explain the use of the Journal proper. What entries, other than the opening entry, would you expect to find in this book?

3 The following errors are discovered in the books of a business concern:

(*a*) £47.50 paid for new office furniture has been charged to office expenses.

(*b*) £39.18, representing a monthly total of discounts allowed to debtors, has been posted from the debit side of the Cash Book to the *credit* of Discount Account.

(*c*) An entry of £10, representing the retail value of goods returned to X & Co., wholesalers, has been made in the Returns Outwards Book and posted. The amount should have been £7, the invoiced value of the goods in question.

Show the entries necessary to correct these errors. The original wrong entries are not to be deleted. Subject to this restriction, make the corrections in whatever form you consider most appropriate.

4 You are required to give the Journal entries necessary to correct the undermentioned errors in the books of a Limited Company:

(*a*) Cost of advertising the Prospectus, £2200, charged to Advertising Account. (A prospectus is the document produced in connection with the sale of shares in a company.)

(*b*) Allowance of £50 made by a supplier of machinery entered in the Returns Outward Book and included in the total posted to Purchases Account.

(*c*) £500 received from a customer for goods yet to be delivered posted to the credit of Sales Account.

(*d*) Imprest of £100 handed to the Petty Cashier debited to General Expenses Account.

5 Give the Journal entries necessary to record the following facts in the books of I. Markham, a manufacturer:

19x4

Jan. 1 I. Markham commenced business with cash in hand, £136; cash at bank, £2141; plant and machinery, £2180; and stock value £1200.

28 Bought plant and machinery on credit from Speed & Co. Ltd, value £1130.

Mar. 3 A debt for £25 owing by B. Sykes proves worthless.

10 The plant and machinery purchased on credit from Speed & Co. was returned as not being according to specification.

31 £25 interest on capital to be allowed.

6 Record by way of Journal entry the following in the books of A., a merchant:

(*a*) X. is both a supplier and a customer. The debit on his Sales Ledger Account is £40, and the credit on his account in the Bought Ledger is £60.

On 28 February 19x6, a cheque in full settlement is sent to him, less 2½% cash discount.

(*b*) Purchase of office fixtures £400, and stationery, etc., £50, from Office Supplies Ltd.

(*c*) Provision on 31 March 19x6 (the date when A. closes his books) for interest at 12% per annum for six months in respect of a loan of £5000 by Mrs A.

(*d*) Sale of delivery van of book value of £4300 in part exchange at the price of £2250, against a new van costing £7500.

7 Give Journal entries to record or correct the following:

19x6

Jan 6 £25 cheque received credited to John White, instead of James White, both being customers.

14 Cuthbert agreed to accept 0.75 in £ in full settlement of the balance of £180 appearing on his account in the Bought Ledger at 21 December 19x5.

17 Matthews, a customer, owed the business £200 on 31 December 19x5. It is agreed to allow him £50 for window display expenses, and 5% gross for special trade discount.

19 Arnold, a customer, to be charged by agreement £40 interest on his overdue account.

24 Wilkins, a supplier, takes over plant and tools valued at £200 as part payment of the balance due to him of £325.

8 The book-keeper employed by John Horton handed you a Trial Balance (see Example 8.1 and p.107) which included on the debit side an item: Suspense Account, £90.90.' He stated that this was the difference between the two sides of the Trial Balance which he could not trace. On investigation you find that the difference is caused by the following errors:

(*a*) The Sales Day Book has been over-cast on page 87 by £100.
(*b*) The Returns Outwards for November, amounting to £30.58 have been posted to personal accounts only.
(*c*) A cheque for £70.32 received from Barton Bros. has been posted to their Sales Ledger account as £73.20.
(*d*) A first and final dividend amounting to £5.88, received from the trustee in bankruptcy of Hubert Wilkins has not been posted to the Sales Ledger account. The full amount of the debt (£19) has been written off as bad during the year.
(*e*) A cheque for £12.24, paid to J. Smithson for goods supplied has been posted to his credit in the Sales Ledger.

Show the entries (Journal *or* Ledger) which are necessary to correct the above errors.

8

Writing Up the Books

We have now become acquainted with the various books of prime entry and the Ledgers to which they serve as a basis, and we have realised in particular that the *double entry is completed within the Ledger*.

The examples that have been taken up to this point have largely dealt with the ordinary purchasing, selling and cash transactions of the business, and have been selected to illustrate the true meaning of double entry.

We ought now, therefore, to be in a position to look at other examples which include all these transactions and aim at the preparation of the Final Accounts, as they are termed, or the **Revenue Account** and **Balance Sheet**.

It is of the utmost importance that in working through them we try to put ourselves in the position of the Book-keeper, and consider *every transaction* from the standpoint of its effect on:

(*a*) The Profit or Loss result of the business, and
(*b*) Its Asset and Liability, or Capital position.

Example 8.1

On 1 February 19x1, R. Ready had the following Assets and Liabilities: Cash in hand £100; Cash at bank £1110; Creditors: B. Bright £75 and C. Clowes £95; Debtors: R. Wright £60, and S. Tune £70; Furniture and fittings £180; Stock on hand £1340.

Open the books by Journal entry, find and credit his capital, and then enter the following transactions in the proper subsidiary books, post to the Ledger and extract a Trial Balance (a list of balances, see p. 107) at 28 February 19x1. The Cash Book and Personal Accounts should be balanced, and the balances brought down.

19x1				£
Feb.	1	Received cash from R. Wright		30.00
	2	Sold on credit to M. Moses goods		50.00 + VAT £7.50
	4	Bought on credit from C. Clowes goods		120.00 + VAT £18.00
	5	Paid wages, cash		112.00
	6	Drew cheque for personal use		125.00
		Cash sales for week		250.00 + VAT £37.50
	9	Paid cash to bank		140.00
	12	Received cash from S. Tune	£67.00	
		Allowed him discount	3.00	
				70.00
		Paid wages, cash		115.00
	13	Paid C. Clowes by cheque	£90.00	
		Discount allowed	5.00	
				95.00
		Cash sales for week		387.00 + VAT £58.05
	17	Sold on credit to R. Wright, goods		252.00 + VAT £37.80
	19	R. Wright returned goods		10.00 + VAT £1.50
		Paid wages, cash		116.00
	20	Cash sales for week		296.00 + VAT £44.40
	22	Paid cash to bank		590.00
	26	Paid wages, cash		119.00
	27	Paid rent, cash		120.00
		Cash sales for week		182.00 + VAT £27.30

Before we begin the work of opening the books for the month, it will be helpful to consider first the transactions and the business practice concerning them.

(*a*) The amount of the proprietor's capital is not stated, but as we know it to be the excess of the Assets over the Liabilities we can easily discover it, *and record it together with the other opening balances*.

(*b*) It is apparent that in the Cash Book there must be columns for 'Cash' as well as for 'Bank'. Cash Discounts also have to be provided for.

(*c*) Both Cash and Credit Sales are made. Only the Credit Sales will be recorded in the Sales Journal, in order to put on record the position of the customer as a debtor to the business, pending payment by him.

(*d*) There is no need to open columnar or analysis Purchase and

Sales Journals. The one word 'goods' is the only indication we have of the purchases and sales as a whole.

(*e*) This illustration includes VAT at the rate of 15%. If VAT was not applicable the only changes would be those connected with the VAT and the VAT account.

R. READY

Journal

Fo. 1

			Fo.	Dr.	Cr.
19x1					
Feb. 1	Sundries	Dr.		£	£
	To Sundries				
	Cash in hand		C.B.2	100.00	
	Cash at bank		2	1110.00	
	R. Wright		S.L.20	60.00	
	S. Tune		25	70.00	
	Furniture and fittings		P.L.65	180.00	
	Stock to hand		70	1340.00	
	To: B. Bright		B.L.15		75.00
	C. Clowes		10		95.00
	Capital		P.L.75		2690.00
	Being Assets, Liabilities and Capital at this date				
				£2860.00	£2860.00

Fo. 3

Purchase Journal

Date	*Supplier*	*Fo.*	*Total*	*Goods*	*VAT*
19x1			£	£	£
Feb. 4	C. Clowes	B.L.10	138.00	120.00	18.00
				I.L.Fo. 30	I.L.Fo. 52

Note:	*Abbreviation*
Cash Book	C.B.
Purchase Journal	P.J.
Sales Journal	S.J.
Sales Returns Journal	S.R.J.
Journal	J.
Bought Ledger (or Suppliers, or Creditors)	B.L.
Sales Ledger (or Customers, or Debtors)	S.L.
Impersonal Ledger (or Nominal)	I.L.
Private Ledger	P.L.

Cash Book

Fo. 2

Date		*Fo.*	*Discount*	*Cash*	*Bank*	*Date*		*Fo.*	*Discount*	*Cash*	*Bank*
19x1			£	£	£				£	£	£
Feb. 1	Balances	J.1		100.00	1110.00	Feb. 5	Wages	I.L.55		112.00	
1	R. Wright	S.L.20		30.00		6	Drawings	P.L.80			125.00
6	Cash sales	I.L.40		250.00		9	Bank	C		140.00	
6	VAT	I.L.52		37.50		12	Wages	I.L.55		115.00	
9	Cash	C			140.00	13	C. Clowes	B.L.10	5.00		90.00
12	S. Tune	S.L.25	3.00	67.00		19	Wages	I.L.55		116.00	
13	Cash sales			387.00		22	Bank	C		590.00	
	VAT	I.L.52		58.05		26	Wages	I.L.55		119.00	
20	Cash sales	I.L.40		296.00		27	Rent	I.L.60		120.00	
	VAT	I.L.52		44.40		28	Balance	c/d		167.25	1625.00
22	Cash				590.00						
27	Cash sales	I.L.40		182.00							
	VAT	I.L.52		27.30							
			3.00	1479.25	1840.00				5.00	1479.25	1840.00
			I.L.46						I.L.50		
Mar. 1	Balances	b/d		167.25	1625.00						

The Journal entries as set out above enable us to post to the various Ledgers the balances outstanding on 1 February.

Thus, the cash items will appear on the *debit* side of the Cash Book; accounts will be opened in the Sales Ledger for Wright and Tune, again as *debits*; and in the Purchase Ledger for Bright and Clowes, but on the *credit* side.

Similarly, *debit* balances will appear in the Private Ledger for Furniture and Stock, while R. Ready's Capital Account will be *credited* with £2690.

Fo. 4

Sales Journal

Date	*Customer*	*Fo.*	*Total*	*Goods*	*VAT*
19x1			£	£	£
Feb. 2	M. Moses	S.L.23	57.50	50.00	7.50
17	R. Wright	S.L.20	289.80	252.00	37.80
			347.30	302.00	45.30
				I.L.Fo. 35	I.L.Fo. 52

Fo. 5

Sales Return Journal
(Returns Inwards)

Date	*Customer*	*Fo.*	*Total*	*Goods*	*VAT*
19x1			£	£	£
Feb. 19	R. Wright	S.L.20	11.50	10.00	1.50
				I.L.Fo. 45	I.L.Fo. 52

Having first written up the Books of Prime Entry *in respect of the transactions during the month*, and brought down the Cash and Bank Balances as instructed, we are able to post as we should in practice, from the Journals to the appropriate Ledger Accounts.

Let us begin with the *Personal* Ledgers, dealing first with that section relating to the Accounts of Suppliers, or **Bought Ledger**. You may find that it is useful to open up and post your own ledger accounts and then compare them with those that follow.

Bought Ledger

Fo. 10

C. CLOWES

Dr. Cr.

Date	Details	Fo.	Amount	Date	Details	Fo.	Amount
19x1			£	19x1			£
Feb. 13	Bank	C.B.2	90.00	Feb. 1	Balance	J.1	95.00
	Discount	C.B.2	5.00	4	Goods and VAT	P.J.3	138.00
28	Balance	c/d	138.00				
			233.00				233.00
				Mar. 1	Balance	b/d	138.00

Fo. 15

B. BRIGHT

Dr. Cr.

Date	Details	Fo.	Amount	Date	Details	Fo.	Amount
				19x1			£
				Feb. 1	Balance	J.1	75.00

As no transactions have taken place on Bright's account, the opening balance on 1 February remains unchanged on 28 February.

Next we may turn to the **Sales Ledger**.

Sales Ledger

Fo. 20

R. WRIGHT

Dr. Cr.

Date	Details	Fo.	Amount	Date	Details	Fo.	Amount
19x1			£	19x1			£
Feb. 1	Balance	J.1	60.00	Feb. 1	Cash	C.B.	30.00
17	Goods & VAT	S.J.4	289.80	19	Returns & VAT	S.J.R.5	11.50
				28	Balance	c/d	308.30
			£349.80				£349.80
Mar. 1	Balance	b/d	308.30				

Fo. 23

M. MOSES

Dr. Cr.

Date	Details	Fo.	Amount	Date	Details	Fo.	Amount
19x1			£				
Feb. 2	Goods & VAT	S.J.4	57.50				

Fo. 25

S. TUNE

Dr. Cr.

Date	Details	Fo.	Amount	Date	Details	Fo.	Amount
19x1			£	19x1			£
Feb. 1	Balance	J.1	70.00	Feb. 12	Cash	C.B.2	67.00
					discount		3.00
			£70.00				£70.00

The **Impersonal**, or as it is usually termed, the **Nominal Ledger**, may now receive attention.

Within this, as we know, we shall expect to find the accounts dealing *with the effect upon the business* of the transactions entered into.

Impersonal or **Nominal Ledger**

Fo. 30

PURCHASES

Dr. Cr.

Date	Details	Fo.	Amount	Date	Details	Fo.	Amount
19x1			£				
Feb. 28	Total for month	P.J.3	120.00				

Fo. 35

CREDIT SALES

Dr. Cr.

Date	Details	Fo.	Amount	Date	Details	Fo.	Amount
				19x1			£
				Feb. 28	Total for month	S.J.4	302.00

Fo. 40

CASH SALES

Dr.							Cr.
Date	*Details*	*Fo.*	*Amount*	*Date*	*Details*	*Fo.*	*Amount*
				19x1			£
				Feb. 6	Cash	C.B.2	250.00
				13	Cash	C.B.2	387.00
				20	Cash	C.B.2	296.00
				27	Cash	C.B.2	182.00
							£1115.00

Fo. 45

SALES RETURNS

Dr.							Cr.
Date	*Details*	*Fo.*	*Amount*	*Date*	*Details*	*Fo.*	*Amount*
19x1			£				
Feb. 28	Total for month	S.R.J.5	10.00				

Fo. 46

DISCOUNTS ALLOWED

Dr.							Cr.
Date	*Details*	*Fo.*	*Amount*	*Date*	*Details*	*Fo.*	*Amount*
19x1			£				
Feb. 28	Total for month	C.B.2	3.00				

Fo. 50

DISCOUNTS RECEIVED

Dr.							Cr.
Date	*Details*	*Fo.*	*Amount*	*Date*	*Details*	*Fo.*	*Amount*
				19x1			£
				Feb. 28	Total for month	C.B.2	5.00

Fo. 52

VAT

Date	*Details*	*Fo.*	*Amount*	*Date*	*Details*	*Fo.*	*Amount*
19x1			£	19x1			£
Feb. 28	Total for month	P.J.3	18.00	Feb. 28	Total for month	S.J.4	45.30
28	Total for month	S.R.J.5	1.50	6	Cash sales	C.B.2	37.50
				13	Cash sales	C.B.2	58.05
				20	Cash sales	C.B.2	44.40
28	Balance	c/d	193.05	27	Cash sales	C.B.2	27.30
			£212.55				£212.55
				Mar. 1	Balance	b/d	193.05

Fo. 55

WAGES

Dr.							Cr.
Date	*Details*	*Fo.*	*Amount*	*Date*	*Details*	*Fo.*	*Amount*
19x1			£				
Feb. 5	Cash	C.B.2	112.00				
12	Cash	C.B.2	115.00				
19	Cash	C.B.2	116.00				
27	Cash	C.B.2	119.00				
			£462.00				

Fo. 60

RENT

Dr.							Cr.
Date	*Details*	*Fo.*	*Amount*	*Date*	*Details*	*Fo.*	*Amount*
19x1			£				
Feb. 27	Cash	C.B.2	120.00				

Lastly, there is the **Private Ledger** to be considered.

Here we shall have first of all two Asset Accounts, for Furniture and Stock respectively, and one Liability Account, for Capital.

Private Ledger

Fo. 65

FURNITURE AND FITTINGS

Dr.							Cr.
Date	*Details*	*Fo.*	*Amount*	*Date*	*Details*	*Fo.*	*Amount*
19x1			£				
Feb. 1	Balance	J.1	180.00				

Fo. 70

STOCK

Dr.							Cr.
Date	*Details*	*Fo.*	*Amount*	*Date*	*Details*	*Fo.*	*Amount*
19x1			£				
Feb. 1	Balance	J.1	1340.00				

Fo. 75

CAPITAL

Dr.							Cr.
Date	*Details*	*Fo.*	*Amount*	*Date*	*Details*	*Fo.*	*Amount*
				19x1			£
				Feb. 1	Balance	J.1	2690.00

If, however, we look at the Cash Book, we see that on 6 February R. Ready, the proprietor, drew a cheque £125 for his personal use. This is a withdrawal from the business of:

(*a*) A part of the amount now standing to his credit on Capital Account, or
(*b*) The profit which he estimates is being earned.

In either event, it must be debited in the Ledger in the Capital Account above, or in a 'Drawings' Account opened for the purpose:

Fo. 80

DRAWINGS

Dr. Cr.

Date	*Details*	*Fo.*	*Amount*	*Date*	*Details*	*Fo.*	*Amount*
19x1			£				
Feb. 6	Bank	C.B.2	125.00				

Having now posted all the transactions to the Ledgers, and recorded *their dual aspect*, it is to be expected that arithmetical agreement has been obtained, in that the sum of the Debit Balances should equal the sum of the Credit Balances on 28 February 19x1.

Let us therefore extract the Balances on the Accounts and list them as Debits or Credits, according to their nature:

Ledger	*Account*	*Fo.*	*Dr.*	*Cr.*
Cash Book	Cash	2	167.25	
	Bank	2	1625.00	
Bought	C. Clowes	10		138.00
	B. Bright	15		75.00
Sales	R. Wright	20	308.30	
	M. Moses	23	57.50	
Impersonal	Purchases	30	120.00	
	Credit sales	35		302.00
	Cash sales	45		1115.00
	Sales returns	46	10.00	
	Discounts allowed	48	3.00	
	Discounts received	50		5.00
	VAT	52		193.05
	Wages	55	462.00	
	Rent	60	120.00	
Private	Furniture and fittings	65	180.00	
	Stock, 1 February	70	1340.00	
	Capital	75		2690.00
	Drawings	80	125.00	
			£4518.05	£4518.05

In total the Double Entry is seen to be completed *within the Ledger Accounts*, regarding the Cash Book as a Ledger for this purpose.

This list, or summary of Ledger Balances, we call a **Trial Balance**.

Its extraction at any time enables us:

(*a*) To satisfy ourselves of the arithmetical accuracy with which the routine work of writing up the Books of Prime Entry, and posting to the Ledgers, has been carried out.

(*b*) To provide a basis for the preparation of the Final Accounts, or **Revenue Account** and **Balance Sheet**.

Because of its importance, we must consider it at greater length in the next chapter.

Questions

1 N. Bell was in business as a wholesale merchant and on 1 January 19x1 he had the following assets and liabilities: Cash in hand, £450; Bank overdraft, £4680; Stock of goods, £7100; Motor vans, £2740; Fixtures and fittings, £920; Sundry Debtors: J. Betts, £640; E. Evans, £600; Sundry Creditors; T. Brown, £840; F. Shaw, £580.

Enter the above and the following transactions into the proper subsidiary books, post to the Ledger and extract a Trial Balance. The Cash Book and, where necessary, the Ledger Accounts should be balanced and the balances brought down. Assume no VAT.

Jan. 4 Received from J. Betts cheque for £628 in full settlement of his account for £640. Paid cheque to bank.
6 Sold goods on credit to E. Evans, £1200.
9 Paid wages in cash, £263.
11 Sold goods for cash, £443.
E. Evans returned goods. Sent him credit note for £48.
15 Sold a motor van for cash, £780.
18 Paid cash into the bank, £800.
23 Paid wages in cash, £263.
Purchased on credit new motor van from the Albion Motor Co. Ltd, for £8450.
25 Received cheque from E. Evans for £1740 in full settlement of the amount due from him. Paid cheque to bank.
Purchased goods on credit from F. Shaw, £800.
27 Paid T. Brown cheque for £820 in full settlement of the amount due to him on January 1.

N.B. – No Trading and Profit and Loss Accounts or Balance Sheet are required.

2 On 1 March 19x1, A. Walker commences business with £10 000 in cash of which he pays £9500 into the bank. Enter the following transactions in the books of original entry, post to Ledger Accounts and extract a Trial Balance.

Mar. 2 Bought premises and paid £1500 by cheque.
4 Purchased on credit from J. Raleigh:
15 gents' cycles at £125.00 + VAT £18.75 each.
20 ladies' cycles at £110.00 + VAT £16.50 each.
20 children's cycles at £77.00 + VAT £11.55 each.
5 Bought at an auction sale sundry goods for £268.00 and paid for them by cash. (No VAT.)
6 Sold to S. Taylor:
1 gents' cycle at £160.00 + VAT £24.00.
1 ladies' cycle at £140.00 + VAT £21.00.
1 child's cycle at £95 + VAT £14.25.
8 Returned to J. Raleigh:
10 children's cycles invoiced on the 4th and received a credit note.
10 Paid J. Raleigh by cheque the amount due, less £167.00 cash discount.
12 Bought office furniture for cash £130.75. (No VAT.)
16 S. Taylor paid by cheque the amount due.
18 Paid by cheque rent £250.00. (No VAT.)
Paid by cash wages £150.60.
Paid by cheque insurance £220.75. (No VAT.)
Cash sales for the period £597 + VAT £89.55.
20 Paid all cash into the bank except £50.

3 R. Simpson was in business as a wholesale cutler and jeweller. On 1 January 19x6, his financial position was as follows: Cash in hand, £440; Cash at bank, £2350; Stock, £2000; Fixtures and fittings, £1160. Sundry Creditors: M. Marsh, £150; D. Steele, £200. Sundry Debtors: H. Robins, £275; J. Long, £175.

Enter the above and the following transactions into the proper subsidiary books, post to the Ledger, and extract a Trial Balance. The Cash Book and, where necessary, the Ledger Accounts should be balanced and the balances brought down. Assume VAT at 15%.

Jan. 2 Received from H. Robins on account, cheque for £200, which was paid to bank.
3 Sold to D. Dennis & Co. Ltd: Goods £240 less 10% trade discount.
4 Paid wages in cash £260.
6 Cash sales paid to bank, £500.
7 Bought from Silversmiths Ltd: Goods £340 subject to trade discount of 15%.
8 Paid M. Marsh by cheque £147.50 in settlement of his account of £150.
11 Paid wages in cash £170.
13 Cash sales paid to bank £250.
15 Withdrew from bank for office cash £200.
17 Sold to J. Long: on credit £130.
18 Paid wages in cash £160.
R. Simpson withdrew £80 for private purposes by cheque.
18 Cash sales paid to bank £285.
20 Received from J. Long in full settlement of the amount due from him, cheque for £307. Paid cheque to bank.

N.B. – No Trading and Profit and Loss Account or Balance Sheet is required.

4 On 1 January 19x1, the financial position of R. Mason, gentleman's outfitter, is as follows: Cash in hand, £45.80; Stock, £3750.00; H. Atherton (Dr.), £31.75; Fixtures and fittings, £750.00; A. Baker (Cr.), £390.00; Bank overdraft £176.75. Assume no VAT. Find and credit his capital. During the month his transactions were as follows:

Jan. 4 Bought goods from G. Henry & Co., to the value of £812.80 less 12½% trade discount.
6 Paid A. Baker the amount owing, less 5% cash discount.
7 Returned to G. Henry & Co., goods to the gross value of £103.25.
9 Sold goods to H. Atherton, £68.60.
9 Received from G. Henry & Co. credit note for the net amount of goods returned.
10 H. Atherton settled his account of 1 January, after deducting £1.75 cash discount.
14 Bought new showcase £75.75 from W. Dixon.
19 Sold goods to N. Dobbin £72.50.
20 R. Mason paid £300 of his own money into the business Bank Account.
23 Sold shop fittings for cash £27.60.
26 Cash sales for the period £311.80.
28 Paid all cash into bank except £50.00.

Enter the transactions in the appropriate subsidiary books – post to the Ledger Accounts and extract a Trial Balance.

N.B. – Trading Account, Profit and Loss Account and Balance Sheet are not required.

5 In the form of a three-column Cash Book, after properly heading each column, enter all the money transactions below and balance the Book. Assume no VAT.

Journalise the opening balances and remaining transactions. (*Note:* Purchases and Sales Books may be used, if preferred.)

Post the entries to the Ledger. Extract a Trial Balance.

Close and balance the Ledger.

On 1 October 19x1, S. Strong reopened his books with the following balances in addition to his Capital Account:

	£
Cash	47.80
K. Knight & Co. (Cr.)	176.90
D. Day (Dr.)	225.75
Bank (overdraft)	217.90
Rent accrued, owing by S. Strong	120.00
Stock of goods	2741.25

During the month his transactions were:

			£
Oct.	3	Received cheque from D. Day to settle account	220.00
	5	Paid same into bank	220.00
	8	Sold to D. Day: Goods	130.00
	10	D. Day returned goods	4.20
	13	Sundry cash sales	183.70
	14	Paid into bank	100.00
	16	Bought of K. Knight & Co.: Goods	91.75
	19	Paid landlord by cheque	120.00
	21	Paid K. Knight & Co. on account	150.00
	22	Sold to D. Day sundry goods and received cheque (banked)	43.75
	26	D. Day's cheque returned dishonoured	43.75
	27	Cash purchases	107.30
	27	Sundry cash sales	249.40
	28	Drew cheque for self	25.00
	30	Wages and expenses for month paid by cheque	50.40
		and in cash	111.50
	31	Rent accrued	120.00
		Bank charges	11.75
		Interest on capital at 6% per annum calculated on balance at 1 October 19x1	
		Stock of goods on hand valued at	2503.25

General note: The following problems may be answered assuming no VAT, or VAT at any rate that is appropriate. Obviously it makes a slight difference to the detailed answers but the general principles remain the same.

6 On 1 January 19x1, R. Baxter commenced business as a fuel merchant with £10 650 in cash. On the same date he opened a current account at the bank and paid in £10 500. His transactions during the month follow:

Jan	1	Bought a second-hand motor lorry by cheque, £1256.00. Bought from the Victory Colliery Co. Ltd: Coal £1970.00.
	4	Cash sales £277.50.
	4	Sold to J. Yates, Coal £184.00.
	6	Paid Victory Colliery Co. £1000 on account by cheque.
	8	Bought from The Shell Oil Co. Plc, Fuel oil £1685.00.
	10	J. Yates settled his account by cheque and allowed him 5% cash discount. Cheque banked.
	12	Sold to W. Jones, Fuel oil £473.00.
	12	Paid carriage by cheque £170.50.
	15	Settled the account of the Victory Colliery Co. by cheque and was allowed 5% cash discount on the original account.
	16	Cash sales £106.
	16	Paid sundry expenses in cash £253.60.
	16	Paid all cash into the bank except £100 retained for business use.

You are required to enter the above transactions in the books of original entry, to post to Ledger Accounts, and to extract a Trial Balance.

No Trading Account, Profit and Loss Account, or Balance Sheet is required.

7 On 1 November 19x1, John Maynard commenced business on his own account, trading under the style of The Bon Marché.

He paid £2000 into the bank account of the business on that date, and also borrowed £5000 from his father, Robert Maynard, to assist him in the venture. He paid £4500 of this sum into the Bank.

The following transactions were entered into during the month of November:

19x1			£
Nov.	1	Paid rent by cheque three months to 31 January 19x2	237.50
	2	Bought material on credit:	
		Forrester & Co.	126.50
		Arnold & Sons	439.75
		H. Meyrick Ltd	112.95
	3	Bought office fittings for cash	220.00
	3	Drew cheque for cash for own use	45.00
	4	Sold goods on credit:	
		E. Walker	221.25
		J. Roberts	51.00
		L. Morley	147.45
		H. Longden	4.85
	10	Paid wages in cash	128.25
	11	Sent cheque to Forrester & Co.	125.00
		and obtained discount	1.50
	16	Received cheque from Roberts, paid into bank	50.00
		and allowed discount	1.00
	19	Received cheque from Morley, paid into bank	146.00
		and allowed discount	1.45
	24	Paid wages in cash	128.25
	27	Sent cheque to Arnold & Sons	435.00
		and obtained discount	4.75
	30	Returned defective goods to H. Meyrick Ltd	9.25

Enter the above transactions in the proper books of prime entry, post to the Ledger, and extract a Trial Balance at 30 November.

9

The Trial Balance

Two advantages have just been claimed for the Trial Balance. The first, that it is evidence of the arithmetical accuracy of the book-keeping work, clearly has reference to the dual aspect from which every transaction may be regarded, each transaction having been looked at from the twofold aspect upon which the double entry system relies.

Are we therefore justified in assuming that the routine work underlying the Trial Balance calls for no further comment? Is arithmetical accuracy alone all with which we need be concerned?

The answer to these two questions is 'no'.

Apparent proof of accuracy is not the same as conclusive proof, and we have to realise that errors may exist in the underlying work which the Trial Balance will not reveal.

If, for example, a *transaction has been altogether omitted* from the books, neither its *debit* nor its *credit* aspect can have been recorded.

Goods may have been purchased from Brown, a supplier, and an invoice duly received. But if, in course of checking prior to entry in the Purchase Journal, the invoice is lost or mislaid, nothing will ultimately appear to the *credit* of the Supplier's Account in respect of it. Similarly as it has never been entered in the Purchase Journal, it cannot form part of the Total Purchases for the month which are posted to the *debit* of Purchases Account.

Such an *error of omission* would be discovered only when the supplier's Statement of Account comes to hand.

Another example would be neglect to record in the Cash Book any discount deducted by a customer.

The customer would be credited with too little in his Personal Account, causing an Asset in the form of a Book Debt to be *overstated*, and the Discounts Allowed Account would be under-debited, resulting in the *understatement* of an expense to the business.

There are also errors which we may describe as *compensating errors*. In this sense, an error in one direction is counterbalanced by an error in another direction of equal amount. Hence, again the lack of agreement is not disclosed by the Trial Balance.

The following are examples of *compensating errors*:

(*a*) The total of Sales Account on one page of the Impersonal Ledger is inadvertently carried forward £10 less than it should be, i.e. there is *short credit* of £10.

At the same time, the addition of Wages Account is made £10 too little, so that there is a *short debit* of £10.

(*b*) In extracting the balances on the Sales Ledger Accounts, an item of £110 is entered on the list of balances as £100, causing a *short debit* of £10, while a cheque for £10 from Jones, a customer, has been debited in the Cash Book but never posted to the credit of his account in the Sales Ledger. The *total book debts* are correctly shown in the List of Balances, *although the detail items are incorrect*.

We may also have to deal with *errors of principle*. Supposing £50 is paid by way of deposit in connection with the supply of electricity to the business. This deposit is refundable if and when the business closes down, and therefore is an Asset. If the amount is debited to Heat, Light and Power Account in the Impersonal Ledger it will in all probability be written off as an *expense* for the particular period, resulting in an *overstatement of working expenses*, and an *understatement of Assets*.

Secondly, should a part of the Fixtures and Fittings be sold to a dealer when the offices are being modernised, and entered as a sale in the Sales Journal, Sales Account will be improperly inflated, *because the goods are not those in which the business is dealing*. Further, the Fixtures and Fittings Account will not record the reduction in value.

Here also the Trial Balance is of no help in the detection of the errors.

We must not, however, assume that its value as a basis for the preparation of the Final Accounts is seriously lessened. So far as accounts in the Impersonal and Private Ledger are concerned, these are not usually numerous, neither are the entries appearing therein, and great care is taken in practice to record the true facts.

Similarly when the Sales and Purchase Ledger Balances are extracted and totalled, it is usual for the work to be checked before the figures are finally accepted.

Errors which the Trial Balance will show

If there is a 'difference' on the Trial Balance, search must be made for the probable cause.

We can compare the names of the accounts appearing in it with those in some previous Trial Balance, and note any omission. We can also scrutinise each item in the light of its description and the definition that:

(*a*) A Debit Balance is either an Asset or an Expense, and
(*b*) A Credit Balance is either a Liability or a Profit.

Thus, if we regard Sales as a Profit, Sales Returns, or Returns Inwards should be considered as an Expense, or Debit Balance. If the returned goods remain in the warehouse unsold we could alternatively look on them as an Asset, but they would still be a Debit Balance.

It will not take long to go through the accounts in the Impersonal and Private Ledgers, if need be, to satisfy ourselves that they are apparently in order, and we should probably do this before re-examining the Sales and Purchase Ledger Accounts. Because they are so rarely met with, Credit Balances on the Sales Ledger and Debit Balances on the Purchase Ledger should also be considered as a likely indication of error.

If nothing is thus brought to light, and assuming the (monthly) totals of the Books of Prime Entry have been checked to the Impersonal Ledger, the following steps can be taken:

(*a*) Check the additions (or casts) of the Books of Prime Entry.
(*b*) Check the postings in detail from the Books of Prime Entry to the Sales and Purchase Ledgers.

The two latter checks involve a great deal of time and labour, but should result in locating the error, and obtaining agreement in the Trial Balance.

Example 9.1

The following Trial Balance was extracted from the books of F. Briers on 31 December 19x1. Do you think that it is correct? If not, rewrite it in its correct form.

	Dr.	*Cr.*
	£	£
Capital Account		11000.00
Stock at 1 January 19x1	3825.00	
Purchases and Sales	21275.00	31590.00
Returns Inwards		80.00
Returns Outwards	70.00	
Discounts Received	80.00	
Discounts Allowed		70.00
Motor Vans		4175.00
Wages and Salaries	10250.00	
Carriage		70.00
Rent and Rates	3185.00	
Sundry Debtors	4760.00	
Sundry Creditors		725.00
Cash in Hand	20.00	
Bank Overdraft	4245.00	
	£47710.00	£47710.00

Although the total debits equal the total credits, the Trial Balance is very far from being correct.

It should instead appear as below:

	Dr. £	*Cr.* £
Capital Account		11 000.00
Stock at 1 January 19x1	3 825.00	
Purchases	21 275.00	
Sales		31 590.00
Returns Inwards	80.00	
Returns Outwards		70.00
Discounts Received		80.00
Discounts Allowed	70.00	
Motor Vans	4 175.00	
Wages and Salaries	10 250.00	
Carriage	70.00	
Rent and Rates	3 185.00	
Sundry Debtors	4 760.00	
Sundry Creditors		725.00
Cash in Hand	20.00	
Bank Overdraft		4 245.00
	£47 710.00	£47 710.00

The adjustments made, and the reasons for them are:

(*a*) *Returns Inwards.* As an expense or Asset (see page 115) this is a Debit Balance.

(*b*) *Returns Outwards,* i.e. to *suppliers*. These are sometimes called Purchase Returns, and are a Credit Balance.

(*c*) *Discounts Received.* As a profit to the business, the amount represents a Credit Balance.

(*d*) *Discounts Allowed.* Clearly an expense, and so a Debit.

(*e*) *Motor Vans* are an Asset of the business and will be a Debit Balance in the Private Ledger.

(*f*) *Carriage.* The cost of carriage is a business expense, and a Debit in the Impersonal Ledger.

(*g*) *Bank Overdraft.* As a liability due to the bank this must be a Credit Balance in the Cash Book.

Questions on the Trial Balance are given at the end of Chapter 10.

10

Four-column Trial Balance

The purpose of this form of Trial Balance is to assist us further in the preparation of the Profit and Loss Account and Balance Sheet. It demonstrates in a manner which is not apparent in the ordinary form of Trial Balance, the fact that:

(*a*) a *Debit* Balance is either an *Asset* or an *Expense*, and
(*b*) a *Credit* Balance is either a *Liability* or a *Profit*.

The expenses and profits comprise the recurring Revenue aspects of the business, whereas the assets and liabilities reflect longer term Capital aspects.

Let us redraft the Trial Balance of R. Ready, shown on page 107, in *four-column* form:

Trial Balance

R. READY 28 February 19x1

			Revenue		*Capital*	
Account	*Ledger*	*Fo.*	*Dr.*	*Cr.*	*Dr.*	*Cr.*
			£	£	£	£
Cash	Cash Book	2			167.25	
Bank		2			1625.00	
C. Clowes	Bought	10				138.00
B. Bright						75.00
R. Wright	Sales	20			308.30	
M. Moses		23			57.50	
Purchases	Impersonal	30	120.00			
Credit sales		35		302.00		
Cash sales		40		1115.00		
Sales returns		45	10.00			
Discounts allowed		46	3.00			
Discounts received		50		5.00		
VAT		52				193.05
Wages		55	462.00			
Rent		60	120.00			
Furniture and fittings	Private	65			180.00	
Stock, 1 Feb.		70	1340.00			
Capital		75				2690.00
Drawings		80			125.00	
			£2055.00	£1422.00	£2463.05	£3096.05

Commencing Stock, although an Asset, is entered in the *Revenue* column because it represents goods in which the business is dealing. The Stock on hand at 28 February 19x1 will be recorded and will be used (see p. 125) in:

(*a*) The Revenue column (Credit), and
(*b*) The Capital column (Debit),

thus enabling us to record:

(*a*) The true Profit, and
(*b*) The existence of the Asset of Stock at this date.

Summary

	Dr.	*Cr.*
	£	£
Revenue	2055.00	1422.00
Capital	2463.05	3096.05
	£4518.05	£4518.05

What we have now done is to show in the *first two columns* all those items which are of a Revenue character, and which alone will concern us in ascertaining Profit or Loss.

In the *third and fourth columns* are found the accounts which relate to Assets except Closing Stock, and Liabilities, and as such comprise the Balance Sheet of the business.

Questions

1 Can the arithmetical agreement of the Debit and Credit Columns in a Trial Balance be considered conclusive proof of the accuracy of the book-keeping work?

Illustrate your answer with at least three suitable examples.

2 Write short notes on:
(*a*) Errors of omission
(*b*) Errors of commission
(*c*) Compensating errors
giving two examples of each.

3 On taking out a Trial Balance from a set of books, a book-keeper found that the Dr. side exceeded the Cr. by £9.

Assuming that this 'difference' was due to a single mistake, mention as many types of error as you can think of, each different in principle, any one of which could have caused it.

4 On preparing a Trial Balance from a set of books the sides are found not to agree, the Dr. total being £2530.20, and the Cr. £2580.60. You are convinced that nothing has been omitted and that all the figures are arithmetically correct, all postings, additions, etc., having been independently checked.

What is the probable nature of the error made and what will be the correct totals of the Trial Balance?

5 The following errors were discovered in a set of books kept by Double Entry:

(*a*) An item of £52 in the Sales Day Book posted to the customer's account as £50.20.

(*b*) Bank interest amounting to £60 charged by the bank on an overdraft, entered on the debit side of the Cash Book in the bank column.

(*c*) An item of £15 for goods returned by a customer entered in the Returns Outwards Book and omitted to be posted.

(*d*) A payment by cheque of £10 to X,Y., entered in the Cash Book on the credit side in the cash column.

State by what amount the totals of the Trial Balance disagreed.

6 The Assets Balances in a Trial Balance amount to £8500, the Capital (less Drawings) to £4000, and the Gross Income or Profits to £6000. The Total Debit Balances amount to £12 000. The only adjustment not appearing in the Ledger is Closing Stock valued at £1000. What is the profit for the year, and what is the amount of the liabilities? Show your workings.

7 State what 'difference' would be caused in the books of a business by each of the following errors:

(*a*) The omission from the list of debtors' balances, compiled for the purpose of the Trial Balance, of a debt of £12.25, due from P. & Co.

(*b*) Omission to post from the Cash Book to the Discount Account the sum of £5.35, representing discounts allowed to debtors during July.

(*c*) Omission to make any entry in respect of an allowance of £8.50 due to Q. & Co. in respect of damaged goods.

(*d*) Posting an item of wages paid, correctly entered as £231.75 in the Cash Book, as £231.25 in the Ledger Account.

(*e*) Posting £20 being cash received from the sale of an old office typewriter, to the debit side of 'Office Equipment' Account.

Note: These errors are to be taken as affecting different sets of books having no relation one to another.

8 The following Trial Balance contains certain errors. You are required to discover them and draw up a correct Trial Balance.

	Dr. £	*Cr.* £
H. Jones, Capital Account		6000.00
Current Account (Cr.)		1091.00
S. Brown, Capital Account		4000.00
Current Account (Dr.)		57.00
Salaries and wages	11140.00	
Rent and rates	2520.00	
Sales, less returns		32556.00
Purchases, less returns	17245.00	
Stock, opening	5472.00	
Trade debtors	10314.00	
Trade creditors		3591.00
Fixtures and fittings	550.00	
Manufacturing expenses	926.00	
Manufacturing expenses (unpaid)	102.00	
Office expenses	341.00	
Carriage inwards	559.00	
Carriage outwards		253.00
Bank overdraft		1956.00
Interest on overdraft		42.00
Bad Debts written off	112.00	
Bad Debts reserve	250.00	
Cash in hand	15.00	
	£49546.00	£49546.00

9 The following is the 'Trial Balance' of Diminishing Returns owned by X.Y. at 31 December 19x1:

	Dr. £	*Cr.* £
Capital		2650.00
Bank	126.00	
Machinery	1452.00	
Fixtures	78.00	
Stock, 1 January 19x1		340.00
Purchases	12242.00	
Wages	7135.00	
Salaries	3312.00	
Rent	1100.00	
Sales		24612.00
Repairs	357.00	
Bad debts	24.00	
Heat and light	748.00	
Bills receivable	118.00	
Debtors	852.00	
Creditors		475.00
	£27544.00	£28077.00

Amend the Trial Balance, taking the following into account:

(*a*) No entry had been made in the ledger in respect of a bill for £24 discounted with the bank on 20 December 19x1. Discounting charges (£1) had, however, been debited to the customer's account.

(*b*) The Sales Day Book had been undercast £89.

(*c*) The bank confirmed the overdraft at the sum shown on 31 December 19x1.

(*d*) X.Y.'s private drawings of £208 had not been posted to the Ledger.

(*e*) A sale of £10 had not been posted to the account of I. Jones, a customer.

10 At 31 December 19x1, the accountant of A.B.C. Ltd. has failed to balance his books of account. The difference has been carried to the debit of a Suspense Account.

Subsequently, the following errors are discovered:

(*a*) The total of the Sales Day Book for June has been posted to Sales Account in the Impersonal Ledger as £2784.25. The Day Book total is £2748.25.

(*b*) For the month of November, cash discounts allowed, £37.10, and Discounts received, £19.85, have been posted to the wrong sides of the Ledger Account.

(*c*) An allowance to a customer of £1.95 has been posted to the debit of his account in the Sales Ledger.

(*d*) A book debt of £14.55, due by L., a customer, has been omitted from the list of Sales Ledger balances.

(*e*) Cash drawings of the proprietor, amounting to £20, have not been posted to the Ledger.

(*f*) Goods purchased costing £21.10 were posted to the credit of the Supplier's Ledger Account, and also to the credit of 'Sundry Purchases' Account in the Bought Ledger.

After the discovery and correction of the errors mentioned, the books balanced. You are required:

1 To show the Suspense Account as it originally appeared.

2 To make the requisite corrective entries.

11

What is Profit or Loss?

Question The profit made seems to be represented by an increase in the Assets of the business during the period. Is this always the case?

Answer Yes. The word 'Profit' has no meaning except in the sense of an increase of Net Assets. You could just as truly say that Profit represents an increase in Capital. Put in another way, if the Capital invested at the commencement is a liability of the business, the liability is greater at the end of the period to the extent of the Profit earned.

Question What, then, is a Loss?

Answer A shrinkage in the Net Assets, or the extent to which they fall short of the initial Capital. If the latter had at one time comprised £100 worth of stock which owing to a general drop in prices had to be sold for £90 cash, an Asset of £90 would replace one of £100 and a Loss of £10 would have been incurred.

Such a loss would be described as a Revenue Loss, because stock is a part of the Current Assets of the business, or its Trading property. But if Fixed Assets, like Plant and Machinery, are sold at a figure below their book value, a Capital Loss is said to have been sustained.

Question Referring again to the example in Chapter 10, the proprietor had withdrawn £125 from the business for his personal use, and yet you put the item in the third, or *Asset* column of the Trial Balance.

Should it not have been entered in the first or *Expense* column?

Answer No, and for this reason. In the majority of businesses the owners will withdraw periodically either cash or goods (sometimes both) for their private use. These withdrawals are probably made to cover their living expenses, and have no relation whatever to the *expenses of the business*. We may regard them as withdrawals *on account of accruing profits*.

Therefore they properly appear elsewhere than in the Revenue columns of the Trial Balance. To enter them in the third or *Asset* column is the only alternative and is justified in point of fact if we look upon the initial Capital as a *Liability*. In withdrawing money or goods from the business, the proprietor has really reduced the Capital invested in the first place, assuming no Profits, or insufficient Profits, have been earned to cover the withdrawals.

Question Should drawings then be set against *Profits*, rather than against Capital?

Answer Often it is found convenient to proceed in this way. The Capital Account, as we have seen, is credited with whatever the proprietor first introduces. Any periodic drawings are then debited to a separate, or *Drawings Account*. This is sometimes called a *Current Account*. Subsequently when the figure of profit is ascertained it is put to the credit of Drawings Account, and any resultant balance probably represents the proprietor's under- or over-estimate of the profits. Of course, withdrawals may be made on account of Capital, and would be debited to Capital Account, but these are somewhat exceptional.

Question Am I right in thinking that the Trial Balance, whether in the ordinary or in the Four-Column Form, gives the whole of the information needed for preparing the Final Accounts?

Answer No. Even in the simple case of R. Ready, in the last example, certain *adjustments* may have to be made. It is true, however, to say, as we did, that it provides a *basis* for their preparation.

Question What are these adjustments?

Answer It will be better for us to consider them after we have become familiar with the ordinary form of *Revenue Account and Balance Sheet*, because they affect both.

The main additional factor we have to take into account is, however, that of *Stock in Trade*.

In ascertaining our profit figure, it is not enough to compare the cost of goods purchased with the proceeds of goods sold. Since a minimum amount of stock has to be held by the business and will usually have been included as part of the cost of purchases, an adjustment is necessary to calculate the cost of goods sold. Thus, at any particular date, e.g. the date to which the business makes up its accounts, allowance must be made for the existence of the stock *then on hand*, and its proper value.

In the case of a new business, if we thought in terms of *quantities* only, we might say *purchases* equal *sales* plus *stock on hand at the end* of the period. Therefore closing stock *must* be included in the second column of the four-column Trial Balance, and as it is a part of the property of the business at the same date, it *appears also* in the third or *Asset* column, i.e. in the former as a credit, and in the latter as a debit, which maintains the 'double-entry'.

12

The Revenue Account: The Trading, Profit and Loss, and Appropriation Accounts

What has just been discussed enables us to proceed to this first section of the Final Accounts.

Our task is to determine, in a suitable way, the Profit or Loss which has resulted from the carrying on of the ordinary transactions of the business.

We have always to remember with regard to the Final Accounts that they must be clear and informative, and free from unnecessary detail.

The period in respect of which they are drawn up will vary according to the requirements of the proprietor. In many cases it is customary to prepare them at yearly intervals, or at the date of the business's financial year end. This may be 31 December, 31 March, the end of the busy season, or some other date when perhaps there is least pressure of work on the office staff.

The **Revenue Account** is usually divided into three sections:

(*a*) The Trading Account.
(*b*) The Profit and Loss Account.
(*c*) The Appropriation Account.

For our present purpose it is the first two sections which are important.

In all three sections, however, we find that the *form* adopted is that of the *ordinary Ledger Account*, using the *Dr.* and *Cr.* symbols which are a feature of the latter.

The Trading Account

The purpose of this account is to determine what is called the **gross profit** or **loss**.

In it, making the due allowance for stocks carried at the beginning and the end of the period, we compare in a merchanting business the proceeds of sales with the cost of goods sold.

Example 12.1

On 1 January 19x7, A. Graham had a stock of goods value £1216. His purchases for the year amounted to £10340, and his sales to £15000. Transport charges on incoming goods amounted to £208. He valued his stock on 31 December 19x7, at £1764. Show his Trading Account.

Trading Account
Year ended 31 December 19x7

Dr.				Cr.
		£		£
Stock, 1 January 19x7		1216.00	Sales	15000.00
Purchases	£10340.00		Stock, 31 December 19x7	1764.00
Carriage inward	208.00			
		10548.00		
Gross Profit		5000.00		
		£16764.00		£16764.00

It is important we should notice the following points:

(*a*) The account is headed 'Year ended 31 December 19x7', implying that it is a summary of the transactions throughout the year.

(*b*) The cost of purchases is increased by the transport charges paid, and represents *delivered cost* to the business. Apart from this no other kind of expense whatever is included as this is a merchanting, or retail business.

(*c*) Gross Profit is seen to be the excess of sales over the purchased cost of the goods sold. It is the first stage in the determination of the final, or net, profit.

Stock in trade

Sometimes a difficulty may arise as to the measurement of the quantity and value of the Stock at 31 December 19x7, which is shown above at £1764.

We saw on page 125 how necessary it was to take it into account and an essential step in this process is to determine the quantities, usually by means of an actual stocktaking.

In this process the goods on hand will be counted, weighed, measured, etc., listed on stock sheets and priced at purchased cost. They cannot be valued at the higher selling price because they are not yet sold, and may never be sold. It is reasonable to value them at cost price, because in doing so we are merely carrying forward *from one period into another* a part of the Cost of Purchases.

It may be that at the date of stocktaking the market price (or present buying price) is less than the cost price. Provided, however, that there is no selling deficiency, i.e. the cost price, together with any selling expenses yet to be incurred, does not exceed the selling price, no adjustment is required. The business is not to be penalised because it failed to buy at the bottom of the market.

A final point to note is that in the Trading Account the ratio of **gross profit** to **sales** or **turnover** is an important one in all businesses. Expressed as a percentage it amounts in this case to 33⅓% of the Sales.

Let us now consider the **closing entries** in the Ledger Accounts concerned.

Private Ledger

STOCK

Dr. Cr.

Date	*Details*	*Fo.*	*Amount*	*Date*	*Details*	*Fo.*	*Amount*
19x7			£	19x7			£
Jan. 1	Balance	b/d	1216.00	Dec. 31	Transfer to Trading A/c		1216.00
Dec. 31	Transfer to Trading A/c		1764.00	Dec. 31	Balance	c/d	1764.00
19x8							
Jan. 1	Balance	b/d	1764.00				

(*a*) On 1 January 19x7, *stock then on hand* of course appears as a Debit Balance and is transferred on 31 December to the *debit* of the Trading Account.

(*b*) At the same time the closing stock figure of £1764 is debited above and posted to the *credit* of Trading Account.

(*c*) The debit of £1764 is then brought down on 1 January 19x8.

As in making these entries in the Stock Account we are transgressing the rule that no first entry shall be made in any Ledger Account, it may be preferred to use the Debit and Credit Journal as the proper Book of Prime Entry. Its use for this purpose was referred to on page 90. The record in this Journal would then be:

			Dr.	*Cr.*
19x7			£	£
Dec. 31	Trading A/c, 19x7	Dr.	1216.00	
	Stock			1216.00
	Being Transfer of Stock at January 1, 19x7			
19x7				
Dec. 31	Stock	Dr.	1764.00	
	Trading A/c, 19x7			1764.00
	Being Stock at this date transferred			

We could also journalise the transfers from the other Accounts which will be found in the Impersonal Ledger. In either case, the closing entries will appear as follows:

PURCHASES

Dr. Cr.

Date	*Details*	*Fo.*	*Amount*	*Date*	*Details*	*Fo.*	*Amount*
19x7			£	19x7			£
Dec. 31	Total purchases for year*		10340.00	Dec. 31	Transfer to Trading A/c		10340.00

* the total of the total for each month.

CARRIAGE INWARDS

Dr. Cr.

Date	*Details*	*Fo.*	*Amount*	*Date*	*Details*	*Fo.*	*Amount*
19x7			£	19x7			£
Dec. 31	Total expenses for year		208.00	Dec. 31	Transfer to Trading A/c		208.00

As regards *Sales* the transfer will be made from the *debit* of Sales Account to the credit of Trading Account.

SALES

Dr. Cr.

Date	*Details*	*Fo.*	*Amount*	*Date*	*Details*	*Fo.*	*Amount*
19x7			£	19x7			£
Dec. 31	Transfer to Trading A/c		15000.00	Dec. 31	Total sales for year		15000.00

In a *manufacturing* business, on the other hand, the Trading Account will be in somewhat different form. In addition to purchases, *wages* paid to workpeople employed in the actual production of the goods will be debited.

Purchases here will include in the main *raw materials* and component parts.

As *gross profit* in a *merchanting* business is ascertained after comparing the proceeds of sales with the cost of goods sold, similarly in a *manufacturing* business the proceeds of sales are compared with the *Direct Cost*, or Prime Cost, of production, which covers *both purchases and workpeople's wages*.

Our justification for dealing with it in this way may be stated as follows:

(*a*) *Merchanting business.* Every sales order booked involves a direct and proportionate increase in Purchases.
(*b*) *Manufacturing business.* Every sales order calls for not only a direct increase in purchases, but also a direct increase in workpeople's wages.

In (*b*), apart from these direct expenses of production, there are also the general factory expenses to be considered. These include rates on the factory premises, repairs to plant and machinery, power costs for operating the plant, and so on. It would be incorrect for us to include these in the Trading Account unless we are instructed to do so, because their inclusion would convert the Account into a Manufacturing, or Production Account.

In practice this will usually mean that a merchanting business will produce a trading account, and a manufacturing business will produce a manufacturing account and a trading account.

The Profit and Loss Account

This follows immediately after the Trading Account, of which it is really a continuation.

It commences with the balance brought down from the Trading Account, which as we have seen is a *gross profit* if a *credit* balance, or a *gross loss* if a *debit* balance.

Its purpose is to ascertain the final or *net profit* of the business for the period by including:

(*a*) The remaining *expenses*, other than those already dealt with in the Trading Account.

(*b*) The *incidental sources of income*, such as
Cash Discounts received,
Bank Interest received, etc.

In form it is precisely similar to the Trading Account, the expenses or debits appearing on the left-hand side, and the incidental sources of income or credits on the right-hand side.

As regards both debits and credits in the Profit and Loss Account, care must be taken that:

(*a*) The expenses are those *of the business only* (*excluding* such items as Proprietor's drawings, or private payments made on his behalf).
(*b*) *The whole of the expenses* relating to the period under review are properly brought in.

We shall see at a later stage the importance of the latter point, but meanwhile let us look at the form and construction of the Profit and Loss Account.

Example 12.2

From the items set out below select those which should appear in the Trading (or Goods) and Profit and Loss Account, prepare those accounts (only) showing the Gross Profit and the Net Profit or Loss.

	£
Capital	22400.00
Freehold Premises	21350.00
Stock at 1 January 19x9	650.00
Debtors	360.00
Creditors	1512.00
Purchases	13500.00
Sales	25000.00
Returns Inwards	20.00
Discounts Allowed	52.00
Salaries	7220.00
Trade Expenses	2753.00
Rates	490.00
Fixtures and Fittings	1062.00
Cash at Bank	450.00

The stock on hand at 31 December 19x9 was £215.

Trading and Profit and Loss Account

Year ended 31 December 19x9

Dr.	£	Cr.		£
Stock, 1 January 19x9	650.00	Sales	£25000.00	
Purchases	13500.00	*Less* Returns	20.00	
Gross profit c/d	11045.00			24980.00
		Stock, 31 Dec. 19x9		215.00
	£25195.00			£25195.00
Salaries	7220.00	Gross profit b/d		11045.00
Trade expenses	2753.00			
Rates	490.00			
Discounts allowed	52.00			
Net profit	530.00			
	£11045.00			£11045.00

The remaining items in the list, with which we have not dealt, are of a Capital nature, and will appear in the Statement of Assets and Liabilities, or Balance Sheet of the business.

The information below the 'Gross Profit' line comprises the *Profit and Loss Account*.

An alternative form of presentation which is increasingly being adopted is a vertical one. The same example is presented below in this form.

Trading and Profit and Loss Account

Year ended 31 December 19x9

	£	£
Sales	25000.00	
less Returns	20.00	
		24980.00
deduct		
Cost of goods sold:		
Stock, 1 January	650.00	
Purchases during year	13500.00	
Available for sale	14150.00	
Stock, 31 December	215.00	13935.00
Gross profit		11045.00
deduct expenses:		
Salaries	7220.00	
Trade expenses	2753.00	
Rates	490.00	
Discounts allowed	52.00	
		10515.00
Net profit		£530.00

The transfers from the Accounts in the **Impersonal** Ledger will be made as follows:

SALARIES

Dr.							Cr.
Date	*Details*	*Fo.*	*Amount*	*Date*	*Details*	*Fo.*	*Amount*
19x9			£	19x9			£
Dec. 31	Total salaries for year		7220.00	Dec. 31	Transfer to Profit and Loss A/c		7220.00

TRADE EXPENSES

Dr.							Cr.
Date	*Details*	*Fo.*	*Amount*	*Date*	*Details*	*Fo.*	*Amount*
19x9			£	19x9			£
Dec. 31	Total for year		2753.00	Dec. 31	Transfer to Profit and Loss A/c		2753.00

RATES AND TAXES

Dr.							Cr.
Date	*Details*	*Fo.*	*Amount*	*Date*	*Details*	*Fo.*	*Amount*
19x9			£	19x9			£
Dec. 31	Total for year		490.00	Dec. 31	Transfer to Profit and Loss A/c		490.00

DISCOUNTS ALLOWED

Dr.							Cr.
Date	*Details*	*Fo.*	*Amount*	*Date*	*Details*	*Fo.*	*Amount*
19x9			£	19x9			£
Dec. 31	Total for year		52.00	Dec. 31	Transfer to Profit and Loss A/c		52.00

Alternatively, instead of making the transfers direct to the Profit and Loss Account, we should use the *Debit and Credit Journal*, with the result that the following Journal entries will appear as *closing entries*:

			Dr.	*Cr.*
19x9			£	£
Dec. 31	Sundries			
	Profit and Loss A/c	Dr.	10515.00	
	Sundries			
	Salaries			7220.00
	Trade expenses			2753.00
	Rates			490.00
	Discounts allowed			52.00
	Being transfer of Expense Account balances to Profit and Loss Account as above.			

If the latter method be adopted the word 'Sundries' with the appropriate Journal reference will describe the credit entries in each of the Ledger Accounts, in place of 'Transfer to Profit and Loss Account'.

Appropriation, or Net Profit and Loss Account

As its name implies, this third section deals with the ascertained Net Profit or Loss, and its distribution among the proprietors of the business.

Thus in a partnership firm the Net Profit figure will here be divided in the ratio in which the partners share profits and losses.

In the case of a Limited Company, the appropriation account shows how the Net Profits are divided in dividend to the shareholders according to their respective rights and interests.

The necessity for such an account rarely, if ever, arises where the position of a sole trader is under consideration, the Net Profit being carried direct to the Capital or Current Account of the proprietor, as already explained.

Questions

1 What do you understand by (*a*) Capital Expenditure; (*b*) Revenue Expenditure?

State some items coming under each of these headings in the case of a Company carrying on business as manufacturers of aeroplanes.

2 What is the object in preparing a Trading Account as distinct from a Profit and Loss Account? Explain what information may be obtained from the former and its importance to a trader.

3 What do you understand by a 'Nominal Account'?

State some exceptions to the general rule that such accounts are closed when the Profit and Loss Account has been prepared, indicating the reasons for any balances which may remain.

4 What are the reasons for dividing the ordinary revenue account of a business into two sections, the Trading Account and the Profit and Loss Account?

5 What is the object of calculating gross profit and net profit? Does gross profit measure the prosperity of a business?

6 On 5 January 19x7, Ambrose sold goods to Applejohn.

The goods had cost Ambrose £100, and the selling price was 50% on cost, payment being due on monthly account less 2% for cash.

On 28 January 19x7, Applejohn returned a part of the goods, and Ambrose sent him a credit note for £30.

The amount due was paid by cheque on 28 February 19x7, but three days later the cheque was returned by the bank unpaid, and ultimately £0.75 in the £ was received from Applejohn and accepted in full settlement.

Show:

(*a*) Applejohn's Account in the books of Ambrose;
(*b*) What profit or loss Ambrose made on the whole transaction.

7 A business has three departments, A, B and C. You are asked to calculate the working profit in each department, by reference to the following:

	£
Opening Stocks, B	1280.00
Opening Stocks, C	640.00
Closing Stocks, B	1320.00
Closing Stocks, C	650.00
Purchases	6000.00
Wages	1800.00
General Expenses	1250.00
Sales, B	6800.00
Sales, C	3200.00

All purchases are made for A department in the first instance. A department (which has no sales) processes the goods and then re-issues them to B and C departments at fixed prices.

The issues to B were valued at £5000 and to C at £2400.

25% of the wages are charged to B, 20% to C, 10% to general expenses, and the balance to A.

The general expenses are recharged as follows:

Department A, 7% on output value,
Department B, 10% on sales value,
Department C, 7% on sales value,

any difference being carried to the Profit and Loss Account.

8 PQ carries on business as a merchant, but, although he has taken stock regularly at the end of December in each year, he has not kept proper books of account. He keeps a Cash Book, Petty Cash Book and Personal Ledger.

Explain briefly how you would proceed if requested by him to ascertain the result of his trading for the past year.

13

The Balance Sheet

Together with the Revenue Account, we have described this as a part of the Final Accounts of the business. It has been fittingly defined as 'a flashlight photograph of the position of affairs of the business at a particular date'.

More precisely we can speak of it as a Statement of Assets and Liabilities, including the balance of the Revenue Account made up to the date at which the Balance Sheet is prepared.

That it is a Statement of Assets and Liabilities justifies us in confining our attention to the 'Capital' columns of the four-column Trial Balance, the *debit balances* in which were seen to represent *Assets*, and the *credit balances, Liabilities.*

The fact that it includes the ascertained balance on the Revenue Account implies that this balance, if a Credit, will be shown as a Liability and if a Debit, as an Asset.

In other words, the business having an *initial liability* to its proprietor for the amount of Capital invested by him, has now a *further liability* in respect of the profit earned. Had a loss been sustained, it would be a Conventional Asset, or Asset in name only, i.e. it would appear on the Assets side of the Balance Sheet as representing the extent to which *the Assets as a whole were deficient in relation to the Capital.*

It is important for us to remember that the Balance Sheet is the complement to the Revenue Account and is indeed an essential part of the Final Accounts, for this reason. When the business was begun Capital was invested in it, perhaps in the first place in the form of cash. Almost at once this cash would be spent in the acquisition of various forms of property, of the kind we have defined as Fixed Assets, or Current Assets.

The former represented property which the business must possess as part of its equipment; the latter consisted of property in which the business was dealing.

If the Current Assets were therefore so dealt in by the proprietor or his manager as to produce a Profit, ascertained by the preparation of a Revenue Account, it would clearly be very desirable to draw up a further Balance Sheet at *the end of each trading period*, showing just what Assets existed in the business at that date. Provided no additions to or withdrawals from Capital had taken place, and each Asset held was reasonably and properly valued in each succeeding Balance Sheet, any increase in the Total Assets would represent a *profit*, and conversely any decrease a *loss*.

In the latter case, as the loss appeared in the Balance Sheet as an 'Asset', it could quite well be deducted from the *liability* of the business to its proprietor on Capital Account, disclosing at that point a *loss of Capital*, which, of course, is in line with the facts.

The form of the Balance Sheet

We have seen that the Revenue Account is prepared very much in the form of the ordinary Ledger Account although before presentation to others it may be redrafted into a vertical format.

In form, it is a summarised Ledger Account to which all the balances appearing in the 'Revenue' columns of the Trial Balance are transferred at the end of the financial year of the business. By so doing, an ultimate balance (either of Profit or Loss) is struck.

But we still have to deal with the balances appearing in the 'Capital' columns. It is these latter remaining balances, **and the balance of the Revenue Account**, which are entered in a 'sheet of balances' or **Balance Sheet**.

We could, if we wished, show this Balance Sheet in the form of an ordinary Ledger Account, debiting to it the Assets, and putting the Liabilities on the credit side.

The opposite, however, is the almost universal practice in this country, the Debit and Credit sides being reversed. Thus, Liabilities are shown on the left-hand or 'Debit' side of the Balance Sheet, and Assets on the right-hand or 'Credit' side, and this is true whether the business be owned by a sole trader, a partnership firm, or a Limited Company.

As a result, in reading the Balance Sheet in the ordinary way, from left to right, we begin with the Liabilities, and then turn to a study of the Assets out of which they are to be met.

We can also regard the Balance Sheet as a *classified summary* of the Ledger Balance, remaining on the books after the preparation of the Revenue Account, and including the balance of this latter Account.

The Balance Sheet and the Trial Balance contrasted

While both are drawn up at a particular date, the former includes only those balances which are, or have become *Assets* and *Liabilities*; the latter includes as well the various Impersonal Ledger balances relating to *expenses* and *gains*.

The Balance Sheet is a properly marshalled statement of the Assets and Liabilities, setting them out in their order of Realisability or Priority. The Trial Balance merely lists the whole of the balances in the order in which they happen to appear in the Ledgers.

Further, the purpose of the Balance Sheet is to give information to the proprietor of the business as to its financial position, whereas the Trial Balance is extracted primarily to prove the arithmetical accuracy of the book-keeping work.

Finally, the Balance Sheet always includes the value of the Stock on Hand at the end of the period; the Trial Balance, unless in four-column form (and not necessarily then) does not show this Asset.

Let us now take two illustrations involving some of the points we have been discussing:

Example 13.1

From the following items construct the Balance Sheet of L. Redfern as on 31 December 19x1.

	£
Capital as at 1 January 19x1	2000
Motor vans as at 31 December 19x1	2200
Cash at bank as at 31 December 19x1	700
Profit for the year	3000
Land and buildings as at 31 December 19x1	4100
Drawings for the year	1500
Stock of goods, 31 December 19x1	2300
Loan from A. Herbert	4000
Debtors as at 31 December 19x1	2000
Sundry creditors as at 31 December 19x1	3800

In this first case, it may be helpful if we list the items as **Assets** (Debits) or **Liabilities** (Credits), i.e.:

	Dr. £	*Cr.* £
Capital, 1 January 19x1		2000.00
Motor vans, 31 December 19x1	2200.00	
Cash at bank, 31 December 19x1	700.00	
Profit for the year		3000.00
Land and buildings, 31 December 19x1	4100.00	
Drawings	1500.00	
Stock of goods, 31 December 19x1	2300.00	
Loan from A. Herbert		4000.00
Debtors as at 31 December 19x1	2000.00	
Sundry creditors as at 31 December 19x1		3800.00
	£12800.00	£12800.00

L. REDFERN

Balance Sheet

as at 31 December 19x1

Liabilities	£	£	*Assets*	£	£
Loan from A. Herbert	4000.00		Cash at bank		700.00
Sundry creditors	3800.00		Debtors		2000.00
		7800.00	Stock of goods		2300.00
Current Account:			Motor vans		2200.00
Profit for year	3000.00		Land and buildings		4100.00
Less Drawings	1500.00				
	1500.00				
Capital Account: As at January 1, 19x1	2000.00				
		3500.00			
		£11300.00			£11300.00

We may then proceed as follows, remembering:

(*a*) That a Balance Sheet is always prepared at some definite date.
(*b*) That the balances on the various Accounts of which it is made up are **not** transferred to it as is the case with the Revenue Account.

It should be noted that:

(*a*) The Assets are stated in their order of realisability beginning with the liquid asset of 'Cash at Bank.'
(*b*) Cash, Debtors and Stock represent Current Assets, while Motor Vans and Land and Buildings are Fixed Assets.
(*c*) Although Profit and Drawings have been shown in a Current Account they might equally well have been recorded in Capital Account only.

As with the Trading and Profit and Loss Account, the Balance Sheet may be presented in a vertical format, for example:

L. REDFERN
Balance Sheet
as at 31 December 19x1

	£	£
Fixed Assets		
Land and buildings	4100.00	
Motor vans	2200.00	
		6300.00
Current Assets		
Stock of goods	2300.00	
Debtors	2000.00	
Cash at bank	700.00	
		5000.00
Total Assets		£11300.00
Capital account		
As at 1 January 19x1	2000.00	
Add profit for year	3000.00	
Deduct drawings	(1500.00)	
		3500.00
Loan from A. Herbert		4000.00
Sundry creditors		3800.00
Total Liabilities		£11300.00

It will be noticed that in this presentation the assets and liabilities are in the order of permanence and not order of realisability.

Example 13.2

From the following particulars construct the Balance Sheet of T. Tomlinson as on 31 March 19x2:

Capital 1 April 19x1 was £5000. The loss for the year to 31 March 19x2 was £1200 and his drawings were £220. On 31 March 19x2 the Stock was £2480, and the Bank Overdraft £1320, the Debtors £3260, the Loan from F. Weston £2200, the Fixtures and Fittings £1480, Creditors £2900, Cash in Hand £50, Machinery £2730.

If you have studied Example 13.1 carefully, it should not be necessary to list the balances again before constructing the Balance Sheet.

Looking at the information given, we see, however, that a *trading loss* of £1200 has been sustained, and in addition there are drawings of £220. The initial Capital has thus *decreased* by £1420.

As regards the Liabilities, we may note here that the first two relate to *cash advances*, the item 'Creditors' referring to the Purchase Ledger Accounts of suppliers for *goods* or *services*.

T. TOMLINSON

Balance Sheet

as at 31 March 19x2

Liabilities	£	£	*Assets*	£	£
Bank overdraft	1320.00		Cash in hand		50.00
Loan from			Debtors		3260.00
F. Weston	2200.00		Stock		2480.00
Creditors	2900.00		Fixtures and fittings		1480.00
		6420.00	Machinery		2730.00
Capital Account:					
1 April 19x1	5000.00				
Less Loss, year to 31 March 19x2 1200.00					
Drawings 220.00					
	1420.00				
		3580.00			
		£10000.00			£10000.00

Having considered separately the Trading and Profit and Loss Accounts, and the Balance Sheet, we may now, as in a practical case, prepare each of them from an ordinary two-column Trial Balance.

Example 13.3

From the following balances prepare the Trading Account, Profit and Loss Account, and Balance Sheet of J. Farmer, a retailer, for half year ended 30 June 19x1:

	£	£
Petty cash	50.00	
Sundry creditors		493.00
Cash at bank	986.00	
Furniture, fixtures and equipment	400.00	
Purchases	8417.00	
Sales		11618.00
Stock, 30 June 19x1	1117.00	
Office expenses	45.00	
Rent and rates	997.00	
Lighting and heating	186.00	
Advertising	75.00	
Delivery expenses	66.00	
Capital		2000.00
Drawings	1560.00	
Carriage on purchases	212.00	
	£14111.00	£14111.00

Stock on 30 June 19x1, £1084.

J. FARMER

Trading and Profit and Loss Account

Six Months ended 30 June 19x1

Dr.	£	£		£	Cr. £
Stock, 1 Jan. 19x1		1117.00	Sales		11618.00
Purchases	8417.00		Stock, 30 June 19x1		1084.00
Carriage on purchases	212.00				
		8629.00			
Gross profit c/d		2956.00			
		£12.702.00			£12702.00
Rent and rates		997.00	Gross profit, b/d		2956.00
Lighting and heating		186.00			
Advertising		75.00			
Delivery expenses		66.00			
Office expenses		45.00			
Net profit, carried to Capital A/c		1587.00			
		£2956.00			£2956.00

J. FARMER

Balance Sheet

as at 30 June 19x1

Dr.			Cr.		
	£	£		£	£
Sundry creditors		493.00	Petty cash	50.00	
Capital Account	2000.00		Cash at bank	986.00	
Add Net profit for half year to date	1587.00				1036.00
	3587.00		Stock		1084.00
Less Drawings	1560.00		Furniture, fixtures and equipment		400.00
		2027.00			
		£2520.00			£2520.00

We should note that as the Trading Account and the Profit and Loss Account are only divisions of the Revenue Account, they may conveniently be shown together, as above, in one statement.

Questions

1 What effect would the following errors made by a book-keeper have upon (*a*) the Trial Balance, (*b*) the annual accounts for a business:

(i) An item of £50 for goods sold to C.D. posted from the Sales Journal to the credit of C.D.'s Ledger Account.
(ii) An item of £212, representing the purchase of a desk, placed in the general expenses column of the Purchase Journal.
(iii) A sum of £15, representing interest allowed by the banker, entered in the correct column on the credit side of the Cash Book.

2 Enumerate the assets you would expect to find on the Balance sheet of A.B., a motor-car manufacturer, grouping them into the different classes.

Why is the distinction between different types of asset important?

3 From the following particulars draw up the Balance Sheet of B. Wilton as on 31 December 19x1: Land and buildings, £51000; Machinery, £7325; Motor vans, £12120; Fixtures and fittings, £3070; Stock on hand at 31 December 19x1, £5950; Sundry debtors, £3856; Cash in hand, £29; Sundry creditors, £7820; Bank overdraft, £1200; Loan from A. Mather, £40000; Capital as at 1 January 19x1, £30230; Loss for the year, £4100.
State briefly your opinion of the financial position of B. Wilton.

4 A.B., an engineer, decides to erect a new machine in his works. He dismantles an old machine and uses material therefrom to the value of £250 in the erection of the new machine. Additional materials are purchased from outside sources at a cost of £840, and the wages amount to £560.

Explain how the foregoing items would be dealt with in his books.

5 In the form of a three-column Cash Book, after properly heading each column, enter all the money transactions below and balance the book.

Journalise the opening balances and remaining transactions.

(Note: Purchases and Sales Books may be used, if preferred.)

Post the entries to the Ledger. Extract a Trial Balance.

Draw up a Profit and Loss Account and Balance Sheet.

On 1 May 19x7, D. Robinson, nurseryman, reopened his books with the following balances in addition to his Capital Account: Cash, £40; Rent outstanding , £80; Bank overdraft, £470; M. Merritt (Cr.), £232; S. Service (Dr.), £327; Stock, £1565.

During the month his transactions were:

			£
May	3	Received cheque from S. Service and paid into Bank	300.00
	5	Sold to S. Service:	
		Rose bushes	146.00
		Rose standards	139.00
		Misc. plants	127.00
	7	S. Service's cheque returned dishonoured	300.00
	10	S. Service paid in cash (banked)	275.00
	14	Bought of M. Merritt:	
		Fruit trees	356.00
		Shrubs	42.00
	18	Paid M. Merritt by cheque to settle account to 1 May	230.00
	21	Returned to M. Merritt damaged shrubs	4.00
	25	Cash sales	48.00
	26	Bought for cash sundry plants at auction	17.00
	27	Paid rent outstanding by cheque	80.00
	29	Drew cheque for self	80.00
	31	Wages and expenses for month:	
		Paid by cheque	120.00
		And in cash	52.00
		Bank charges	6.00
		Rent accrued	40.00
		Interest on capital at 6% p.a.	
		Stock on hand valued at	1701.00

6 The following balances were extracted from the books of D. Wright on 31 December 19x1. You are required to prepare a Trading Account, Profit and Loss Account and Balance Sheet as on that date.

	Dr.	*Cr.*
	£	£
Cash in hand	17.00	
Bank overdraft		175.00
Stock, 1 January 19x1	6794.00	
Purchases and sales	14976.00	26497.00
Wages	3719.00	
Insurance	155.00	
Bank charges	110.00	
Furniture and fittings	1115.00	
Returns inwards and outwards	309.00	237.00
Sundry Drs. and Crs.	1753.00	615.00
Land and buildings	20000.00	
Discount		154.00
Capital		21270.00
	£48948.00	£48948.00

Stock at end £1169.00.

7 From the following Trial Balance of J. Lowe, prepare Trading and Profit and Loss Accounts for the year ended 31 March 19x2, and a Balance Sheet as on that date.

The stock on hand at 31 March 19x2, was valued at £5500.00.

	£	£
Purchases	21300.00	
Carriage inwards	350.00	
Sales		36600.00
Stock, 1 April 19x1	4000.00	
Trade expenses	850.00	
Fixtures and fittings	2000.00	
Discounts allowed	900.00	
J. Lowe: Capital		6000.00
Returns inwards	750.00	
Cash in hand	150.00	
Sundry debtors	2400.00	
Salaries	7200.00	
J. Lowe: Drawings	2500.00	
Discounts received		400.00
Sundry creditors		4000.00
Cash at bank	2700.00	
Rent	500.00	
Rates	1400.00	
	£47000.00	£47000.00

8 The following Trial Balance was extracted from the books of R. Parr on 31 December 19x1:

	Dr. £	*Cr.* £
Capital		35000.00
Drawings	1450.00	
Stock at 1 January 19x1	26000.00	
Purchases and sales	45000.00	65000.00
Returns outwards		600.00
Returns inwards	1000.00	
Salaries	4750.00	
Trade expenses	2050.00	
Bad debts	230.00	
Discount account (balance)		350.00
Sundry debtors	35750.00	
Sundry creditors		19600.00
Insurance	220.00	
Fixtures and fittings	1850.00	
Motor vans	2650.00	
Rent and rates	3550.00	
Bank overdraft		3950.00
	£124500.00	£124500.00

The value of the stock on hand was £17950.

You are required to prepare Trading and Profit and Loss Accounts for the year ended 31 December 19x1, and a Balance Sheet as on that date.

9 The following balances were extracted at 30 April 19x2, from the books of C.D.:

(*a*) Prepare therefrom a Trading and Profit and Loss Account for the year ended on that date, and also a Balance Sheet.

(*b*) Do the results of the business for the year justify the drawings of £350 by C.D.?

	£
Office salaries	7628.00
Insurance of plant	61.00
Discounts received	33.00
Sales	27350.00
Bad debts	69.00
Plant and machinery	7430.00
Commission	127.00
Investment Interest received	30.00
Stock, 1 May 19x1	1110.00
Repairs	98.00
Sundries	46.00
Goods returned by customers	100.00
Discounts allowed	115.00
Rent and rates	1322.00
Purchases	4290.00

Sundry debtors	3143.00
Travelling expenses	263.00
Wages and National Insurance	13004.00
General insurance	34.00
Carriage inwards	87.00
Sundry creditors	1426.00
C.D.: Capital, 1 May 19x1	13250.00
Cash at bank	109.00
Coal, gas and water	2177.00
Goods returned to suppliers	74.00
Investment in Utopia Ltd	600.00

The stock at 30 April 19x2, was valued at £1275.00.

10 The following is the Trial Balance extracted at 31 December 19x2, from the books of S. Printer, who carries on business as a manufacturer of sports equipment:

	Dr. £	*Cr.* £
Petty Cash Book	28.00	
Nominal Ledger:		
Carriage outwards	504.00	
Carriage inwards	266.00	
Travelling expenses	2169.00	
Discount allowed	933.00	
Discount received		218.00
Repairs and incidentals	820.00	
Rent and rates	872.00	
Factory wages	10655.00	
Heating and lighting	137.00	
Sales, less Returns		30750.00
Factory National Insurance	318.00	
Packing and dispatch expenses	1252.00	
Purchases, less Returns	10546.00	
Salaries and National Insurance	2735.00	
Private Cash Book		853.00
Private Ledger:		
Stock, 1 January 19x2	3915.00	
S. Printer: Capital at 1 January 19x2		10000.00
S. Printer: Drawings	1200.00	
Office fixtures and general equipment 1 January 19x2	1567.00	
Equipment sold		136.00
Equipment purchased	608.00	
Bank interest account	46.00	
Sales Ledgers:		
Accounts receivable	6002.00	
Purchase Ledger:		
Accounts payable		2616.00
	£44573.00	£44573.00

The stock at 31 December 19x2, was valued at £5200.
You are required to:

(*a*) Prepare a Trading and Profit and Loss Account for the year ended 31 December 19x2, and a Balance Sheet at that date.

(*b*) State the percentages of Gross Profit and of Net Profit to Turnover.

(*c*) Show the office Fixtures and General Equipment Account as it would appear in the Private Ledger.

11 The following is the Trial Balance extracted from the books of J.B. as at 31 December 19x1.

	Dr. £	*Cr.* £
Private Ledger:		
Capital, 1 January 19x1		4137.00
Drawings	1000.00	
Stock, 1 January 19x1	2035.00	
Fixtures and fittings, 1 January 19x1	2119.00	
Bills payable		268.00
Bills receivable	238.00	
Nominal Ledger:		
Purchases	5911.00	
Sales		30782.00
Discounts allowed	223.00	
Discounts received		104.00
Packing expenses	192.00	
Office expenses	74.00	
Salaries	7826.00	
Repairs	58.00	
Lighting and heating	1087.00	
Rates	1146.00	
Rent	1200.00	
Wages (workpeople)	11644.00	
Sundry expenses	61.00	
Cash book		781.00
Petty cash book	27.00	
Creditors (Personal Ledger)		1433.00
Debtors (Personal Ledger)	2664.00	
	£37505.00	£37505.00

The stock on hand at 31 December 19x1, was valued by J.B. in the sum of £3157.

Prepare Trading and Profit and Loss Account, and Balance Sheet.

12 The following 'Statement of Affairs' has been drawn up to give the financial position, as on 31 March 19x1, and 31 March 19x2, respectively, of A. Brown, who keeps his books on a single entry basis:

Statement of Affairs, 31 March 19x1

	£		£
Capital	6192.00	Fixtures	250.00
Creditors	742.00	Stock	2305.00
		Debtors	4176.00
		Cash	203.00
	£6934.00		£6934.00

Statement of Affairs, 31 March 19x2

	£		£
Capital	5933.00	Fixtures	230.00
Creditors	817.00	Stock	2562.00
		Debtors	3777.00
		Cash	181.00
	£6750.00		£6750.00

Brown has transferred £100 a month regularly from his business banking account to his private banking account by way of drawings, and he has taken £25 worth of stock for his private use. The alteration in the value of the fixtures represents an amount written off by way of depreciation.

Calculate Brown's trading profit for the year.

13 The only books kept by Brown are Personal Ledgers. At 1 January his position is as follows:

	£		£
Cash	17.00	Creditors	635.00
Debtors	3109.00	Capital	3023.00
Stock	102.00		
Equipment at cost	430.00		
	£3658.00		£3658.00

At 31 December following, he informs you that the following are the figures concerning his Assets and Liabilities:

	£
Cash	15.00
Bank (overdraft)	230.00
Stock	98.00
Debtors	3036.00
Creditors	502.00

He has had his equipment valued, and thinks that it is now only worth £350. He has taken notes as to his drawings, and informs you that he has spent £1332 for household purposes, etc., £140 for a life assurance premium, and £110 for fire insurance for business assets. In addition, he has taken home goods, of which the cost price was £90 and the sale price £120.

Prepare a Statement showing Brown's profit for the year, and his general position at 31 December.

14 **Balance Sheet**

	£		£
Creditors	721.00	Freehold premises	21560.00
Capital	33150.00	Machinery and plant	7420.00
		Stock	2876.00
		Debtors	1982.00
		Cash	33.00
	£33871.00		£33871.00

The above is a copy of Samuel Wood's Balance Sheet as on 31 December 19x1. The only books kept are a Cash Book and a Ledger. The following is a summary of his receipts and payments for the year ended 31 December 19x2:

Receipts	£	*Payments*	£
Cash on account of credit sales	4276.00	Creditors for goods purchased	3954.00
Cash sales	12863.00	Wages	10743.00
Capital paid in	4200.00	General expenses	627.00
		Additions to machinery	4160.00
		Drawings	536.00
	£21339.00		£20020.00

On 31 December 19x2, the amount due to Creditors was £816, and the Debtors and Stock amounted to £2918 and £1854 respectively. You are required to prepare Trading and Profit and Loss Accounts for the year ended 31 December 19x2, and a Balance Sheet as on that date, after making adjustments in respect of the following:

(*a*) Depreciation of 10% is to be written off the Machinery and Plant, including additions during the year.

(*b*) £150 is to be provided as a Reserve for Doubtful Debts.

(*c*) The sum of £38 for goods supplied to the proprietor was included in the Debtors' balances at 31 December 19x2.

14

Adjustments in the Final Accounts

Question You said on page 124 that certain adjustments may be necessary in preparing the Final Accounts, and that the Trial Balance does not show what they are. Can we consider them now?

Answer As we have dealt with the simple form of Revenue Account and Balance Sheet, in which no adjustments were called for, we may now look a little more closely at the problem of ascertaining *true Profit and Loss* as it arises in practice.

In the first place, our task is not merely to prepare the Final Accounts from the information given in the books of the business as they may stand. We must examine the Ledger Accounts, particularly the accounts in the Impersonal or Nominal Ledger, with a view to seeing that they are *complete for the period under review*.

Question Is there any likelihood of their being incomplete?

Answer When we speak of the function of the Revenue Account, for example, as the statement of the Profit or Loss over a definite period, it is essential that we include in it *all the expenses incurred as well as the whole of the gross income* of the business.

If any expenses *attributable to the period* were inadvertently omitted, the final figure of Profit would be untrue, and would be *overstated*. Similarly, Profit is *understated* if we neglect to bring in every kind of income, however incidental to the main purpose of the business, which has been *earned* during the period and for which it may properly take credit.

Question Can you give me examples of such items, and explain why they are termed 'adjustments'?

Answer One of the biggest single items of expense in a manufacturing business is the *wages* of the workforce. In an ordinary case wages may be paid on Fridays in respect of the week ended on the preceding Wednesday. The wage sheets or cards for the week have to be checked and certified, the pay roll prepared, deductions made for National Insurance, and so on. Consequently, if the financial year ended on a Thursday, wages for a whole week and one day would be outstanding, no payment would have been made, and there would be no Credit entry in the Cash Book, and no Debit entry in the Wages Account for the amounts involved when the books were closed.

In effect, the *expense* figure for wages would be less than the true amount, and the fact that the workpeople were *creditors* of the business would be ignored. The former clearly has a bearing on the Revenue Account and the latter on the Balance Sheet. Therefore we must make an adjustment raising the wage figure to its true level (an additional Debit), and at the same time record the liability for wages in the Balance Sheet (an additional Credit).

Another instance arises in connection with the Book Debts, or 'Sundry Debtors', as we have more recently described them.

At the end of the financial year, a certain amount will be due from customers under this head for goods sold to them. The value of these goods appears as 'Sales' in the Trading Account, as we have seen, and is the main source of Profit. Unless we are quite convinced that our customers are willing and able to pay what they owe, a part of the Book Debts may become Bad Debts, and any loss that is likely to arise in this way must be charged by way of *estimate* against the Profit earned in the period. Otherwise, such estimated loss, if and when it becomes an actual or ascertained loss, is a burden on the Profits of the *subsequent* trading year. Neglect to reserve an estimated sum for Bad or Doubtful Debts has then the effect of *overstating Profits*, and *overstating Assets also*, in that they appear in the Balance Sheets of the business at more than they will ultimately realise.

The adjustment required in this case is to *debit* a sum to *Revenue* by way of 'Provision for doubtful debts', along with the debts actually written off as Bad during the period.

The corresponding Credit balance so created can be shown on the Liabilities side of the Balance Sheet, or better, as a *deduction* from the total Sundry Debtors on the Assets side, thereby reducing them to their estimated collectible value.

Question With all these adjustments, then, both the Revenue Account and the Balance Sheet are affected?

Answer Yes, either as a Debit to Revenue and a Credit on the Balance Sheet, with what is called a **Liability Provision**, or as a Credit to Revenue and a Debit on the Balance Sheet, in the form of an **Asset Provision**. The following are illustrations:

Example 14.1

Merryweather & Co. pay a rent of £2400 per annum for their business premises, which are rated at £2000 per annum. The local rates are £1.50 in the £ payable half yearly in advance on 31 March and 30 September.

The rent is payable on the usual quarter days, but on 30 September 19x6, the firm sublet a part of the premises to Tenant & Co. at £800 per annum, the first half-yearly payment being due on 31 March 19x7.

The Rent and Rates Account in Merryweather's books was as follows on 1 January 19x6:

19x6		£	19x6		£
Jan. 1	Balance b/d, Rates prepaid	750.00	Jan. 1	Balance b/d, Rent due 25 December	600.00

You are required:

(*a*) To write up the account for the year, bringing down any necessary balances at 31 December 19x6.

(*b*) To state in which section of the Final Accounts for the year 19x6 these balances would appear, giving reasons in brief.

Before we begin, let us take the information given, and consider it. The following points must be borne in mind:

(*a*) The financial year end of the business is 31 December 19x6.

(*b*) In the year ended on that date we shall expect to find in the Profit and Loss Account:

1 An expense for rent payable of £2400.
2 An expense for rates of £3000 (2000 × £1.50).
3 A profit for rent receivable from Tenant & Co. of £200 (3 months at £500 per annum).

MERRYWEATHER & CO.

Rent and Rates

Dr. | Cr.

Date		*Rent*	*Rates*	*Date*		*Rent*	*Rates*
19x6		£	£	19x6		£	£
Jan. 1	Balance b/d, Rates prepaid		750.00	Jan. 1	Balance b/d, Rent due December 25	600.00	
2	Cash, Rent	600.00		Dec. 31	Provision for 3 months' Rent		
Mar. 25	Cash, Rent	600.00			accrued from Tenant & Co. at		
31	Cash, Rates 6 months to 30 September 19x6		1500.00		this date at £800.00 per annum c/d	200.00	
June 24	Cash, Rent	600.00		31	Provision for 3 months' Rates		
Sept. 29	Cash, Rent	600.00			paid in advance c/d		750.00
30	Cash, Rates 6 months to 31 March 19x7		1500.00	31	Transfer to Profit and Loss A/c:		
Dec. 25	Cash, Rent	600.00			Rent Payable	2400.00	
31	Transfer to Profit and Loss A/c				Rates		3000.00
	Rent Receivable	200.00					
		£3200.00	£3750.00			£3200.00	£3750.00
19x7							
Jan. 1	Balance b/d:						
	Rent accrued due	200.00					
	Rates prepaid		750.00				

(*c*) And in the Balance Sheet:

4 An Asset or Debit Balance of £750 representing *rates paid in advance for the 3 months to 31 March 19x7.*

5 A similar Asset of £200, being rent accrued due at 31 December 19x6.

(*d*) The opening balances represent half the rates paid on 30 September 19x5 (one half of 2000 × £0.75) and the rent due (one quarter £2400).

The Rent and Rates Account in the Impersonal Ledger will then appear as shown on p. 154 assuming all payments are made on the due dates.

We notice in the above account that two columns may usefully be provided for rent and rates respectively, and that the *two provisions* carried down appear as the opening figures for the year 19x7. Since they are Debit Balances they may rightly be described as Asset Provisions.

It is not usually the practice to journalise these provisions (as by entry in the Debit and Credit Journal) and to this extent we find one exception to the general rule that 'nothing should be recorded in a Ledger Account which has not first appeared in a Book of Prime Entry.'

One more illustration may be taken of a provision, which is in the reverse direction.

Example 14.2

During 19x5, his first year of business, a merchant wrote off Bad Debts amounting to £100, and at 31 December made a provision for Bad and Doubtful Debts, amounting to £50.

During 19x6, a final dividend, £30, was received in respect of one of the debts (£40) written off in 19x5, further debts amounting to £60 were written off, and at 31 December 19x6, the merchant considered it prudent to make a provision against existing debts of 60% for one of £40, and 30% for one of £30.

In addition it was estimated that a final dividend of £0.75 in the £ would be received in 19x7 in respect of a debt standing in the books at £28.

You are required to produce, for the two years, the Bad Debts Account, Provision for Bad and Doubtful Debts Account, and (as far as possible) Profit and Loss Account.

Impersonal Ledger

BAD DEBTS

Dr.			Cr.		
19x5		£	19x5		£
Dec. 31	Sundry customers' debts written off	100.00	Dec. 31	Transfer to Profit and Loss A/c	100.00
19x6			19x6		
Dec. 31	Sundry customers' debts written off	60.00	Jan. 1	Cash, final dividend of £0.75 in £ on debt of £40.00 written off in 19x5	30.00
			Dec. 31	Transfer to Provision for Bad and Doubtful Debts A/c	30.00
		£60.00			£60.00

Impersonal Ledger

PROVISION FOR BAD AND DOUBTFUL DEBTS

Dr.				Cr.		
19x5			£	19x5		£
Dec. 31	Provision c/d, being provision at this date		50.00	Dec. 31	Transfer to Profit and Loss A/c	50.00
19x6				19x6		
Dec. 31	Transfer from Bad Debts A/c		30.00	Jan. 1	Provision b/d	50.00
31	Provision c/d, being provisions at this date:			Dec. 31	Transfer to Profit and Loss A/c	20.00
	X. 60% of £40.00	£24.00				
	Y. 30% of £30.00	9.00				
	Z. 25% of £28.00	7.00				
			40.00			
			£70.00			£70.00
				19x7		
				Jan. 1	Provision b/d	40.00

Profit and Loss Accounts (extract)

Year ended 31 December 19x5

Dr.		Cr.
	£	
Bad debts, including Provision	150.00	

Year ended 31 December 19x6

Dr.	£	Cr.
Bad debts, less Recoveries, and including Provision	20.00	

In this illustration, we are instructed to open separately an account for the Provision for Bad and Doubtful Debts.

The recovery of £30 during 19x6 serves to reduce the expense of £60 for debts written off during that year, and the balance is transferred at the year end to the Provision Account. The Provision required at 31 December 19x6, is brought down as a Credit Balance on 1 January 19x7, and may as such be termed a Liability Provision.

Alternatively, the Profit and Loss Account for 19x6 could show a debit (charge) for Bad Debts of £30 and a credit of £10, being the difference between the opening provision of £50 and the required closing provision of £40. This would be a more accurate use of the two accounts.

Questions

1 Explain briefly the object of a bad debts reserve. Upon what basis is it usually formed? How does it affect the Profit and Loss Account and the Balance Sheet? Illustrate your answer with a specimen account.

2 During the year ended 31 December 19x9, C. P. Kilham made the following bad debts: A.B., £13.13; X.Y., £5.49; and R.Z., £12.91.

Submit the entries Kilham should make when closing his books as on 31 December 19x9.

3 X. sets up in practice as a doctor on 1 January 19x2. During 19x2 he received fees amounting to £33 545, and at the end of the year £237 was owing to him. During 19x3 the fees received amounted to £33 831, and at the end of the year £364 was owing to him. His expenses amounted to £11 265 in 19x2 and £11 320 in 19x3, there being no liabilities outstanding at the end of either year.

Ascertain his profit for each of these years.

4 On 1 October 19x5, the Bad Debts Reserve Account of a business stood at £3768. During the ensuing twelve months bad debts amounting to £3389 were written off. On 30 June 19x6, a payment of £80 was received on account of a debt which had been treated as irrecoverable two years previously. The debts outstanding at 30 September 19x6, were examined, and the book-keeper was instructed to make a reserve of £3400 to cover the anticipated loss.

You are required to show the Ledger Account or Accounts as they appear after the closing of the books had been completed.

5 On 1 January 19x6, H. Jacks owed J. Dixon £220. On 31 March Jacks purchased goods from Dixon valued at £246, of which he returned goods to the value of £16 on 3 April. On 6 April Jacks paid Dixon £120 on account. On 1 July Dixon received notice of the bankruptcy of

Jacks, and on 5 October he received first and final dividend of £0.35 in the £ from the Trustee in Bankruptcy. Show the account of H. Jacks in the Ledger of J. Dixon as it should appear after Dixon had balanced his books at 31 December 19x6.

6 The Rates Account of G. Baker is shown in his Ledger as follows:

RATES ACCOUNT

19x4
31 Dec. To Balance, in advance, b/f £360.
19x5
31 May To Cash, half-year to 30 September 19x5, £734.50.
18 Nov. To Cash, half-year to 31 March 19x6, £734.50.

Balance the account by transfer to Profit and Loss Account at 31 December 19x5, bringing forward the appropriate amount in advance. (Remember that rates are due on 31 March and 30 September.)

7 At 31 December 19x1, the Ledger of T. Atkins contained the following balances for debts due to him:

	£
Arthur	436.08
Charles	215.50
Henry	314.09
Percy	120.50

The estate of Arthur is being administered in Bankruptcy, and it is feared, pending realisation, that not more than £0.50 in the £ will be recoverable. Henry has died and his estate has no assets whatever. For the sake of prudence 5% is to be reserved on the debts of Charles and Percy.

Show the four accounts, together with Bad Debts Account and Reserve for Doubtful Debts Account. Journal need not be given.

8 In 19x2 a trader, X, wrote off as a bad debt £319.77, the balance of an account due to him by Y.

In 19x3 Y paid the debt in full. Show by means of Journal entries how the recovery of this debt would be dealt with in closing X's books for 19x3, on the assumption that:

(*a*) The cash received was posted to the credit of Y's account.
(*b*) The cash was posted to a nominal account.

9 The payments made by X Ltd to its travellers on account of commission and salaries during 19x4 amounted to £121 547.18 and during 19x5 to £141 752.67. The amounts accrued and unpaid under this heading were as follows:

	£
31 December 19x3	2036.96
31 December 19x4	3441.18
31 December 19x5	3122.89

Draw up a statement showing the amount to be charged against profits in 19x4 and 19x5 respectively, and show what would have been the effect of accidentally omitting to make the proper reserve at the end of 19x4.

10 The Rent and Rates Account in the Ledger of Riley Bros. showed that on 31 December 19x5, the rent for the quarter to Christmas was outstanding, and that the rates for the half-year ending 31 March 19x6, amounting to £876.38 had been paid. During the ensuing year the following payments relating to rent and rates were made:

		£
Jan. 4	Rent for Christmas quarter	590.00
Mar. 29	Rent for Ladyday quarter	590.00
June 26	Rates for half-year ending 30 September 19x6	974.73
July 7	Rent for Midsummer quarter	590.00
Sept. 30	Rent for Michaelmas quarter	590.00
Dec. 28	Rent for Christmas quarter	590.00

The rates for the half-year ending 31 March 19x7, which amounted to £980.88 were paid on 6 January 19x7.

You are required to show the Rent and Rates Account as it would appear after the books for the year ended 31 December 19x6 had been closed. Make any calculation in months.

11 The financial year of Sanctions Ltd ended on 31 December 19x5.

At that date, the following balances appeared, among others, in their Impersonal Ledger:

Rates, £3225 (15 months to 31 March 19x6).
Wages, £47098 (to 27 December 19x5).
Stationery, Advertising, etc., £864.
Bad and Doubtful Debts, written off, £126.

The wages for the week ending 3 January 19x6, were £2562 (7 day week).

Stationery stocks for which an adjustment is required amounted to £117.

The Sundry Debtors totalled £5660, and a reserve is to be made of 5% for doubtful debts, and 2% for discounts.

Show the Ledger Accounts involved after giving effect to the above.

12 XY, who owed £200 to AB for goods supplied on 1 June 19x4, became unable to pay his debts in full and offered a composition of £0.25 in the £ to his creditors and this was accepted. A cheque for the dividend was received by AB on 1 December 19x4.

When XY called his creditors together, AB had on his premises a machine belonging to XY and claimed a right of lien in respect thereof. This was admitted and the machine was valued at £80. AB's claim was consequently reduced by this amount.

AB decided that instead of selling the machine he would retain it as part of his plant. When making up his annual accounts on 31 December 19x4, the balance of XY's account was written off as a bad debt.

You are required to show, by means of Journal entries and Ledger Accounts, how the foregoing transactions would be recorded in AB's books.

13 In the books of Harry Holborn at 31 December 19x6, the financial year end, the Ledger Account for 'Heat, Light, Power and Water' shows a Debit Balance of £1253. Investigation discloses the following points:

(*a*) A deposit of £100 (returnable on cessation of supply) was paid on 1 April 19x6, in respect of electric power.

(*b*) The charge for electric power is made quarterly, and the last debit in the account is for the three months to 30 November 19x6. The demand note for the three months to 28 February 19x6, amounted to £135.

(*c*) A half-year's water rate, amounting to £94, was debited to the account in October 19x6, in respect of the period to 31 March 19x7.

Make such adjustments in the Ledger Account as appear to you to be necessary and state how, if at all, they would be shown in Holborn's Balance Sheet at 31 December 19x6.

14 On 1 January 19x3, A and B go into business as advertising consultants, on the footing that each contributes £1000 cash as capital, profits and losses to be shared equally.

The £1000 provided by A is borrowed by him privately from his bankers at 8% p.a. interest.

It is agreed that B, who devotes his whole time to the business, shall receive prior to the ascertainment of profit a management salary of £1250 p.a.

Office accommodation is acquired on 1 February 19x3, at a rent of £300 p.a., payable quarterly, the first payment to be made on 31 March 19x3.

Furniture and fittings are purchased on the latter date from O.F. Ltd, for a sum of £72 cash, and B introduces other similar equipment of a value of £36 to be credited to his Capital Account.

Apart from the above items, at 31 December 19x3, there has been received in cash by A and B as consultants' fees the sum of £6150, and at that date fees totalling £340 are outstanding and due to them.

Heating, lighting, etc., amounted to £575 during the period, and A and B incurred travelling and entertaining expenses of £763 in connection with visits to clients, all of which has been duly paid.

Prepare a Revenue Account of the business of A and B for the year ended 31 December 19x3, and a Balance Sheet at that date.

15

Depreciation

We have seen in the preceding chapter how very important it is that all matters affecting the ascertainment of true profit shall be properly taken into account whenever an attempt is made to produce a Trading and Profit and Loss Account and Balance Sheet. Thus, any outstanding income, even though not actually received in cash, and any expense incurred but not yet paid must, if relating to the period under review, be provided for either as an *Asset or a Liability Provision*.

In so doing, we are taking steps to ensure *the genuineness of the profit figure* which the Revenue Account discloses, but we should not forget that the Balance Sheet drawn up at the end of the period likewise calls for attention. If the Balance Sheet is concerned with the proprietor's Capital, and the property or Assets by which it is represented, it is just as necessary to consider the correctness of the values put upon these Assets. Generally speaking, it is sufficient for the Assets as a whole to be shown at their 'going concern' values, i.e. at a figure which reflects their worth to the business as an established concern, producing a normal and reasonable profit on the total Capital invested. By way of contrast we can speak of *break-up* values of the property, representing its realisable value if sold in the market for what it will fetch. Between the two, there is a very wide gap, particularly noticeable with Fixed Assets, as distinct from Current Assets.

Examples of Current Assets, as we know, are:

(*a*) Stock in Trade, and
(*b*) Book Debts,

and we have seen that they are typical of the property *in which the business is dealing from day to day*. The Stock held by the business must be capable of sale at the prevailing market price; Book Debts must also be capable of collection from customers at their full value, subject to any provision made for debts which are considered to be doubtful.

We can, therefore, appreciate that as regards Current Assets, the test of their *realisable value* is all-important, and their *book value* (as shown in the Books of Account) should be in line with it.

In the case of Fixed Assets, however, being property *purchased for retention* and *not* for resale, altogether different considerations apply. Of this class of property, examples are:

(*a*) Plant and Machinery,
(*b*) Motor Vehicles for delivering goods to customers.

Without them, the business cannot begin to function, and they are clearly an essential part of its Capital equipment.

Because they represent property *used* for the purpose of the business, we have to recognise that there is in them *an element of impermanence*, and although they are retained within the business, a limit must be set to their *effective working life*, or the period of time during which they can be economically operated. Beyond that period, no matter how carefully they have been repaired and overhauled, it will probably be found that charges for renewals and replacements of parts to an increasingly large extent have to be met, so much so that, quite apart from the risk of their becoming obsolete, or out of date, *these Assets as a whole must be replaced.*

The effective working life will naturally vary as between one class of Fixed Asset and another; sometimes it may be from 20 to 30 years, while with motor vehicles 3 years is often the maximum period during which useful service can be rendered to the business.

As a result, we can recognise a progressive shrinkage in value of these classes of property, which we term *depreciation*, and it is very important that we take a note of it as *a shrinkage of value caused by the use of the property for the purpose of profit-earning.*

We can even take the matter further, and argue that against the profits earned in each trading year should be put as an expense the depreciation estimated to have taken place.

In other words, we may say that the loss in value is just as truly a business expense as the wages paid to workpeople, or the charge for rent and rates.

The real working expenses will be understated if the factor of depreciation is ignored year by year, and ultimately, when the machinery is worn out, or obsolete, the proprietor of the business may have to introduce fresh Capital to replace it, or else shut down.

This point of view brings us to the second reason for charging depreciation. Net Profit as ascertained by the preparation of the Trading and Profit and Loss Account is the yield upon the Capital invested, and may be wholly withdrawn by the proprietor in the form of cash. If depreciation is charged as a business expense, this Profit figure will be accordingly reduced, and also the amount of *cash withdrawable from the business* on account of it. Put in yet another way, cash or its equivalent, representing the charge for depreciation, will be retained within the business, and may, over a period of time, accumulate to provide the moneys required for eventual replacement.

For these reasons, it is the general practice to depreciate or *write down* the Fixed Assets, usually on a percentage basis, at all times when the Final Accounts are to be prepared.

The result is that we have:

(*a*) A Debit to Profit and Loss Account, and
(*b*) A Credit to the particular Asset Depreciation Account.

The two methods most generally employed are:

1 The Straight Line, or Fixed Instalment method.
2 The Diminishing Balance, or Reducing Instalment method.

They have in common the fact that a percentage of either the cost or book value of the Asset is written off against profits period by period, with or without allowance for any *residual* or *scrap* value.

Straight line method

The straight line method relies on writing off yearly a part of the *original or purchase cost.* When the Asset is bought its effective working life is estimated as being a certain number of years, and the cost is recovered rateably over this period.

Example 15.1

Sanders and Son have a motor lorry which cost £13 185 on 1 January 19x5. Depreciation is to be provided using the Straight Line method over a period of 3 years, at the end of which it is expected that it will be bought back by the supplier for £2400. Show the Ledger Account of the Asset and the Asset Depreciation Account in the firm's books.

Calculation of depreciation

		£	
original cost		13 185	
resale value		2 400	
loss in value	=	10 785	
over 3 years, i.e.		£3 595	per annum

At 31 December 19x5 the lorry would appear in the Balance Sheet as below:

Assets

	£	£
Motor Lorry, at cost	13 185.00	
Less Depreciation	3 595.00	
		9 590.00

i.e. its book value would then be £9590 only.

Private Ledger

MOTOR LORRY

Dr.							Cr.
Date	*Details*	*Fo.*	*Amount*	*Date*	*Details*	*Fo.*	*Amount*
19x5			£	19x5			£
Jan. 1	Cash, Purchase cost		13 185.00	Dec. 31	Balance	c/d	13 185.00
			£13 185.00				£13 185.00
19x6				19x6			
Jan. 1	Balance	b/d	£13 185.00	Dec. 31	Balance	c/d	£13 185.00
19x7				19x7			
Jan. 1	Balance	b/d	£13 185.00	Dec. 31	Cash		2 400.00
				31	Transfer to disposal of motor lorry A/c		10 785.00
			£13 185.00				£13 185.00

MOTOR LORRY DEPRECIATION

Dr.							Cr.
Date	*Details*	*Fo.*	*Amount*	*Date*	*Details*	*Fo.*	*Amount*
19x5			£	19x5			£
Dec. 31	Balance	c/d	3595.00	Dec. 31	Transfer to Profit & Loss A/c		3595.00
19x6				19x6			
Dec. 31	Balance	c/d	7190.00	Jan. 1	Balance	b/d	3595.00
				Dec. 31	Transfer to Profit & Loss A/c		3595.00
			£7190.00				£7190.00
19x7				19x7			
Dec. 31	Transfer to disposal of motor lorry A/c		10785.00	Jan. 1	Balance	b/d	7190.00
				Dec. 31	Transfer to Profit & Loss A/c		3595.00
			£10785.00				£10785.00

Diminishing balance method

In this case, *a fixed percentage is written off the book value* of the Asset as it appears *at the commencement of each year*. This method is sometimes used by smaller firms, usually for assets with a small value. Most firms would keep a detailed register for each particular motor car or lorry and for each item of plant and machinery.

Example 15.2

At 1 January 19x6, the balance on the Plant and Tools Account was £4730. During the year a lathe was purchased costing £575, and on 31 March 19x7, three drilling machines which cost £900 when purchased 3 years ago were sold for £520.

Show the Asset Account, reckoning depreciation at 10% per annum on the Diminishing Balance method.

Private Ledger

PLANT AND TOOLS

Dr.							Cr.
Date	*Details*	*Fo.*	*Amount*	*Date*	*Details*	*Fo.*	*Amount*
19x6			£	19x6			£
Jan. 1	Balance	b/d	4730.00	Dec. 31	Profit & Loss A/c Depreciation 10% of £4730.00		473.00
June 30	Cash Lathe		575.00	31	Balance	c/d	4832.00
			£5305.00				£5305.00
19x7				19x7			
Jan. 1	Balance	b/d	4832.00	Dec. 31	Cash 3 Drilling Machines sold		520.00
				31	Profit & Loss A/c Loss on sale		136.10
				31	Profit & Loss Depreciation 10% on £4832.00		483.20
				31	Balance	c/d	3692.70
			£4832.00				£4832.00
19x8							
Jan. 1	Balance	b/d	£3692.70				

N.B. –

Cost 3 years ago	900.00
1st year 10%	90.00
	810.00
2nd year 10%	81.00
	729.00
3rd year 10%	72.90
	656.10
Selling price	520.00
Loss:	£136.10

At 31 December 19x6, the following would appear in the Balance Sheet:

Assets

	£	£
Plant and Tools		
At 1.1.19x6	4730.00	
Add Additions at Cost	575.00	
	5305.00	
Less Depreciation at 10% per annum	473.00	
		4832.00

Although this is the net book value it does not show the aggregate cost and depreciation provided which 'best practice' would consider desirable.

The reducing instalment method is open to the criticism that Fixed Assets so depreciated tend to be dealt with in groups, and that with ordinary rates of depreciation its slowness in writing down the values is not sufficiently recognised. If the life of the asset is short the percentage required may be prohibitively high; e.g. to depreciate a tool having a life of three years only would require a 90% rate.

Sometimes the Debit and Credit Journal is used so as to avoid making a Prime Entry in the particular Ledger Account:

Example 15.3

19x6			*Dr.*	*Cr.*
Dec. 31			£	£
	Profit and Loss A/c	Dr.	473.00	
	Plant and Tools Depreciation A/c.			473.00
	Being depreciation at 10% p.a. now written off.			

As the illustration shows, an account for Depreciation as a business expense may be opened in the Impersonal Ledger, *but the Debit Balance on it must ultimately be transferred to Profit and Loss Account.*

Questions

1 How is the shrinkage in the value of fixed assets provided for in accounts kept on the double entry principle?

Illustrate your answer by showing an account relating to an asset which has been written down in accordance with your suggestions.

2 Explain briefly, but as clearly as you can, why it is generally necessary, when preparing the accounts of a business, to make provision for depreciation of the fixed assets.

If you know of any exceptions to this general rule, mention them and give your reasons.

Note: Goodwill is, for the purpose of this question, not to be regarded as a fixed asset.

3 On 1 January 19x1, a business purchased a motor delivery van for £8800.

Show how the account would appear in the books of the business for the four following years assuming that depreciation is written off (*a*) by the fixed instalment method, and (*b*) by the diminishing balance method, the rate of depreciation being 20% in each case.

State, giving your reasons shortly, which method of depreciation you consider is more appropriate for an asset of this sort.

4 On 1 January 19x2, Dix Ltd purchased machinery costing £1240. For the years 19x2, 19x3 and 19x4 depreciation was written off at the rate of 5% on the diminishing balance. During 19x5, it became apparent that the machinery would not be of service after 31 December 19x6, and for these latter two years the fixed instalment method was substituted to write off the remaining balance. In December 19x6, the machinery realised £15 on sale. You are required to write up the Machinery Account from the commencement, reckoning depreciation to the nearest £.

5 X Ltd purchased a seven-year lease of certain shop premises for £8000. A further sum of £2000 was expended in various alterations, and it was estimated that at the end of the lease the cost of restoring the premises to their original condition (for which the company was liable) would be about £500.

Show the Ledger Account for the first two years, providing for depreciation.

6 From the following particulars, write up the Machinery Account for the year ended 30 November 19x6.

The balance from the previous year was £26 882.

On 31 May 19x6, new machinery was purchased for £1164, and wages amounting to £124 were paid for its erection. The old machinery replaced by the above was sold for £144, which was its written-down value on 30 November 19x5.

Depreciation at the rate of 12½% per annum is to be written off (for this question half a year is significant).

7 The Balance Sheet of P.Q. & Co. Ltd, drawn up as on 31 March 19x7, showed plant and machinery valued, after writing off depreciation, at £25 500.

Depreciation had been written off regularly, from the dates of purchase of the various items, at the rate of 10% per annum on the diminishing value.

On 1 June 19x7, a motor, which had been bought on 1 November 19x2, for £5750, was sold for £1250 and replaced by a new one costing £7700.

Show the Plant and Machinery Account as it would appear in the Company's books for the year ended 31 March 19x8, after writing off the appropriate depreciation for the year. (For this question work in months.)

8 C.D. purchased factory premises (subject to a lease of 10 years from 30

June 19x0) from the Liquidator of H Ltd on 30 June 19x4, the purchase price being £3000.

To enable him to complete the purchase, he borrowed £1650 from Happy Bank Ltd, the loan being repayable in three years by equal annual instalments of principal, reckoning interest at 10% per annum.

Provide depreciation on the fixed instalment basis, and show the Property Account and the Loan Account in C.D.'s books for the three years to 30 June 19x7.

9 On 1 January 19x4, a manufacturer acquired a machine at a cost of £1200.

During 19x4 repairs to the machine cost £50 and a new attachment, which cost £250, was added to it.

The repairs during the year 19x5 amounted to £180.

It was decided to depreciate the machine at the rate of 10% per annum on the reducing instalment method.

From the foregoing particulars you are required to write up the Machinery Account for the two years ended 31 December 19x5.

10 The following is the Trial Balance extracted from the books of J. Falconer at 31 December 19x6:

	Dr. £	*Cr.* £
Salaries	12414.00	
Discounts received		132.00
Repairs and renewals	318.00	
Sales		68505.00
Carriage outwards	163.00	
Creditors		674.00
Wages	26116.00	
Sundry expenses	86.00	
Sundry debtors	3445.00	
Commission	196.00	
Capital, 1 January 19x6		7200.00
Stock, 1 January 19x6	1572.00	
Discounts allowed	578.00	
Returns outwards		295.00
Plant and machinery, 1 January 19x6	7460.00	
Cash in hand	2.00	
Purchases	7336.00	
Rates	3575.00	
Warehouse expenses	4537.00	
Office fixtures, etc., 1 January 19x6	4220.00	
Cash at bank	1200.00	
Rent of premises	2788.00	
Drawings	1000.00	
Bad debts reserve, 1 January 19x6		200.00
	£77006.00	£77006.00

You are required to prepare:

(*a*) Trading and Profit and Loss Account for the year to 31 December 19x6.

(*b*) Balance Sheet at 31 December 19x6, showing per cent net Profit to Capital at 1 January 19x6.

(*c*) The following adjustments are necessary:

(1) The stock on hand at 31 December 19x6, was valued at £1769.

(2) 3 months rates are prepaid in the sum of £715.

(3) The rent of premises is £3717 per annum, payable quarterly, and has been paid to 29 September 19x6.

(4) Depreciation is to be charged at 5% on plant and machinery, and 10% on office furniture, etc.

11 Give the Journal entries necessary to record the following transactions:

Dec. 2 Bought fixtures and fittings value £345 on credit from S. Maxton and Sons.

15 A cheque value £76.25 received from Perkins Ltd was wrongly posted to Brampton Bros.' Account.

19 Exchanged one motor-car value £1120 for three typewriters value £200 each and the balance in cash.

31 Plant and machinery is to be depreciated by £2173.

31 O. Carfax, a debtor for £55, having become insolvent, pays £0.2 in the £ settlement of the amount owing.

12 A firm acquired a 25 years' lease of its business premises for £18 000. The firm's bankers advanced £12 000 towards the purchase price on the security of the lease.

Repayment of the Bank loan is made by quarterly instalments of £250 which the bank debit to the firm's current account together with interest at the rate of 10% per annum.

You are required to make the entries in the firm's books at the end of the first year to record the above arrangements, including depreciation of the lease according to the method you consider most suitable in the circumstances.

16

Partnership

In the chapters that have gone before we have considered the business to be owned by a sole proprietor, or, as he is termed, a **sole trader**. This was the earliest form of proprietorship, and still exists in the typical small business, often of the merchanting and distributive type.

With the growth in the size of the business unit, the Capital required to provide the necessary equipment and to finance ordinary trading is usually found to be in excess of the resources of any one individual. A further handicap must be recognised in the fact that, in the event of the business failing, the proprietor is liable to his last penny for the payment of his business creditors. His liability is said to be **unlimited**, in contrast to that of the shareholders in a Limited Company, which is restricted to the amounts, if any, unpaid on the shares they have contracted to take.

Between these two extremes we have the partnership relation which, just as in the case of the Sole Trader, involves each partner in unlimited liability as regards the whole of the debts of the **partnership firm**.

It is a very suitable form of business proprietorship where:

(*a*) A large amount of Capital is not required.
(*b*) Liabilities to suppliers and others are unlikely to be considerable.
(*c*) The business is of a size in which each partner can take part in the general supervision.

For these reasons, partnerships are often found in the professions and in the smaller merchanting and manufacturing businesses.

Partnership Act 1890

A measure of statutory control was imposed by this Act, which defines partnership as *the relation which subsists between persons carrying on business in common with a view to profit.*

The Act of 1890 provides certain rules which, in the absence of written or verbal arrangement between the partners, can be applied in defining the duties of the partners to each other, and their responsibility to persons outside the firm with whom they have business dealings.

As it is in all respects desirable to make special arrangements in each individual case, and to have a permanent record of what is agreed upon, a **Deed**, or **Articles of Partnership**, is often drawn up by which each of the partners consents to be bound. These also provide for such modifications of the Act of 1890 as may be thought necessary.

The Deed may state:

(*a*) The term for which the partnership is entered into.
(*b*) The nature of the business to be carried on.
(*c*) The amount of Capital to be introduced and in what circumstances it may be withdrawn.
(*d*) The ratio in which Profits and Losses shall be shared.
(*e*) How much each partner shall be entitled to draw on account of accruing profits.
(*f*) Whether Interest shall be allowed on Partners' Capitals.
(*g*) The salaries, if any, to be paid to individual partners.

As regards (*a*), if no term is stated, or the partnership is continued without any fresh agreement after the original term has expired, it is said to be a **Partnership at Will**.

Of the above, items (*c*), (*d*), (*e*), (*f*) and (*g*) have a special bearing on the *accounts*, and must therefore be considered separately.

Capital

The Capital brought in may take the form of cash, or property in kind, such as machinery, buildings, stock, etc.

In any event, the agreed value must be credited to the Partner's Capital Account, and the proper Asset Account debited. If the Capitals are **fixed** the profit shares and drawings on account thereof will be dealt with in separate Current Accounts. The form of the latter is exactly similar to what was described on page 141.

Profits and losses

Partners may share Profits and Losses on any agreed basis. In the last resort the Partnership Act provides that they are entitled to share equally. Sometimes Profits and Losses may be divided in the ratio of the Fixed Capitals; in other cases where one partner takes a more active part than another, he may be rewarded with a bigger proportionate share.

Drawings

It is better to agree at the outset upon a limit for each partner's drawings. As the cash so withdrawn depletes the circulating Capital, interest may be charged thereon from the date withdrawn to the end of the firm's financial year. To avoid this calculation the agreement may stipulate that drawings on account of profit throughout the year will be in the profit-sharing proportion. Drawings may be in the form of goods as well as cash, in which event the Purchases Account will usually be credited and the partner's Current Account debited.

Interest on capitals

Prior to the division of the Net Profit, the Deed may provide for charging Interest on the Capital of each partner. If this were not done in a case where, for example, Capital Accounts were unequal, but Profits and Losses were divided equally, the partner having the larger (or largest) Capital would lose.

Such Interest on Capital is in no sense a business expense, and would be debited in the Appropriation, or Net Profit and Loss Account.

Partnership salaries

A management salary may be paid to one or more of the partners if they devote more time to the business than their co-partners, or if they are *active*, as distinct from *sleeping* (or *dormant*), partners. The latter may be regarded as those who have contributed Capital, but take no part in the daily supervision of affairs.

Salaries paid or payable to the partners will, like interest on Capital, be debited in the Appropriation Account. They are, in effect, and as regards each partner, a part of the ascertained profit due to him as a proprietor.

Partners' advances

If a partner, to assist the firm, advances cash by way of *loan*, it is probable that he will require it to be treated in the books in a manner different from the Capital invested by him. The amount should therefore be credited to a separate Loan Account.

The Act of 1890 provides that the partner making the *advance* shall be entitled to interest thereon at the rate of 5% per annum from the date of the advance, but a more appropriate rate is usually agreed.

Goodwill

Goodwill is a business Asset, which may be defined as the worth inherent in an established business producing a normal and reasonable profit on the Capital employed in it.

It is *worth* or *value* over and above that represented by the *Tangible* Assets, such as buildings, plant, stock and book debts, and can so be termed an *Intangible* Asset.

If the business were sold, it would clearly be to a purchaser's advantage to pay something for the right to enjoy a continuity of the profits arising, and this is well brought out in the case of a *partnership*.

An incoming partner can be expected to pay the existing partners for the goodwill represented by his profit share, and an outgoing partner is entitled to have goodwill taken into account in determining the sum due to him. The Deed of Partnership will often indicate how the value of the goodwill is to be ascertained, in these and similar circumstances, as by reference to past profits or an estimate of future maintainable profits.

Example 16.1

A joins B in partnership on 1 January 19x5. The Capital is provided as to £15 000 by A, who is a dormant partner, and £5000 by B, who devotes his whole time to the business and is wholly dependent on it.

Assuming the gross receipts for 19x5 are £40 000, and the working expenses £19 000, prepare a Revenue Account incorporating these items, and also the distribution of profit, allowing 10% Interest on Capital, and dividing the balance equally.

A AND B

Profit and Loss Account

Year ended 31 December 19x5

Dr.			Cr.	
		£		£
Working expenses		19 000	Gross receipts	40 000
Balance, Net profits c/d		21 000		
		£40 000		£40 000
Interest on capital:			Net profit b/d	21 000
A. 10% on £15 000		1 500		
B. 10% on £5 000		500		
		2 000		
Balance:				
A. ½ share	£9 500			
B. ½ share	9 500			
		19 000		
		21 000		21 000

In the above we see the benefit to A of charging interest on Capital. B would perhaps think it appropriate that he should be paid a salary, but if the agreement does not include a reference to it, none will be due.

The interest due to each partner and the amount of his profit share can be carried direct to Capital Account, or alternatively credited to a Current Account.

Example 16.2

Rogers and Shaw enter into partnership on 1 January 19x7, and agree to divide Profits and Losses equally, after charging Interest on Capital at 10% per annum.

On 31 December 19x7, the following Balances are extracted from their Books:

	Dr. £	*Cr.* £
Rogers: Capital		13000.00
Drawings	1156.00	
Shaw: Capital		12000.00
Drawings	1156.00	
Sales		34257.00
Discounts received		81.00
Purchases	5413.00	
Discounts allowed	187.00	
Salaries	11497.00	
Wages	12500.00	
Sundry debtors	4200.00	
Rates	1075.00	
Printing and stationery	292.00	
Travelling expenses	596.00	
Bad debts	24.00	
Repairs and renewals	133.00	
Cash in hand	11.00	
Bank overdraft		34.00
Subscriptions	8.00	
Bank charges	46.00	
Sundry creditors		662.00
Factory and warehouse premises	19234,00	
Plant and machinery	2506.00	
	£60034.00	£60034.00

The stock at 31 December 19x7 was valued by the partners at £1125.

You are required:

(*a*) To prepare Trading and Profit and Loss Account for the year to 31 December 19x7, and a Balance Sheet at that date.
(*b*) To state the percentage of Gross Profit to turnover.
(*c*) To show the Partners' Current Accounts.

The following adjustments are necessary:

1. Provide £150 for wages accrued due.
2. Provide 1% on the amount of the Sundry Debtors for Bad and Doubtful Debts.
3. Provide £500 depreciation in respect of Plant and Machinery.

ROGERS AND SHAW

Trading and Profit and Loss Account

Year ended 31 December 19x7

		£		£
Purchases		5413.00	Sales	34257.00
Wages	£12500.00		Stock, 31 December 19x7	1125.00
Add Provision	150.00			
		12650.00		
Gross profit c/d (50% to turnover)		17319.00		
		35382.00		35382.00
Salaries		11497.00	Gross profit b/d	17319.00
Travelling expenses		596.00	Discount received	81.00
Printing and stationery		292.00		
Discounts allowed		187.00		
Repairs and renewals		133.00		
Rates		1075.00		
Bad debts	£24.00			
Add Provision	42.00			
		66.00		
Bank charges		46.00		
Subscriptions		8.00		
Depreciation of plant and machinery		500.00		
		14400.00		
Net profit c/d		3000.00		
		17400.00		17400.00
Interest on capitals:			Net profit b/d	3000.00
Rogers 10% on £13000		1300.00		
Shaw 10% on £12000		1200.00		
		2500.00		
Rogers, ½ share	£250.00			
Shaw, ½ share	250.00			
		500.00		
		£3000.00		£3000.00

Note: In practice, the Provisions are seldom shown separately in the Revenue Account, e.g. Wages would be shown in the one sum of £12650.00 only.

ROGERS AND SHAW

Balance Sheet

As at 31 December 19x7

Liabilities			*Assets*		
		£			£
Sundry creditors	£662.00		Cash in hand		11.00
Wages due	150.00		Sundry debtors	£4200.00	
			Less Provision	42.00	
		812.00			
Bank overdraft		34.00			4158.00
Current Accounts:			Stock in trade		1125.00
Rogers:			Plant and machinery	£2506.00	
Interest on capital	£1300.00		*Less* Depreciation	500.00	
One half profit	250.00				
					2006.00
	1550.00		Factory and warehouse		
Less Drawings	1156.00		premises		19234.00
		394.00			
Shaw:					
Interest on capital	1200.00				
One half profit	250.00				
	1450.00				
Less Drawins	1156.00				
		294.00			
Capital Accounts:					
Rogers	£13000.00				
Shaw	12000.00				
		25000.00			
		£26534.00			£26534.00

Private Ledger

ROGERS – CURRENT ACCOUNT

Dr.			Cr.		
19x7		£	19x7		£
Dec. 31	Drawings	1156.00	Dec. 31	Interest on capital 10% on £13000	1300.00
31	Balance c/d	394.00	31	One half Profit, year to date	250.00
		1550.00			1550.00
			19x8		
			Jan. 1	Balance b/d	394.00

SHAW – CURRENT ACCOUNT

Dr.			Cr.		
19x7		£	19x7		£
Dec. 31	Drawings	1156.00	Dec. 31	Interest on capital 10% on £12000	1200.00
31	Balance c/d	294.00	31	One half profit, year to date	250.00
		£1450.00			£1450.00
			19x8		
			Jan. 1	Balance b/d	294.00

In this example we should be careful to note how the provisions for **wages, doubtful debts** and **depreciation** are dealt with in the Balance Sheet.

When two sole traders amalgamate to form a partnership it is usually necessary to value the assets that each is contributing to the new business. They may agree the values themselves or employ a professional valuer, and goodwill (as described on p. 174) should be taken into account.

Similarly when a new partner is joining the firm, or an old one is leaving, a revaluation of assets will usually be necessary so that the correct amount can be attributed to each partner.

Questions

1 Give some reasons why interest is generally charged against the drawings of individual members of a firm, and also credited to their Capital Accounts.

2 Give two reasons why interest on Capital Accounts should be taken into account in dividing the profits of a partnership.

Mention a case, if you know of one, where one of these reasons does not apply.

3 Earle and Yeoman contemplate the establishment of a dairy to be carried on by them in partnership. Earle is to provide nine-tenths of the capital required, but, having no practical knowledge of the work, is not expected to take much active part in it. Yeoman is experienced in this direction and upon him will devolve the management of the undertaking.

If consulted by them with regard to the financial provisions to be embodied in the Partnership Deed, enumerate your suggestions.

4 In the absence of agreement, to what extent are partners entitled to interest on capital in and loans to the firm?

Illustrate your answer by reference to the following:

	£
A. Capital	10000.00
B. Capital	5000.00
A. Loan	3000.00

Profits of the firm (before charging any interest), £2500.

5 On 1 January 19x6, A and B entered into partnership but without any formal deed of partnership, A provided £10000 as capital, and B provided £500. On 1 July, 19x6, A advanced £2000 on loan to the firm.

Accounts were prepared and disclosed a profit of £6000 for the year to 31 December 19x6, but the partners could not agree as to how this sum should be divided between them. A contended that the partners should receive 5% interest on capital and that he should receive 6% interest on his loan to the firm, and the balance then available should be divided equally. B contended that, as he did most of the work, he should be paid a salary before any division of profit was made.

You are required to show how the profits of the firm should be divided and to state what different division, if any, would be made if A had written a letter to B agreeing that a partnership salary of £1500 should be paid to him.

6 A, a sole trader, prepared accounts as on 31 March 19x4, when his Capital Account showed a balance of £9000. On 1 April he took in B as a partner on the terms that before B's entry a Goodwill Account for £4000 should be raised, that B should bring in £3000 in cash as his capital, interest at 5% per annum should be allowed on Capital Accounts and the balance of profit be divided between A and B, in the proportion of 3 to 1.

The profit for the year to 31 March 19x5, before charging interest, was £4050. Show the division of this between A and B. Show also what the division would have been had no provision been made as to goodwill, the other arrangements being as stated above.

7 X and Y are partners, and they admit Z as a partner, profits to be shared as follows: X four-ninths, Y three-ninths, Z two-ninths.

Y is credited with a partnership salary of £4500 per annum, and X and Y guarantee that Z's share of profits shall not be less than £8000 in any year.

The profits for the year ended 31 December 19x9, prior to providing for Y's salary, amounted to £38214.

Prepare the Appropriation section of the firm's Profit and Loss Account.

8 A, a sole trader owning an established business, took B into partnership on 1 January 19x3, at which date the goodwill of the business was agreed to be worth £6000. A's capital (exclusive of goodwill) was £10000, and B brought in £3000 as his capital. Interest on Capital

Accounts was to be allowed at 5%, and A and B were to divide the remaining profit in the ratio of 2 to 1.

The profit for 19x3 before charging interest, was £5600.

Calculate the division of this sum between A and B on the alternative assumptions that:

(1) Goodwill was ignored on B's entering the business.
(2) Goodwill was taken into account at its correct value.

9 Bright and Smart carry on business in partnership, sharing profits in the proportion of three-fifths and two-fifths respectively.

On 1 January 19x6, the Capital Accounts showed the following credit balances: Bright, £8000; Smart, £6000.

The Partnership Agreement provides that the partners shall be allowed interest on capital at 5% per annum and that Bright shall be entitled to a salary of £6000 per annum and Smart to one of £4000 per annum. During the year ended 31 December 19x6, the partners' drawings were: Bright, £3550; Smart, £2425.

The profit for the year, prior to making any of the foregoing adjustments, was £23 500.

You are required to write up the Profit and Loss Appropriation Account and to show how the Capital Accounts of the partners would appear on the Balance Sheet at 31 December 19x6.

10 A and B entered into partnership on 1 January 19x6, sharing profits and losses equally.

A contributed £5000 as capital, comprising £2000 in cash, and fixtures and plant valued at £3000.

B could only introduce £1000 in cash, but it was agreed he should be given credit in the sum of £1500 for his sales connection, and also receive a salary at the rate of £4800 per annum.

On 30 June 19x6, B paid in an additional £500, and at the same date C entered the firm, paying £1600 for a quarter share of the profits and goodwill and bringing in £1000 cash as his capital, all of which it was agreed should be left in the business.

A and B continued to share profits in the same relative proportions as before, and it was arranged that as from the date of C's entry, B's salary should cease, but 10% per annum interest on capitals should be allowed.

The profits for the year to 31 December 19x6, prior to charging such interest and B's salary, were £16 800. Draw up a Statement showing the division of this amount between the partners, making any necessary apportionments on a time basis, and open Ledger Accounts to record the whole of the foregoing.

11 James and John entered into partnership as merchants on 1 January 19x6. James brought in cash £500 and stock-in-trade £1000; John brought in cash £2300 and a motor lorry £8700. The agreement provided that John was to have a salary from the firm of £2250 per annum and that each partner might draw (on account of salary and profit) £100 per month plus £5000 each on 15 December; otherwise the terms of the Partnership Act, 1890, were to apply.

At the end of 19x6 the following Trial Balance was extracted from the books:

Trial Balance
31 December 19x6

	Dr. £	*Cr.* £
Capital Accounts		12500.00
Debtors	950.00	
Cash	25.00	
Carriage inwards	500.00	
Bank		135.00
Stock	1000.00	
Rent paid	1550.00	
Sales		36000.00
Motor lorry	8700.00	
Carriage outwards	130.00	
Discounts received		575.00
Petty cash expenditure	52.00	
Purchases	11500.00	
Drawings	12400.00	
Creditors		697.00
Discounts allowed	50.00	
Rates paid	1200.00	
Salaries (not Partners)	10850.00	
Fixtures and fittings (cost)	1000.00	
	£49907.00	£49907.00

Notes: (1) Stock 31 December 19x6, valued at £1800.
(2) Rent accrued but not paid, £150.
(3) Rates paid in advance, £140.
(4) Depreciate the motor lorry at 10% per half-year on the diminishing balance system, and the Fixtures and Fittings at 5% per half-year on original cost.
(5) Bank charges not yet entered in books, £50.

Prepare Trading and Profit and Loss Accounts for 19x6 and a Balance Sheet at the end of the year.

12 The following Trial Balance has been extracted as at 31 March 19x7, from the books of C. Spargo and W. Penna – partners sharing profits and losses in the proportion of 2 to 1 respectively.

	Dr.	*Cr.*
	£	£
Stock, 1 April 19x6	3690.00	
Purchases and sales	36892.75	89469.97
Bad Debts written off	291.67	
Plant and machinery (cost £7000)	6650.00	
Furniture and fittings (cost £1200)	1164.00	
Returns	371.56	297.54
Discounts	351.71	403.69
Drawings: C. Spargo	3560.00	
W. Penna	2380.00	
Debtors and creditors	5620.00	4872.68
Light and heat	1397.80	
Rent and rates	3650.63	
Insurances	1131.50	
Salaries	11215.68	
Wages	26394.93	
General expenses	445.62	
Bad Debts reserve		200.00
Commissions		363.97
Capital: C. Spargo		5800.00
W. Penna		3800.00
	£105207.85	£105207.85

Value of stock on 31 March 19x7, £1793.

You are asked to draw up Trading and Profit and Loss Accounts for the year, using the following data for making necessary adjustments:

(*a*) Depreciate plant and machinery 10% on cost.
(*b*) Depreciate furniture and fittings 5% on cost.
(*c*) Amount of insurance pre-paid, £131.75.
(*d*) Amount of wages due but unpaid, £511.65.
(*e*) The Bad Debts Reserve is to be increased to an amount equal to 5% of debtors' balances.
(*f*) Amount of commissions due but not received – £34.94.
(*g*) Capital Accounts to be credited with interest at 5% per annum.

(No interest to be charged on drawings.)

No Balance Sheet is to be drawn up.

Instead, you are to show the following accounts in full for the year ended 31 March 19x7:

(i) Plant and Machinery Account.
(ii) Insurance Account.
(iii) Bad Debts Reserve Account.
(iv) Commission Account.

13 The firm of John Smith & Sons, makers of engineering equipment, consists of John and Magnus Smith. They share profits equally, after each has been credited with interest at 5% on his capital at the beginning of the year.

At 31 January 19x7, the end of the firm's financial year, the following are the balances in the Ledger:

	£	£
Purchases: Raw materials	18562.00	
Finished goods	860.00	
General office expenses	934.00	
Returns inwards	413.00	
Creditors, including an unsecured loan of £500, maturing in 19x9		2617.00
Bad Debts provision		205.00
Stock: Raw materials	3906.00	
Finished goods	101.00	
Wages (factory)	48687.00	
Salaries (factory)	11252.00	
Rent, insurance, etc. (factory)	1246.00	
Rent, insurance, etc. (factory), prepaid	25.00	
Net rents from workmen's cottages		97.00
Fire expense	750.00	
Carriage outwards	909.00	
Factory equipment and machinery	14315.00	
Factory equipment and machinery depreciation provision		2000.00
Cash	14.00	
Sales		85200.00
Interest paid on overdraft, etc.	61.00	
Debtors	4135.00	
Capital: John Smith		12420.00
Magnus Smith		3740.00
Drawings: John Smith	837.00	
Magnus Smith	371.00	
Bank		1099.00
	£107378.00	£107378.00

The stock of raw materials at 31 January 19x7 was valued at £4310. There were then no finished goods on hand.

The 'Fire Expense' Account shows the balance of a heavy loss from fire in 19x2. £150 of this amount is now to be written off.

£22 of bank overdraft interest is accrued and has not been allowed for.

The Equipment Depreciation Provision is to be increased by £315.

A claim for £150 has been made against the firm under the Redundancy Payments Act 1965.

Prepare suitable Final Accounts and Balance Sheet.

17

The Criticism and Interpretation of Accounts

Much of what has been already written concerns the recording of business transactions from the earliest stage in the Books of Prime Entry to the preparation of the Final Accounts.

We must never lose sight of the fact that accounts are kept in order that they may assist the proprietor or manager of the business, and it will be time well spent to consider the work we have done from the point of view of those who are to make use of it.

If the accounts, or any part of them, have no meaning to us, they can have no meaning to others, and we must try to regard the records made as telling a story of what has happened, and telling it in a clear and intelligible manner.

A very simple instance of this is seen in the ordinary Ledger Account. Having regard to the subject-matter of the account as indicated by its heading, we should be able to describe not only the nature of the entries appearing in it, but also the final result of the transactions, both from the personal and the impersonal aspect.

Example 17.1

Overleaf is a customer's account as shown in the Sales Ledger. At the beginning of the year £50 was owing by him, and a month later he returned goods to the value of £10, further goods being supplied to him on 28 February.

On 10 March, he remits a sum of £20, which is stated to be 'on account' – in itself often a sign of weakness. Despite this, goods are again invoiced to him on 3 May, and on 4 June a cheque is received for the balance of what was due as far back as 1 January.

The bank subsequently reports that the cheque has not been met, and Brown is accordingly debited with the amount of the cheque *and* discount.

Between then and 8 August, he either compounds with his creditors as a whole, or is made bankrupt. A first and final dividend of £0.25 in the £ is received, and £0.75 in the £ has to be written off as a Bad Debt.

H. BROWN

Dr. Cr.

Date	*Details*	*Fo.*	*Amount*	*Date*	*Details*	*Fo.*	*Amount*
19x7			£	19x7			£
Jan. 1	Balance	b/d	50.00	Feb. 1	Returns		10.00
Feb. 28	Goods		25.00	Mar. 10	Cash on A/c		20.00
May 3	Goods		15.00	June 4	Bank		19.50
June 7	Bank, cheque returned		19.50		Discount		0.50
7	Discount		0.50	Aug. 8	Bank, First and Final Dividend of £0.25 in the £		15.00
				31	Bad Debts		45.00
			£110.00				£110.00

Criticism of the Final Accounts

It is, however, in regard to the Trading and Profit and Loss Account and Balance Sheet, as representing the logical conclusion of the book-keeping work, that the principal points for criticism arise.

To deal firstly with the Trading Account, the following may have to be considered:

(*a*) How does the sales figure compare with that of the previous year, or other period, and how far have alterations in selling prices contributed to any difference noted?

(*b*) Similarly as regards *purchases* and the cost of materials bought.

(*c*) Are the *closing stocks* much in excess of those held at the beginning of the year, and if so, in a manufacturing business, to what extent do they consist of raw material or the finished product? In the former case, have purchases been made in anticipation of a rise in the price of materials? In the latter case, is the turnover partly seasonal so that a large part of the stock is sold early in the following trading period? What is the average stock carried, and what is its relation to the turnover?

(*d*) Does the business earn a fairly consistent rate of Gross Profit, expressed as a percentage to turnover? *If less than the usual Gross Profit is earned*, is it because selling prices have declined or because the closing stock is valued at the then market price which is below the original cost?

Should the Gross Profit percentage rise, is the cause to be found in more favourable selling prices, or in an improper inflation of closing stock values?

The following illustration may be helpful:

Example 17.2

At 1 January 19x7, T. Peters had a stock of 1000 articles then valued at £1 per unit. During the year he purchased 10000 articles at the same average cost. To arrive at his selling price he adds 50% to cost, his Gross Profit thus being 33⅓%. The sales amount to 9000 articles. Show his Trading Account for the year assuming two different circumstances:

1 Selling prices were advanced 10%, stock values remaining constant, and, as a separate situation
2 Stock values at 31 December 19x7 had fallen by 10%, which is to be provided for.

In the first case the Trading Account shows a Gross Profit of 39.4%, as follows:

Dr.	Units	£		Units	£ Cr.
Stock, 1 Jan., 19x7	1000	1000.00	Sales (at £1.65 per unit)	9000	14850.00
Purchases	10000	10000.00	Stock (at cost, £1.00 per unit)	2000	2000.00
Gross Profit (39.4% to Sales)		5850.00			
	11000	£16850.00		11000	£16850.00

In the second case, the stock provision may appear as a separate expense contra in the Profit and Loss Account:

Dr.	Units	£		Units	£ Cr.
	Units	£		*Units*	£
Stock, 1 Jan. 19x7	1000	1000.00	Sales (at £1.50 per unit)	9000	13500.00
Purchases	10000	10000.00	Stock (at current market price)	2000	1800.00
Gross profit (33⅓% to sales)	—	4500.00	P/L A/c contra, Stock Provision	—	200.00
	11000	£15500.00		11000	£15500.00

In practice it is probable that no separate entries would be made for the £200, and the Gross Profit would be shown as £4300.

The Profit and Loss Account

This section of the Revenue Account includes, as we have seen, the *indirect* or 'overhead' expenses of the business.

To a large extent these do not vary in sympathy with the sales or turnover figure, and therefore it is always necessary to watch carefully the individual items, and the total to which they amount.

Broadly speaking, the Profit and Loss Account is concerned with the reconciliation of **Gross** and **Net Profit**. Stated in another way, Gross Profit may be said to consist of (*a*) the indirect expenses and (*b*) Net Profit.

Indirect expenses

To assist scrutiny, some suitable arrangement of these expenses is most desirable. *Subheadings* may be inserted, such as:

1 *Production Expenses*
Factory Rent, Rates, etc.
Repairs to Plant.
Depreciation of Plant, etc.
2 *Selling and Distribution Expenses*
Travellers' Salaries and Commission.
Travelling Expenses.
Rent of Show Rooms, etc.
3 *General or Administrative Expenses*
Office Salaries.
Bank Interest.
Depreciation of Office Furniture, etc.

A classification of the Profit and Loss Debits in this way is much more helpful than a mere haphazard listing of the balances on the various Ledger Accounts.

Net profit

This is of importance because it represents:

1 The amount which the proprietor may withdraw in the form of cash, *and still leave his Capital intact.*
2 The net yield on the Capital invested, which may conveniently be stated as *a percentage return on that Capital.*

The net earnings of the business can only be ascertained after including all expenses, and all forms of income, as we saw in Chapter 14, and clearly the proprietor will expect to receive something in excess of the rate of interest obtainable from the investment of an equivalent amount of capital in, say, gilt-edged securities. How much more will largely depend on the degree of risk to which his business Capital is exposed in each particular case.

The Balance Sheet

A point constantly to be borne in mind is that the Revenue Account and the Balance Sheet must be read together. Each serves to explain and interpret the other. As an example, if a profit is disclosed at the end of the period, it must be reflected in an increase of the Net Assets. If a loss has been sustained, these Assets will be less at the end of the period than they were at the beginning. Further, when depreciation is charged in the Profit and Loss Account, not only will the profit figure be reduced, but the book value of the Fixed Asset in question will similarly be reduced in the Balance Sheet.

The Balance Sheet is concerned with showing the position of the business *at a particular date*. That position may substantially alter on the day after its preparation, or it may be materially different on the day before it was prepared. The most informative Balance Sheet is that which gives the typical or average state of affairs.

In criticising a Balance Sheet we may well begin with the Liabilities.

Who is interested in the business as a provider of Capital? Apart from the liability to the proprietor *on* Capital Account, there may be amounts due to trade creditors, and to bankers. The latter liabilities rank ahead of the former, and the proprietor must wait until all these claims are met before he can recover any part of his original investment.

The proportion of the Proprietor's Capital to other liabilities should also be noted. If relatively large sums are due to suppliers and others, the position must be further investigated by reference to the total Assets available, and their division between *Fixed,* and *Current or Floating Assets*.

Just as liabilities may be divided as between Fixed or Deferred Liabilities – those in favour of the proprietors, and Current Liabilities – or the claims of creditors, so it is from the Current or Floating Assets that the creditors primarily look for payment.

We have already considered the distinction between Fixed and Current Assets, but as a final illustration, the following introduces other points:

The Balance Sheet of T, a haulage contractor, at 28 February 19x6, is as set out below.

		£			£
T Capital:			Leasehold warehouse,		
Balance forward	£7350.00		offices, sheds, etc., at		
Add Profit for			cost, 1 March 19x0		3511.00
year	1750.00		Motor vehicles,		
			at cost		
	9100.00		*less* Depreciation,		
Less Drawings	1600.00		1 March 19x5	£5700.00	
		7500.00	*Less* Depreciation	2037.00	
Trade creditors		2118.00			3663.00
Accrued expenses		432.00	Stocks of fuel, oil, waste,		
Western Bank Ltd		269.00	etc., as estimated by T.		495.00
			Book debts, gross		2606.00
			Insurance prepaid		15.00
			Cash in hand		29.00
		£10319.00			£10319.00

You are required:

1 To comment carefully upon the position disclosed.
2 To draw up a statement showing the amount of the:
  (*a*) Fixed Assets.
  (*b*) Net Current Assets.

1 Criticism of position disclosed

The **Profit** for the year is rather more than 20% on the Capital. Before accepting it, we should look at the **Assets** of the business and the basis of their valuation.

The first item, Leasehold Warehouse, Office, etc., is stated at cost six years ago. No provision for depreciation has been made by reference to the term of the lease.

By contrast, Motor Vehicles have been depreciated, but we do not know the rate. A proper figure for depreciation would probably be from 15 to 20% of the original cost, i.e. on the straight line method (see page 163).

The Stocks are shown 'as estimated.' Estimates may be of two kinds, good and bad, and information should be sought as to whether the quantities or values, or both, have been estimated, and whether the values are in line with cost or market price, whichever was the lower at the date of the Balance Sheet.

As the Book Debts are described 'gross', their full face value has clearly been taken, and there is no provision for Doubtful Debts. The amount should be related to the value of sales during the year, or in January and February.

It would thus seem that the profit for the year is over-stated because of possible over-valuations of the Assets mentioned.

Lastly, there is a pressing need for the collection of the Book Debts to provide moneys out of which to pay the trade creditors and accrued expenses. The extent of this urgency will in part depend on the limit set to the Overdraft facilities.

2 Statement of Fixed Assets and Net Current Assets
This may be drawn up as follows:

(*a*) **Fixed Assets**

		£
Leasehold warehouse, offices, shed, etc., at cost 1 March 19x0		3511.00
Motor vehicles, at cost, less depreciation		3663.00
Total Fixed Assets		£7174.00

(*b*) **Net Current Assets** (or net working capital)

	£	£
Stocks of Fuel, oil, etc., as estimated		495.00
Book debts (gross)		2606.00
Insurance prepaid		15.00
Cash in hand		29.00
		£3145.00
Deduct:		
Trade creditors	2118.00	
Accrued expenses	432.00	
Western Bank Ltd	269.00	2819.00
Total net current assets		326.00
Fixed Assets		7174.00
Net Current Assets		326.00
		£7500.00
Representing		£
Capital introduced by proprietor		7500.00

The insurance prepaid is an asset at the date of the balance sheet. If the business was discontinued it could be recovered from the insurance company and if the business carries on then the following period will receive the benefit of it.

Questions

1 A trader's Capital appears on the 'liabilities' side of his Balance Sheet. In what sense is it true that the Capital is a liability of the business?

What would you infer if the trader's Balance Sheet (assumed correctly drawn up) showed his Capital on the 'Assets' side?

2 Give an example of one of each of the following:

(*a*) Fixed Asset.
(*b*) Current Asset.

Explain the difference (if any) in the purposes for which such Assets are held by a trader or manufacturer.

3 Suppose that you have been newly appointed to an administrative position in a wholesale merchanting business. What data would you call for, and what tests would you apply to this, in order to find out if the general financial position of the business is sound and healthy?

4 The following is an account taken from the Sales Ledger of Herbert Charleston. Explain clearly what information this account gives you.

LEONARD BRYAN

Dr. 19x4		£	19x4		Cr. £
Jan. 1	Balance	102.00	Feb. 3	Returns	21.00
Mar. 3	Goods	336.00	April 4	Cheque	401.00
				Balance carried forward	16.00
		£438.00			£438.00
April 4	Balance forward	16.00	Sept. 22	Cheque	164.00
June 23	Goods	141.00			
Aug. 3	Interest Charged	7.00			
		£164.00			£164.00
Sept. 26	Cheque Dishonoured	164.00	Nov. 15	Bad Debts A/c	164.00
		£164.00			£164.00

5 Briefly explain the meaning of the items shown in the following Ledger Account.

E. SIMPSON – CAPITAL ACCOUNT

Dr. 19x2		£	19x2		Cr. £
June 30	Cash drawings	2200.00	Jan. 1	Balance	3636.00
Sept. 30	Purchases, motor car for self	9060.00	June 30	Cash	500.00
Nov. 30	Balance	4116.00	Sept. 30	Freehold property	11225.00
			Nov. 30	A. Graham	15.00
		£15376.00			£15376.00

Note: On 20 November, A. Graham, a creditor, for goods supplied had agreed to accept a cash payment of £0.5 in the £ in full discharge of his account of £30.

6 Each year a firm calculates the following percentages:
(*a*) Gross profit per cent on sales.
(*b*) Net profit on gross profit.
(*c*) Net profit per cent on capital.
What information do you think is obtained from these calculations?

7 From the under-mentioned figures which were extracted from the books of a manufacturer you are asked to prepare an account or statement in a form which will give the proprietor the maximum information as to his trading results, including the percentages of the various items to turnover, and to state what conclusions can be drawn from the figures:

	Year ended 30 September,	
	19x4	*19x5*
	£	£
Purchases of material	45823.00	56494.00
Wages: Productive	25064.00	36768.00
Non-productive	10620.00	10984.00
Returns inwards	472.00	1903.00
Discount received	180.00	36.00
Salaries	11560.00	15584.00
Selling expenses	1720.00	2784.00
Discount allowed	420.00	492.00
Works expenses	3176.00	3456.00
Office expenses	6370.00	8420.00
Stock at commencement of year	2189.00	2876.00
Sales	120472.00	165903.00

The stock of material at 30 September 19x5 was valued at £1882.

8 Criticise, under the appropriate headings, any five of the items of the Balance Sheet of B. M. Downfield. In your opinion, is his financial position satisfactory? Give reasons for your answers.

Balance Sheet of B. M. Downfield
for 19x5–19x6

Liabilities		*Assets*		
	£			£
Sundry creditors	12500.00	Cash		1300.00
Bank	3200.00	Bills receivable		2680.00
Capital	1040.00	Sundry debtors		3200.00
		Stock		6860.00
		Plant	£2000.00	
		add cost of repairs	200.00	
				2200.00
		Fittings, cost price in 19x0		500.00
	£16740.00			£16740.00

9 The following accounts showing the result of a year's trading, with comparative figures for the preceding year, have been submitted to the proprietor of a manufacturing business, who has forwarded them to you for criticism. Rearrange the accounts in the form you consider will give the maximum information (showing also the percentages of the various debits on turnover), and state any conclusions which can be drawn from the figures.

Trading and Profit and Loss Accounts

	Year ended 31 Dec. 19x0	19x1		*Year ended 31 Dec.* 19x0	19x1
	£	£		£	£
Stock	2105.00	2001.00	Sales	50000.00	48000.00
Purchases	5576.00	5524.00	Stock	2001.00	1495.00
Wages (productive)	15500.00	15400.00			
Works expenses	960.00	909.00			
Gross profit c/d	27860.00	25661.00			
	£52001.00	£49495.00		£52001.00	£49495.00
Rent and rates	3700.00	3720.00	Balance b/d	27860.00	25661.00
Wages (non-productive)	7800.00	7990.00			
Salaries	11808.00	11818.00			
Travellers' commission and expenses	920.00	900.00			
Office expenses	272.00	270.00			
Bad debts	200.00	414.00			
Net profit	3160.00	549.00			
	£27860.00	£25661.00		£27860.00	£25661.00

10 In the course of your audit of the accounts of a trading company, the following comparisons are noted:

	19x9	*19x0*
	£	£
Sales	40000.00	30000.00
Stocks, closing	10000.00	14000.00
Gross profit	8000.00	7800.00
General expenses	2500.00	1800.00
Selling expenses	1000.00	1100.00
Discounts to customers	400.00	450.00
Bad and doubtful debts	200.00	100.00
Debtors	10000.00	11000.00
Trade and sundry creditors	5000.00	3000.00

Comment on the figures set forth above and indicate what, if any, special inquiries you consider the facts necessitate.

18

Limited Companies and the Companies Acts

The limited company, as an artificial body corporate, owes its existence to registration under the provisions of the Companies Act, 1948, and must be considered apart from changing generations of shareholders. The latter, when subscribing for shares, are able to limit their liability to the nominal or 'face' value of the shares taken by them. An applicant for 100 shares of £1 each offered for sale by the company at £1 each has, when his offer is accepted by the company, a liability to pay £100 *and no more*, even if the company should in future be unable to meet the claims of its creditors. The creditors have contracted with the company, to which alone they can look for payment.

Thus limited liability has furnished an immense stimulus to the development of business because:

(*a*) *The company*, unlike the Sole Trader, or Partnership firm, can obtain capital funds from a very large number of persons.
(*b*) *The individual shareholder* can take as many, or as few shares as he desires, and when once he has paid for them is protected from any further liability.

Public and private companies

All Companies incorporated under the Companies Acts 1948 to 1981 are bound by its provisions and comprise two main classes: Public Companies and Private Companies.

A **Public Company** is one whose name ends with the words 'public limited company' or 'plc'. It must have a minimum allotted share capital of £50 000.

A **Private Company** is any company which is not a Public Company, and it is prohibited from offering its shares or debentures to the public.

The book-keeping and accounting requirements are the same for all companies but the disclosure requirements are greater in respect of the Public Company.

A broad distinction is that a Public Company is one in which the public are substantially interested as providers of capital, whereas in a Private Company management and proprietorship are often identical, the company having been formed chiefly to obtain the benefit of limited liability rather than the provision of new money.

Restrictions on the transfer of shares in a Private Company may mean that a would-be seller must first offer his shares to an existing shareholder, or accept a price determined in accordance with the Articles, etc.

The Memorandum and Articles of Association

Any seven or more persons, or, where the company to be formed will be a Private Company, any two or more persons, may form an incorporated Company by subscribing their names to a Memorandum of Association and otherwise complying with the requirements of the Companies Act.

The Memorandum of Association is, in effect, the Charter of the Company, and must state:

(*a*) The name of the company, with 'Limited' as the last word of the name.
(*b*) The situation of the Registered Office of the company.
(*c*) The objects of the company.
(*d*) That the liability of the members is limited.
(*e*) The amount of the Share Capital with which the company proposes to be registered, and the division thereof into shares of a fixed amount.
(*f*) A public limited company will also state this fact.

No subscriber of the Memorandum may take less than one share.

As regards the Memorandum, note:

(*a*) The name chosen for the new company must not so closely resemble that of an existing company as to deceive or cause confusion in the mind of the public.

(*b*) The applicants for registration must state the objects which it is proposed to carry out. The company may only act in fulfilment of the objects stated. If the substratum of the business disappears, particularly where the company is a Public Company, it is only right that the directors should not be able to turn unhindered to some quite unrelated form of business with the residue of the funds originally subscribed.

Usually the opportunity is taken to provide for eventualities by adding to the main object a number of others which may be regarded as reasonably incidental to it.

(*c*) The Capital stated in the Memorandum of Association is variously styled the Registered, Authorised or Nominal Capital, but may be altered from time to time by the company in general meeting.

Articles of Association, or a series of regulations prescribed for the company, may be registered with the Memorandum, but failing this, a model set of articles, known as Table A (and given as an appendix to the Companies Act, 1948), is applicable.

The Articles may be likened to the rules of a club or society, and provide for the general conduct of the company's affairs.

All members of the company are bound by the Articles in force, even if they subsequently acquire their shares by purchase in the market, and were not original subscribers.

The Articles may be altered or added to by passing a special resolution of members in general meeting, a three-fourths majority being required and not less than 21 days' notice of the intention to propose the resolution as a special resolution having been given.

The Articles will concern the following, *inter alia*:

Shares Issue, transfer and voting rights.
Directors Appointment, powers and remuneration.
Meetings Procedure, and business thereat.
Finance Preparation and circulation of Accounts, payment of dividends, etc.

Share capital

Shares, as units of proprietorship, may be generally classified as Ordinary and Preference Shares. The latter carry a fixed rate of dividend. Before payment of this dividend, income tax at the basic rate will be deducted by the company, and the net rate payable is used to describe the shares. If the rate before tax was 8%, tax at 30% is 2.4% and the shares would be described as 5.6% Preference Shares. Preference Shareholders have a priority for this dividend to the extent there are profits available. Ordinary Shares, subject to the placing to reserve of any part of the profits, take what remains, and may earn very large dividends in prosperous years. The Ordinary Shareholders have thus the opportunity of capital appreciation through an increase in market price.

With Cumulative Preference Shares any arrears of dividend are carried forward to the ensuing period.

Redeemable Preference Shares are those which are to be redeemed either out of *profits*, or from the proceeds of a fresh issue of *capital*: otherwise the shareholder of any class may only realise his investment by sale in the market.

The two latter classes represent variations of the simple Preference Share, and are usually of importance in the case of a Public Company, whose appeal to the investor it is desired to frame in the broadest possible way.

Voting rights are commonly restricted to the Ordinary Shareholders. Preference Shareholders may enjoy voting rights during any period when their dividend is unpaid.

It must be carefully observed that with both Public and Private Companies the boon of limited liability is conferred only on the understanding that the capital fund of the company is maintained intact.

The capital must not be returned to shareholders in dividend.

Dividends should only be paid out of profits periodically ascertained by preparing accounts, and as recommended by the directors and approved by the members in general meeting.

The Articles may give the directors power to pay *interim* dividends.

Dividends are usually paid according to the amounts from time to time *paid-up* on the Shares.

Debentures

In addition to issuing shares, a company may issue debentures, which are acknowledgments of *loans* made to the company. The debenture-holder, unlike the shareholder, is a *creditor*, with all a creditor's remedies.

Debentures issued by companies incorporated under the Companies Act are usually redeemable at a future date. Meantime the debenture-holder is entitled to receive interest at a fixed rate per cent whether or not profits exist out of which to pay it.

A further feature of debentures is that the holders are almost always *secured* creditors. This means that the company pledges or charges some part of its property (e.g. its factory premises)in favour of such creditors specifically, who may, on default by the company, appoint a Receiver (Receiver for debenture-holders), realise the security to the best advantage and repay themselves out of the proceeds.

It will thus be appreciated that an issue of debentures, because of the minimum risk of loss to the holder, may enable money to be *borrowed* at a rate of interest relatively low in comparison with the rate of dividend paid on Preference and Ordinary *Shares*.

Unsecured Loan Stock

Many companies, particularly well-known public companies, are able to borrow without the necessity of providing any security. There will be negotiated rates of interest and repayment terms but the liability is sufficiently different from that associated with debentures for a separate classification to be justified.

Books of account

Statutory Books

The Companies Act, 1948, requires every company to keep proper books of account to record its:

(*a*) Cash receipts and payments.
(*b*) Trading purchases and sales.
(*c*) Assets and liabilities.

Proper books of account are such as are necessary to give a true and fair view of the state of the company's affairs and to explain its transactions. They may be kept in bound books, loose cards, or on magnetic tapes or discs so long as they provide an accurate accessible record of the transactions.

The *Statutory Books* of the company similarly required, chiefly comprise:

(*a*) The Register of Members.
(*b*) The Register of Charges (e.g. Debentures).
(*c*) The Register of Directors and Managers.
(*d*) Separate Minute Book for meetings of directors, and of shareholders.

The Register of Members is the principal statutory book, in which particulars are to be kept of members, their share-holdings, transfers, etc.

Access to the Register of Charges is clearly a help to an unsecured creditor or other person giving credit to the company, enabling him to see what part of the company's property is already charged.

Accounts and audit

The directors of both Public and Private Companies must once in each year lay before the company in general meeting a Profit and Loss Account made up to a date not earlier than the date of the meeting by more than nine months.

A Balance Sheet made up to the same date must also be presented, together with a report of the directors as to their dividend recommendations and the general state of the company's affairs.

The Balance Sheet must contain a summary of the Authorised and Issued Share Capital of the company, and particulars of the general nature of its Assets and Liabilities. The Companies Acts, 1948 to 1981, lay down detailed requirements as to the contents of Balance Sheets and Profit and Loss Accounts.

Every company must at each annual general meeting appoint an Auditor, or Auditors, who must in general belong to a body of accountants recognised by the appropriate government department. The Auditors are to report to the members on the accounts examined by them, and have a right of access at all times to the books, accounts and vouchers of the company.

Example 18.1

From the following particulars, prepare a Balance Sheet of Wick Ltd at 30 November 19x6, grouping the Assets and Liabilities in the form you think most desirable:

	£
4% Debentures, repayable 1990/95	20000.00
Cash at bank	4911.00
Stock-in-trade, 30 November 19x6	34009.00
Goodwill, at cost	30800.00
40000 5.6% Preference shares	40000.00
80000 Ordinary shares	80000.00
Doubtful Debts provision	500.00
Contingent liability on bills discounted	250.00
Sundry debtors	12350.00
Freeholds, at cost	32750.00
Creditors	6962.00
Profit and Loss Account, 1 December 19x5 (Cr.)	14900.00
Plant and machinery, at cost, less depreciation, provided to date (£20000) 1 December 19x5	54600.00
Deposit with Local Authority	9800.00
Additions to plant and machinery, at cost	742.00
Profit for the year, *less* Dividends on Preference shares	7600.00
Depreciation for the year	10000.00

The Authorised Capital of the company is 50000 5.6% Preference Shares of £1, and 100000 Ordinary Shares of £1.

Solution to Example 18.1

WICK LTD

Balance Sheet

at November 19x6

Share Capital	*Authorised* £	*Issued and Fully Paid* £
5.6% Preference Shares of £1.00	50000.00	40000.00
Ordinary Shares of £1.00	100000.00	80000.00
	150000.00	120000.00
Reserves		
Profit and Loss Account		22500.00
Share Capital and Reserves		142500.00
Loan		
4% Debentures repayable 1990/95		20000.00
Current Liabilities		
Trade Creditors		6962.00
		£169462.00

Fixed Assets	*Cost* £	*Depreciation* £	*Net Book Value* £
Intangible Asset			
Goodwill	30800.00	—	30800.00
Tangible Assets			
Freehold land	32750.00	—	32750.00
Plant and machinery	75342.00	30000.00	45342.00
Total Fixed Assets	£138892.00	£30000.00	108892.00
Current Assets			
Stock		34009.00	
Debtors, less doubtful debts provision (£500.00)		11850.00	
Local Authority Deposit		9800.00	
Cash and Bank Balance		4911.00	
			60570.00
			£169462.00

Note: There is a Contingent Liability of £250.00 in respect of Bills discounted

Note: There should also be presented the corresponding amounts at the end of the immediately preceding financial year for all items shown in the balance sheet.

Example 18.2

The following is the Balance Sheet at 30 June 19x0, of Bleak House & Co.:

	£	£		£
Sundry creditors		8 440.00	Cash	120.00
Bankers		18 600.00	Sundry debtors	20 780.00
			Stock-in-trade	42 140.00
Capital Accounts:				
B. Bleak	74 000.00		Plant and machinery	63 000.00
H. House	29 000.00		Goodwill	4 000.00
		103 000.00		
		£130 040.00		£130 040.00

The partners shared profits and losses as to three-fifths to B. Bleak and as to two-fifths to H. House.

A private limited company, Bleak House Ltd, was formed to acquire the business as from 1 July 19x0, the purchase consideration being £106 000. All the Assets and Liabilities were taken over at book values, except as regards the Goodwill and the Plant and machinery, which last were valued for the purpose of the Sale and Purchase Agreement of £58 000.

In respect of the amount due to him, B. Bleak received 20 000 5.6% Preference Shares of £1 each, valued at £1 each, in the new company, and the balance in cash.

H. House received the whole of his share in £1 Ordinary Shares, allotted at par, except for £3 200 paid to him in cash.

In addition to the foregoing, 30 000 Preference Shares were issued to the public at par for cash, and 60 000 Ordinary Shares at a premium of £0.1 per share; these issues were subscribed and paid up in full.

You are required to record the above in the books of Bleak House Ltd and to give the commencing Balance Sheet of the new company.

Solution to Example 18.2

Books of Bleak House Ltd

B. BLEAK AND H. HOUSE – VENDORS

Dr.		£	£			£	Cr. £
19x0				19x0			
July 1	Sundry creditors		8440.00	July 1	Sundry Assets:		
	Bankers		18600.00		Cash	120.00	
	Balance c/d		94000.00		Sundry debtors	20780.00	
					Stock-in-trade	42140.00	
					Fixed assets	58000.00	
							121040.00
			£121040.00				£121040.00
July 1	*B. Bleak:*			July 1	Balance b/d		94000.00
	5.6% Preference shares	20000.00			Goodwill		12000.00
	Cash	55800.00					
			75800.00				
	H. House:						
	Ordinary shares	27000.00					
	Cash	3200.00					
			30200.00				
			£106000.00				£106000.00

GOODWILL

Dr.					Cr.
19x0					
July 1	B. Bleak and H. House	£12000.00			

5.6% PREFERENCE SHARES

Dr.					Cr. £
			19x0		
			July 1	B. Bleak	20000.00
			1	Application and allotments	30000.00
					£50000.00

ORDINARY SHARES

Dr.			19x0		Cr. £
			July 1	H. House	27000.00
			1	Applications and allotments	60000.00
					£87000.00

APPLICATIONS AND ALLOTMENTS

Dr. 19x0		*Ordinary* £	*Preference* £	19x0		*Ordinary* £	Cr. *Preference* £
July 1	Share capital A/cs	60000.00	30000.00	July 1	Cash	66000.00	30000.00
1	Share premium A/c	6000.00	—				
		£66000.00	£30000.00			£66000.00	£30000.00

SHARE PREMIUM ACCOUNT

Dr.		19x0		Cr. £
		July 1	By Applications and Allotments	£6000.00

CASH BOOK

Dr. 19x0		£	£	19x0		Cr. £
July 1	B. Bleak and H. House		120.00	July 1	B. Bleak and H. House	18600.00
1	Applications and Allotments:			1	B. Bleak	55800.00
	Ordinary shares	66000.00		1	H. House	3200.00
	Preference shares	30000.00		1	Balance c/d	18520.00
			96000.00			
			£96120.00			£96120.00
	Balance b/d		18520.00			

There would also be accounts for sundry creditors, sundry debtors, stock and fixed assets.

BLEAK HOUSE LTD

Balance Sheet

at 1 July 19x0

	Authorised	Issued and Fully Paid				
	£	£	£		£	£
Share Capital and Reserve				*Fixed Assets*		
				Intangible asset		
				Goodwill	12000.00	
5% Preference shares of £1.00	50000.00	50000.00		Tangible assets		
Ordinary shares of £1.00	100000.00	87000.00		Plant and machinery at cost	58000.00	
						70000.00
	£150000.00		137000.00	*Current Assets*		
				Stock	42140.00	
Share premium account			6000.00	Debtors	20780.00	
				Cash	18520.00	
Share Capital and Reserve			143000.00			
Current Liability						81440.00
Creditors			8440.00			
			£151440.00			£151440.00

Note: in future years comparative figures will also be shown.

Note to student

	B. Bleak	*H. House*
	£	£
Prior to sale the partners' Capitals are They share profits and losses as 3 is to 2.	74000.00	29000.00
They *lose* £9000.00 on revaluation of Goodwill, etc.	5400.00	3600.00
	68600.00	25400.00
The net worth of their business is thus reduced to £94000.00.		
But the Purchase Price is £106000.00, a *profit* of (in effect, Goodwill of £12000, shared on the profit-sharing ratio)	7200.00	4800.00
	£75800.00	£30200.00

Alternatively; the partners were paid £106000 in respect of capital of £103000, a net gain of £3000, being a loss of £5000 on plant and a gain of £8000 to £12000 on goodwill. This gain of £3000 will be shared in the original profit-sharing ratio. The issue of shares to the public follows the normal debit to cash book, credit to liability accounts. The share premium, £0.1 per share, is credited to a separate account and the nominal amount, £1.0 per share, to the ordinary and preference share accounts.

Questions

1 A.B. & Co. Ltd has an authorised Capital of £8000, divided into 8000 Ordinary Shares of £1 each. On 31 December 19x3, 6000 shares had been issued and fully paid, and there were also balances on the books of the Company in respect of the following:

	£
Sales	40350.00
Purchases	14128.00
Wages	13084.00
Stock (1 January 19x3)	746.00
Salaries	6525.00
Rent	2135.00
Rates	1348.00
Insurance	729.00
Repairs	37.00
Debenture interest	75.00
Bank charges	14.00
Travelling expenses	197.00
Sundries	188.00
Goodwill, at cost	3000.00
Patents, at cost	2506.00
Plant and machinery, at cost	1240.00
Experimental account (asset)	1777.00
Trade debtors	2316.00
Trade creditors	846.00
Bank overdraft	187.00
5% Debenture	2000.00
Preliminary expenses	142.00
Profit and Loss Account (liability) at 1 January 19x3	804.00

Stock, as taken on 31 December 19x3, amounted to £911, but includes an item of £65 for catalogues, the invoice for which has not yet been passed through the books.

The charges for Carriage Inwards, amounting to £102, have been debited to Sundries Account.

You are requested to prepare a Trading and Profit and Loss Account for the year ended 31 December 19x3, providing 5% depreciation on Plant and Machinery, and £84 for Bad Debts. It is also required to provide 2½% for discounts to be allowed to Debtors, ignoring any provision of a similar kind for Creditors.

2 Tompkins, the accountant of Gloria Tubes Ltd, submits to you the following Revenue Account of the Company for the year ended 28 February 19x5.

Dr.				Cr.
		£		£
Wages		28 200.00	Balance of Profit, 1 March 19x4	1 250.00
Purchases		12 500.00	Stock, 28 February 19x5	2 350.00
Salaries		13 468.00	Rates, prepaid	21.00
Commission		2 803.00	Sales	61 550.00
Rates		3 105.00	Discounts received	125.00
Carriage inwards		180.00		
Repairs and maintenance		217.00		
Stock, 1 March 19x4		2 120.00		
Depreciation	£			
Plant, 10%	710.00			
Fixtures, 5%	195.00			
Lorries, 20%	280.00			
		1 185.00		
Directors' fees		105.00		
Packing and carriage		486.00		
Insurance		87.00		
Debenture interest		60.00		
Bank interest		22.00		
Sundry expenses		308.00		
Profit		450.00		
		£65 296.00		£65 296.00

The authorised capital of the Company is £15 000, in shares of £1 each. Of these, 14 951 have been issued as fully paid to the vendor, who is the managing director, and his wife.

A 6% Debenture for £1000 is outstanding favour of the managing director's wife.

£1452 is owing to suppliers, and £2500 by customers, in respect of which latter 2% is to be provided. At 28 February 19x5, the Company had £1767 in the Bank, while at 1 March 19x4, the book values and original cost of the Fixed Assets were:

	£	£
Plant	7100.00	7500.00
Fixtures	3900.00	4200.00
Lorry	1400.00	2000.00

Prepare in proper form Trading and Profit and Loss Account for the year ended 28 February 19x5, and a Balance Sheet at that date.

3 The authorised capital of the Waterloo Engineering Co. Ltd is £80 000 in £1 shares. The Trial Balance on p. 210 was extracted from the Company's books as on 31 March 19x4.

You are required to prepare the Manufacturing Account, Profit and Loss Account and Balance Sheet of the Company after taking into consideration the following matters:

(*a*) The item 'Delivery Expenses' include £175 in respect of the subsequent trading period.

(*b*) Wages £515 and Directors' Fees £100 are outstanding.
(*c*) No provision has been made for the half-year's Debenture Interest due on 31 March 19x4.
(*d*) The Machinery and Plant is to be depreciated at the rate of 10% on the original cost of £36 450 and the Motor Lorry is to be written down to £3000 being half of the original cost.
(*e*) The Bank Pass Book shows on 31 March 19x4, a credit of £15 for Interest on Deposit, but this item has not been entered in the Company's books.
(*f*) The General Reserve is to be increased by £2000.
(*g*) The Stock held on 31 March 19x4, was valued at £8765.
(*h*) Ignore income tax.

	Dr. £	*Cr.* £
Issued capital (60000 shares)		60000.00
Sales		138980.00
Land and buildings	30000.00	
Machinery and plant	29530.00	
Sundry debtors and creditors	30059.00	8131.00
Purchases	46150.00	
Interim dividend	3000.00	
Delivery expenses	3910.00	
Stock, 31 March 19x3	5782.00	
Discounts	1537.00	729.00
Returns inwards	1110.00	
Salaries	2697.00	
Travellers' commission and expenses	3740.00	
Profit and Loss Account, 31 March 19x3		2530.00
Motor lorries	3987.00	
5% Debentures		20000.00
Rent and rates (factory £1650, office 224)	1874.00	
Wages	61846.00	
General expenses	892.00	
Factory power and light	2839.00	
Debenture interest	500.00	
General reserve		6000.00
Repairs to machinery	1421.00	
Directors' fees	300.00	
Bank deposit	3500.00	
Bank current account	1696.00	
	£236370.00	£236370.00

Answers to Questions

For reasons of space, the answers provided here are limited to double-entry and numerical answers only. Answers to other questions are exemplified in the text and in the sample solutions to examination papers (see next section).

Questions on Chapter 3 (pp. 51–3)

3 (a) Debit.
(b) Debit.
(c) Credit.
(d) Debit, if allowed: Credit, if received.
(e) Credit.

5 (*b*) £101.23.
(*c*) Brown is indebted.

6 Balance £7502.52.

7 (*b*) Credit Bank. Debit Bank charges.
(*c*) Credit Motor Vans £25.00.
Debit Loss on Sale A/c £25.00.

8 (*a*) Plant A/c. Debit.
(*b*) Robinson's personal A/c. Credit.
Cash £170.00 and Discount allowed £2.60.
(*c*) Fire Loss A/c. Credit.
(*d*) Motor Van A/c. Credit.
(*e*) Fitter's personal A/c. Debit.
Cash £250.00 and Discount received £10.75.

Questions on Chapter 4 (pp. 70–3)

4 (*a*) Credit landlord.
Debit rent.
Debit cash.
Debit landlord.

(*b*) Credit cash.
Debit rent.

5 Dr. Bals. Cash £63.50.
Bank £94.85.
Discount. Dr. £1.00. Cr. £2.35.

6 Dr. Bals. Cash £35.00. Bank £612.00.
Discount. Dr. £6.75. Cr. £2.00.

7 Cheque payment £354.90.

8 Cash Dr. balance £8.75.
Bank Cr. balance £11.75.

9 (*a*) Dr. side Personal
Impersonal
Private
Cr. side Impersonal
Personal
Personal
Impersonal

10 Dr. Bal. Cash £124.60
Cr. Bal. Bank £267.15
Discount Dr. £1.25. Cr. £2.50

Questions on Chapter 5 (pp. 81–3)

2 (*a*) Favourable Bal. £65.82
(*b*) Unfavourable Bal. £233.96

3 Favourable Bal. £80.39

Questions on Chapter 8 (pp. 108–12)

1 Balances in T.B.:

Capital Cr.	£6350.00
Cash Dr.	£347.00
Bank Cr.	£2332.00
T.B. Totals	£20155.00

2 Balances in T.B.:

Capital Cr.	£10000.00
Cash Dr.	£50.00
Bank Dr.	£3165.95
T.B. Totals	£11159.00

3 Balances in T.B.:

Capital Cr.	£6050.00
Cash Dr.	£50.00
Bank Dr.	£3464.50

	Discount Cr.	£2.50
	Discount Dr.	£17.50
	T.B. Totals	£7974.40
4	Balances in T.B.:	
	Capital Cr.	£4310.80
	Cash Dr.	£50.00
	Bank Dr.	£117.95
	Discount Cr.	£19.50
	Discount Dr.	£1.75
	T.B. Totals	£5466.90
5	Balances in T.B.:	
	Capital Cr.	£2500.00
	Cash Dr.	£162.10
	Bank Cr.	£255.05
	Discount Dr.	£5.75
	T.B. Totals	£6131.30
	(including opening and closing stock)	
6	Balances in T.B.:	
	Capital Cr.	£10650.00
	Cash Dr.	£100.00
	Bank Dr.	£4556.70
	Discount Dr.	£9.20
	Discount Cr.	£98.50
	T.B. Totals	£13474.00
7	Balances in T.B.:	
	Capital Cr.	£2000.00
	Cash Dr.	£23.50
	Bank Dr.	£5853.50
	Discount Dr.	£2.45
	Discount Cr.	£6.25
	T.B. Totals	£7543.75

Questions on Chapter 10 (pp. 120–2)

5 Short Credit £103.20

7 (*a*) Short Dr. £12.25
(*b*) Short Dr. £5.35
(*c*) None
(*d*) Short Dr. £0.50
(*e*) Short Cr. £40.00

8 T.B. Totals £49546.00

9 T.B. Totals £27952.00

10 Original Balance short Dr. £122.25

Questions on Chapter 12 (p. 135)

6 (*b*) £10.00

7 Net Profit. Dept. A £72.00
B £710.00
C £226.00
Dr. P/L A/c £8.00 Balance of general expenses

Questions on Chapter 13 (pp. 143–50)

1 (*a*) Short Debit. £100.00: None: Short Debit £30.00
(*b*) Debtors understated £100.00: Fixtures understated £212.00: Profit understated £242.00: Bank balance understated £30.00.

3 Balance Sheet Totals £83 350.00

5 T.B. Totals £2717.00
Gross Profit £13.00. Net Loss £100.00
Balance Sheet Totals £2184.00

6 Capital £23 264.00
Net Profit £1994.00
Bal. Sheet Totals £24 054.00

7 Gross Profit £15 700.00. Net Profit £5250.00
Bal. Sheet Totals £12 750.00

8 Gross Profit £11 550.00. Net Profit £1100.00.
Bal. Sheet Totals £58 200.00

9 Gross Profit £10 108.Net Loss £1769
Bal. Sheet Totals £12 557

10 Gross Profit £10 250.00 (33⅓%)
Net Profit £1000.00 (3¼%)
Bal. Sheet Totals £13 269.00

11 Gross Profit £14 349.00. Net Profit £2586.00
Bal. Sheet Totals £8205.00.

12 £986.00 less £20.00 depreciation: £966.00

13 Profit £1306.00. Bal. Sheet Totals £3499.00

14 Gross Profit £2261.00. Net Profit £326.00
Bal. Sheet Totals £37 918.00.

Questions on Chapter 14 (pp. 157–60)

3 Profits 19x2 £22 517.00. 19x3 £22 638.00

4 P/L Debit £2941.00

5 P/L Debit £214.50

6 P/L Debit £767.75

7 Bad Debts £314.09. Reserve £234.83.

9 P/L Dr. 19x4 £1551.40
19x5 £1734.38
Omission overstates 19x4 Profits and understates Liabilities £3441.18

10 P/L Dr. Rent £2360.00. Rates £1903.31

11 P/L Dr. Rates £2580.00. Wages £48 562.00
Stationery, etc. £747.00
Bad Debts and Reserve £409.00
Discounts £107.54

12 P/L Dr. £90.00

13 P/L Dr. £1151.00. Prepayments etc. £147.00
Accrued expenses £45.00

14 Profit £3627.00
Bal. Sheet Totals £5663.00

Questions on Chapter 15 (pp. 168–70)

4 P/L Dr. 19x2 £62.00
19x3 £59.00
19x4 £56.00
19x5 £532.00
19x6 £516.00 (net)

5 P/L Dr. £1500.00 p.a.

6 Depreciation £3432.00 (calculating depreciation for a half-year where appropriate).
Profit on sale £9.00.

7 Depreciation (nearest £) £2890.00
Loss on sale £2305.00

8 Depreciation £500.00 p.a.
Interest 19x5 £165.00
19x6 £110.00
19x7 £55.00

9 Depreciation (opening Balances): 19x4 £120.00
19x5 £133.00

10 Gross Profit £35 545.00. Net Profit £10 013.00
139% on Capital.
Bal. Sheet Totals £17 816.00

Questions on Chapter 16 (pp. 179–84)

4 Interest on Loan £150.00
Profit Shares £1175.00

5 (*a*) Interest on Loan £50.00
Profit Shares £2475.00
(*b*) Salary £1500.00
Interest on Loan £50.00
Profit Shares £2225.00

6 (*a*) A. £2437.50. B. £812.50
(*b*) A. £2587.50. B. £862.50

7 X. £14964.00. Y. £11020.00. Z. £4500.00 + 8000.00 = 12500.00

8 (*a*) A. £3800.00. B. £1800.00
(*b*) A. £1900.00. B. £1700.00

9 Profit Shares
Bright £11530.00. Smart £6995.00

10 A. Profit £5951.25. Interest £290.00
B. Profit £5951.25. Interest £190.00. Salary £2400.00
C. Profit £1967.50. Interest £50.00.

11 Gross Profit £24800.00. Net Profit £9780.00
Bal. Sheet Totals £10912.00

12 Gross Profit £23699.62
Net Profit (before Interest) £5308.36.
Balances carried forward:
Plant A/c £5950.00. Insurance A/c £131.75
Bad Debts Reserve £281.00
Commission A/c £34.94

13 Manufacturing A/c £39561.00
Gross Profit £4265.00
Net Profit (before Interest) £2189.00
Bal. Sheet Totals £21029.00

Questions on Chapter 18 (pp. 208–10)

1 Gross Profit £13136.00. Net Profit £1763.20
Bal. Sheet Totals £11690.20

2 Gross Profit £20900.00. Net Loss £850.00
Bal. Sheet Totals £17803.00

3 Gross Profit
(Manufacturing A/c) £22787.00
Net Profit £8319.00
Bal. Sheet Totals £103095.00

Examination Papers and Sample Solutions

It is suggested that you attempt to produce your own solutions to these problems and then compare your solution with the one provided.

The examination papers are reproduced here by permission of the Royal Society of Arts and the London Chamber of Commerce and Industry; the sample solutions have been provided by the author, who accepts sole responsibility for their content.

THE ROYAL SOCIETY OF ARTS EXAMINATIONS BOARD

BOOK-KEEPING
Stage I (Elementary)

[TWO HOURS ALLOWED]

You have TEN *minutes to read through this question paper before the start of the examination.*

Two *questions in Section A and* FOUR *questions in Section B are to be attempted.*

Marks will be lost for untidy work.

Answers must be written in pen or ball pen.

SECTION A

Answer any TWO *questions in this section.*

1 (*a*) What is meant by double-entry book-keeping?
Explain the principles concerning debit and credit entries.

(*b*) The accounts given below appeared in the books of P. Wilkes a hardware retailer on 1 January 1981:

	£
Stationery (balance of stock in hand)	220
Cash in hand	800
N. Roper – a debtor	490
P. Potts – a creditor	650
Capital	18000

Transactions during January 1981 are summarised below:

	£
Bought stationery from P. Potts	230
Goods sold to N. Roper	510
Cash paid on account by N. Roper	250
Paid cash for stationery	140
Cash paid in by P. Wilkes from his private funds	2000
Total credit sales (includes sales to Roper)	8600
Total sales returns	500
Total credit purchases	3800
Cash purchases	400
Sold surplus stationery for cash	30

You are required to:

(i) prepare the accounts for stationery, sales, purchases, proprietor's capital, N. Roper, P. Potts and sales returns;

(ii) balance the accounts for stationery, cash, N. Roper and P. Potts.

(25 marks)

2 Owen Williams prepared the following trial balance at 31 December 1981 after drafting his Trading Account:

	£	£
Trade debtors	9300	
Trade creditors		11650
Bank		4500
Capital		48300
Rent and rates	2600	
Drawings	9000	
Freehold premises	30600	
Heat and light	1650	
Wages and salaries	7550	
Cash in hand	1700	
Motor vehicle expenses	2500	
Carriage outwards	800	
Motor vehicles	5200	
Advertising	2000	
Gross Profit		21000
Stock 31 December 1981	12550	
	£85450	£85450

You are given the following information:

(*a*) Provide for carriage outwards owing £200.

(*b*) An electricity bill for £300 for the quarter ended 31 December 1981 had not been paid.

(*c*) The advertising expenditure shown above includes £1600 for a television contract due to commence on 1 January 1982.

You are required to prepare:

(i) the Profit and Loss account for the year ended 31 December 1981.

(ii) a Balance Sheet as at 31 December 1981.

(25 marks)

3 (*a*) In the case of a retailer selling and repairing domestic electrical appliances, state which of the following items should appear in :

(i) the Trading Account,

(ii) the Profit and Loss Account,

(iii) the Balance Sheet.

Income from repairs to customers' appliances
Purchase of second-hand van
Book-keeper's salary
Wages of mechanics
Showroom expenses
Returns and allowances to customers
Petty cash in hand

(*b*) F. Watts runs a school of motoring. He informs you that his net profit for the year ended 31 December 1981, except for items 1 to 8 below, is £9200. He is not sure what effect certain transactions will have on his net profit and asks you to help him to distinguish between Capital Expenditure and Revenue Expenditure, and between Capital Receipts and Revenue Receipts. Mr Watts provides you with his list of items as shown below:

		£
1.	Motor car repairs	1800
2.	Telephone rental and charges	800
3.	Cash received in settlement of insurance claims for damage to cars used for instruction	1600
4.	Rent received from sub-letting flat above office	2000
5.	Purchase of new car for instruction purposes	4500
6.	Proceeds from sale of old car replaced by the new vehicle	500
7.	Cost of petrol and oil	1750
8.	Commission received from motor car manufacturers	280

You are asked to:

(i) enter the items under one of four headings:

Capital Expenditure	Revenue Expenditure
Capital Receipts	Revenue Receipts

(ii) Draw up a statement showing what effect, i.e. increase/decrease, each item will have on the net profit of £9200 as originally calculated, and give your revised figure of net profit. If you consider that an item will have no effect write 'no effect'.

(25 marks)

SECTION B

Answer any FOUR *questions in this section.*

4 The information below appeared on the wages record of Miss E. Wren for the week ending 5 March 1982.

Name of employee: Miss E. Wren *Grade:* Machinist
Works No. 3546

Piecework rates: Type A units £1 per 100
Type B units £1 per 150

Week ending: 5 March 1982

	No. of units produced	*Type*
Monday	1600	A
Tuesday	1400	A
Wednesday	1800	B
Thursday	1500	B
Friday	1300	A

No. of times late: Nil

Employees work 40 hours per week and an additional bonus of £3 per week is paid to those who commence work on time every day.

You are required to:

(*a*) calculate Miss Wren's total piecework earnings showing separately the amount earned for each type of unit produced;

(*b*) give the payroll entry for Miss Wren for the week ending 5 March 1982 taking into account the additional information below:

Contribution to pension fund is at the rate of 5% of the employee's gross earnings

PAYE £7 National Insurance £5.50

Cumulative deductions made up to the previous pay day were:

Income tax £359 National Insurance £234.50
Pension fund £280

(12 marks)

5 The bank columns of your cash book for the month of February 1982 are shown below.

1982		£			Cheque No.	£
Feb. 1	Balance	480	Feb. 4	Wages	335	180
22	A. Ball	250	5	F. Lowe	336	60
22	C. Lamb	136	11	G. Dow	337	110
22	E. Mann	208		J. Iles	338	244
26	L. Day	85	23	K. Peel	339	401
			28	Balance		164
		1159				1159
Mar. 1	Balance	164				

The following bank statement was received for the month of February:

		Dr.	*Cr.*	*Balance*
Feb. 1	Balance			600
3	Cheque No. 334	120		480
8	335	180		300
16	338	244		56
17	336	60		4 o/d
23	Sundries		594	590
26	D. May credit transfer		65	655
	Ace Insurance standing order	26		
	Charges	18		611

(*a*) Make the necessary entries in the cash book and ascertain the correct balance as on 28 February 1982.

(*b*) Reconcile your revised cash book balance with the balance shown in the bank statement.

(12 marks)

6 J. Jones extracted the following trial balance from his books on 31 January 1982.

	£	£
Capital		7450
Drawings	3000	
Stock 1 February 1981	2500	
Trade debtors	2950	
Trade creditors		2684
Shop fittings	1530	
Purchases	5140	
Sales		7460
General expenses	860	
Discount ureceived		40
Cash at bank	1660	
Returns outwards		40
	17640	17674

The following errors and omissions were subsequently discovered:

(*a*) A purchase of shop fittings £320 had been debited to purchases account.

(*b*) A sales invoice of £150 entered in the sales day book had not been posted to the customer's personal account.

(*c*) A credit note for £30 issued by J. Jones to a customer had been completely omitted from the books.

(*d*) A credit balance of £16 in the purchases ledger had been omitted from the trial balance.

(*e*) The Sales day book was undercast by £100 in December 1981.

Draw up a corrected Trial Balance. Show all workings.

(12 marks)

7 (*a*) Explain what is meant by proprietor's drawings.

(*b*) G. Beacham commenced business as a building contractor on 1 January 1981. On that date he transferred £8000 of his personal savings into a business bank account and also borrowed £2000 from a finance company to be repaid by the business.

During the year ended 31 December 1981 G. Beacham made regular cash drawings for his own use of £50 per week for 50 weeks. On 1 June 1981 he used a quantity of building materials taken from stock for building an extension to his house. These materials were valued at cost £200.

Net profit for the year to 31 December 1981 amounted to £9000 but no entries had been made in the accounts for interest at the rate of 10% per annum on the loan.

From the information given above you are required to draft the Capital account of G. Beacham for the year ended 31 December 1981 and carry down the closing balance.

(12 marks)

8 (*a*) Clearly distinguish between VAT inputs and VAT outputs.

(*b*) A. Wise made the following purchases and sales on credit during the three months ended 31 December 1981.

	Purchases	
1981	October	£6000 + VAT
	November	£8000 + VAT
	December	£9000 + VAT
	Sales	
	October	£9000 + VAT
	November	£10000 + VAT
	December	£15000 + VAT

VAT is to be taken at the rate of 10%

Prepare the VAT account of A. Wise for the three months ended 31 December 1981. Any outstanding amount payable to the Customs and Excise should be remitted by cheque on 31 December 1981.

(12 marks)

Sample solutions

1 (*a*) See pages 2–4
(*b*) (i)

STATIONERY

1981				1981			
Jan. 1	Stock		220	Jan. 31	Sundry sales		30
31	Purchases (P. Potts)		230	31	Balance	c/d	560
31	Cash purchases		140				
			590				590
	Balance	b/d	560				

SALES

			1981		
			Jan. 31	Sales (Roper)	510
			31	Sales (other)	8090
					8600

PURCHASES

1981					
Jan. 31	Purchases on credit	3800			
31	Cash purchases	400			

PROPRIETOR'S CAPITAL

			1981		
			Jan. 1	Balance	18000
			31	Cash	2000

N. ROPER

1981				1981			
Jan. 1	Balance		490	Jan. 31	Cash		250
31	Goods		510	31	Balance	c/d	750
			1000				1000
	Balance	b/d	750				

P. POTTS

1981				1981			
	Balance	c/d	880	Jan. 1	Balance		650
				31	Goods		230
			880				880
					Balance	b/d	880

SALES RETURNS

1981							
Jan. 31	Returns		500				

(ii)

CASH

1981				1981			
Jan. 1	Balance		800	Jan. 31	Stationery		140
31	N. Roper		250	31	Purchases		400
31	P. Wilkes		2000	31	Balance	c/d	2540
31	Stationery		30				
			3080				3080
	Balance	b/d	2540				

N.B. You are not asked for other debtors accounts/creditors.

2

OWEN WILLIAMS
Profit and Loss Account
for the year ended 31 December 1981

	£	£
Gross profit, brought forward		21000
Wages and salaries	7550	
Rent and rates	2600	
Heat and light	1950	
Motor vehicle expenses	2500	
Carriage outwards	1000	
Advertising	400	
		16000
Profit		5000

Balance Sheet
at 31 December 1981

	£	£
Fixed assets		
Freehold premises		30600
Motor vehicles		5200
		35800
Current assets		
Stock	12550	
Debtors and prepayments	10900	
Cash in hand	1700	
	25150	
less Current Liabilities		
Creditors and accrued expenses	12150	
Bank overdraft	4500	
	16650	
Net current assets		8500
		44300
Represented by:		
Capital	48300	
add Profit for year	5000	
	53300	
less Drawings	9000	
		44300

3 (*a*)

(i)	Trading a/c	Income from repairs to customers' appliances Wages of mechanics Returns and allowances to customers
(ii)	Profit & Loss a/c	Book-keeper's salary Showroom expenses
(iii)	Balance Sheet	Purchase of second hand van (part of motor vehicles total) Petty cash in hand

(*b*) (i)

	Expenditure	*Receipts*
Capital	Purchase of new car	Sale proceeds of old car
Revenue	Motor Car repairs Telephone rental and charges Cost of petrol and oil	Rent received *Commission from motor car manufacturers Cash received insurance claim

* Basis of calculation assumed to be for the continued use of a particular make. If it was merely commission (discount) related to the new car bought during the year it would be a capital receipt.

(ii)

	£	£
Profit as originally stated		9200
add Rent received		2000
Insurance claims		1600
Commission received		280
		13080
deduct Motor car repairs	1800	
Telephone rental & charges	800	
Petrol and oil	1750	
		4350
Adjusted profit		8730

4 (*a*) Piecework earnings for Miss E. Wren

		£
A	1600	
	1400	
	1300	
	4300 @ £1 per 100	43.00
B	1800	
	1500	
	3300 @ £1 per 150	22.00
		65.00

(*b*)

		£	
Gross this week (65 + 3)		68.00	
Total gross to date			(no data)
Total tax due	366.00		
Tax deducted previously	359.00		
Tax due this week		(7.00)	
National Insurance this week		(5.50)	
total to date	240.00		
Pension contribution this week		(3.45)	
total to date	283.45		
Net pay		52.05	

(*Note:* Depending on the system used, it is possible that only the column of figures relating to the current week would appear on the payroll.)

5 (*a*)

		£		£
Mar. 1	Balance, per q.	164		
Feb. 26	Credit transfer	65		
			Standing order	26
			Bank charges	18
			Balance (revised)	185
		229		229
Mar. 1	Revised balance	185		

(*b*)

		£
Balance per bank statement		611
add lodgement not yet credited		85
		696
deduct cheques not yet presented		
337 G. Dow	110	
339 K. Peel	401	
		511
Balance per cash book		185

6

	Original		*Adjustments*			*Revised*	
Capital	—	7450					7450
Drawings	3000	—				3000	
Stock	2500					2500	
Trade debtors	2950		(*b*)	150		3070	
			(*c*)		30		
Trade creditors		2684	(*d*)		16		2700
Shop fittings	1530		(*a*)	320		1850	
Purchases	5140		(*a*)		320	4820	
Sales		7460	(*c*)	30			7530
			(*e*)		100		
G. Expenses	860					860	
D. received		40					40
Cash	1660					1660	
Returns outwards		40					40
	17640	17674				17760	17760
Difference	34	—	(*b*)		150	—	—
			(*d*)	16			
			(*e*)	100			
	17674	17674				17760	17760

7 (*a*) See p. 124
(*b*)

Capital Account of G. Beacham
for year to 31 December 1981

Jan. 1	Initial transfer		8000
Dec. 31	Profit for year,		
	before interest	9000	
	10% p.a. on 2000	200	
			8800
			16800
Dec. 31	Drawings during year		
	50 weeks @ £50	2500	
	Materials for own use	200	
			2700
			14100

Redraft

CAPITAL ACCOUNT – G. BEACHAM

1981			£	1981			£
Dec. 31	Drawings		2500	Jan. 1	Capital		8000
June 30	Goods for own use		200	Dec. 31	Profit for year		8800
Dec. 31	Balance	c/d	14100				
			16800				16800
				1982			
				Jan. 1	Balance	b/d	14100

8 (*a*) See page 50
(*b*)

VAT ACCOUNT

1981		£	1981		£
Oct.	on purchases for month	600	Oct.	on sales for month	900
Nov.	on purchases for month	800	Nov.	on sales for month	1000
Dec.	on purchases for month	900	Dec.	on sales for month	1500
	cheque to C & E	1100			
		3400			3400

THE LONDON CHAMBER OF COMMERCE AND INDUSTRY

BOOK-KEEPING
Elementary Stage

[TWO HOURS ALLOWED]

(*a*) *All questions may be attempted.*
(*b*) *Marks may be lost by lack of neatness.*
(*c*) *Journal entries are not required unless requested.*

1 L. Gibson and H. Powell are in partnership sharing profits and losses in the proportion of two thirds and one third respectively. The following Trial Balance was extracted from their books at the close of business on 28 February 1982:

		Dr.	*Cr.*
		£	£
Capital accounts	Gibson		5000
1 March 1981	Powell		3000
Current accounts	Gibson		240
1 March 1981	Powell		190
Drawings	Gibson	1200	
	Powell	700	
Purchases and sales		7630	13990
Stock 1 March 1981		1780	
Wages and salaries		2860	
Debtors and creditors		3830	1910
Office furniture		660	
Balance at bank		4560	
Cash		80	
Discounts		390	170
Rent and rates		440	
Sundry expenses		370	
		£24500	£24500

Notes:

(1) Stock at 28 February 1982 is valued at £2120.
(2) Rent and rates prepaid at 28 February 1982 – £60.
(3) Wages and salaries accrued at 28 February 1982 – £70.
(4) No provision is to be made for depreciation.
(5) Interest is to be allowed on the capital accounts at the rate of 5% per annum.
(6) The Capital Accounts are to remain unchanged, at the figures shown in the Trial Balance. All entries in respect of Drawings, interest on capital and share of profits are to be made in the partners' Current Accounts.

Required:

Prepare the Trading and Profit and Loss Accounts of the partnership for the year ended 28 February 1982, together with a Balance Sheet as at that date.

(30 marks)

2 William Prentice, a sole trader, bought a new delivery van for his business on 1 January 1982. He wishes to write off depreciation of the van over 3 years but cannot decide whether to use the straight line method or the diminishing balance method. The cost of the new van was £2800 and Prentice's year end is 31 December.

Notes:

(1) Identify each account *clearly* – 'Straight line method' and 'Reducing balance method'.
(2) Each account should be balanced at the end of each year.
(3) The rate of depreciation in *both cases* is to be 10% and calculations should be made to the nearest £.

Required:

To assist Prentice in making his decision, draw up the delivery van account as it would appear in the ledger of William Prentice for three years from the date on which the van was acquired, using:

(i) The straight line method.
(ii) The reducing balance method.

(20 marks)

3 Andrew Mason, a sole trader, had the following transactions during the month of February 1982:

(i) Mason purchased goods on credit from Thomas Shipley. The cost of the goods was £84 but, in error, the transaction was entered in both Mason's ledger and Purchases Day Book as £48.
(ii) Mason took goods from his warehouse for his own private use. The *cost* of these goods, to Mason's business, was £55.
(iii) Mason purchased a new office machine for £370. In part exchange he gave an old office machine which, for this purpose, was valued at £114. The balance of the purchase price was paid by cheque. In Mason's ledger the old machine appeared at a figure of £135.
(iv) Mason owes John Temple the sum of £288 in respect of goods supplied. In full settlement of this debt Mason 'accepts' a Bill of Exchange for £270 drawn on him by John Temple.

Required:

Draw up the Journal entries to record (ii), (iii) and (iv) and to correct the error in (i).

Note: The cash entries should be journalised.

(25 marks)

4 George Johnson, a sole trader, had the following transactions during February 1982:

2 Feb.	Purchased on credit from Frank White 20 bottles of white wine at £2.50 per bottle and 30 bottles of red wine at £3 per bottle. Trade discount was allowed at 10% on the whole transaction.
8 Feb.	Purchased on credit from Wine Suppliers Ltd. 40 bottles of rosé wine at £2 per bottle less 5% trade discount.
15 Feb.	Sold on credit to James Smithson 15 bottles of white wine at £4 per bottle less 5% trade discount.
18 Feb.	Purchased on credit from Frank White 70 bottles of soda water at 60p each.
22 Feb.	Sold on credit to Charles Gardner 30 bottles of soda water at £1 each and 20 bottles of rosé wine at £3 each. Trade discount was allowed at 10% on the whole transaction.

Required:

(i) Enter the above transactions in the Purchases Day Book and Sales Day Book of George Johnson. You must also post the items to the personal accounts in his ledger.

(ii) Post the totals of the two day books to the appropriate nominal accounts in Johnson's ledger.

(25 marks)

Sample solutions

1

Trading and Profit and Loss Account
for the year ended 28 February 1982

	Gibson	*Powell*	£	£
Sales				13990
Cost of sales				
opening stock			1780	
Purchases			7630	
			9410	
deduct closing stock			2120	
				7290
Gross profit				6700
Discount received				170
				6870
Wages and salaries (2860 + 70)			2930	
Rent and rates (440 − 60)			380	
Discount allowed			390	
Sundry expenses			370	
				4070
	Gibson	*Powell*		2800
	£	£		
Interest on capital	250	150		400
				2400
Share of profit	1600	800		2400
				—

Balance Sheet
at 28 February 1982

			£	£
Fixed assets				
Office furniture				660
Current assets				
Stock			2120	
Debtors & prepayments (3830 + 60)			3890	
Cash & Bank balances			4640	
			10650	
deduct Creditors & accruals			1980	
				8670
				9330
	Gibson	*Powell*		
Partners accounts	£	£		
Capital	5000	3000		8000
Current				
opening balance	240	190		
interest	250	150		
share of profit	1600	800		
drawings	(1200)	(700)		
	890	440		
				1330
				9330

2 *Note:* It is assumed that the 'Delivery van account' will include Depreciation, although in practice there would probably be separate accounts for 'cost' and 'depreciation'.

(i) **Straight-line method**

DELIVERY VAN ACCOUNT

Dr.							Cr.
1.1.82	Cost of new van	CB	2800	31.12.82	Depn. charge for year	P&L a/c	280
				31.12.82	Net book value	c/d	2520
			2800				2800
1.1.83	NBV	b/d	2520	31.12.83	Depn charge for year	P&L a/c	280
				31.12.83	NBV	c/d	2240
			2520				2520
1.1.84	NBV	b/d	2240	31.12.84	Depn charge for year	P&L a/c	280
				31.12.84	NBV	c/d	1960
			2240				2240
1.1.85	NBV	b/d	1960				

(ii) **Reducing balance method**

1.1.82	Cost of new van	CB	2800	31.12.82	Depn charge for year	P&L a/c	280
				31.12.82	NBV	c/d	2520
			2800				2800
1.1.83	NBV	b/d	2520	31.12.83	Depn charge for year	P&L a/c	252
				31.12.83	NBV	c/d	2268
			2520				2520
1.1.84	NBV	b/d	2268	31.12.84	Depn charge for year	P&L a/c	227
				31.12.84	NBV	c/d	2041
			2268				2268
1.1.85		b/d	2041				

3 (i)

		Dr.	*Cr.*
Purchases	*Dr.*	36	
Thomas Shipley			36
being correction of cost of £84 originally recorded at £48			

(ii)

Drawings (or Mason)	*Dr.*	55	
purchases for resale			55
being goods taken for own use			

(iii)

New office machine	*Dr.*	256	
Bank account			256
New office machine		114	
old office machine			114
Loss on sale of old office machine		21	
old office machine			21

being purchase of new office machine for £256 plus trade in of old machine at £114, and writing off the loss on the old machine.
(*Note:* The two entries for the new machine could be added together 114 + 256 = 370.)

(iv)

Creditors	*Dr.*	288	
Bills payable			270
Discount received			18

(being settlement of debt owed of £288 by bill for £270, remaining £18 treated as discount received).

4 *Note:* It is assumed that VAT is not applicable. If it was, at say 10%, the additional column would be needed.

(i) **Purchase Day Book**

				Goods £	*VAT* £
Feb.					
2	Frank White	20 White wine @ £2.50	= 50.00		
		30 Red wine @ £3.00	= 90.00		
			140.00		
		Trade discount 10%	14.00		
				126.00	12.60
8	Wine Suppliers Ltd	40 Rosé wine @ £2.00	= 80.00		
		Trade discount 5%	4.00		
				76.00	7.60
18	Frank White	70 Soda @ £0.60	= 42.00	42.00	4.20
				244.00	24.40

Sales Day Book

Feb.					
15	James Smithson	15 White wine @ £4.00	60.00		
		Trade discount 5%	3.00		
				57.00	5.70
22	Charles Gardner	30 Soda @ £1.00	30.00		
		20 Rosé @ £3.00	60.00		
			90.00		
		Trade discount 10%	9.00		
				81.00	8.10
				138.00	13.80

Personal Accounts in Creditors Ledger

FRANK WHITE

					1982			Goods	VAT
								£	£
					Feb. 2	Goods	P.D.B.	126.00	12.60
					Feb. 18	Goods		42.00	4.60

WINE SUPPLIERS LTD

					Feb. 8	Goods		76.00	7.60

CHARLES GARDNER

1982			*Goods*	*VAT*					
Feb. 22	Goods	S.D.B.	81.00	8.10					

JAMES SMITHSON

1982			*Goods*	*VAT*					
Feb. 15	Goods	S.D.B.	57.00	5.70					

(ii) Nominal Ledger Accounts

PURCHASES

Feb.	Goods for resale	P.D.B.	£ 244.00				

SALES

				Feb.	Goods sold	S.D.B.	£ 138.00

VAT

Feb.	Paid on purchase	P.D.B.	£ 24.40	Feb.	Charged on sales	S.D.B.	£ 13.80

THE LONDON CHAMBER OF COMMERCE AND INDUSTRY

BOOK-KEEPING
Intermediate Stage

[THREE HOURS ALLOWED]

(*a*) *All questions may be attempted.*
(*b*) *Candidates are advised to study the Required Section of each question carefully. They should then extract from the information supplied the data required for their answers.*
(*c*) *Marks may be lost by lack of neatness.*
(*d*) *Candidates may use silent cordless and non-programmable calculators in this examination. The provision of batteries and responsibility for their condition must rest with the candidate. The steps taken in calculations must be shown.*

1 The Authorised Capital of The Erewhon Trading Co. Ltd consists of: 100 000 10% Preference Shares of £1 each and 200 000 Ordinary Shares of £1 each. The following balances remain at 31 December 1981 after the preparation of a Trading Account:

	£	£
Wages	48 800	
Carriage outwards	3 400	
Rates	2 700	
Discounts received		7 100
Bad debts written off	300	
Stock at 31 December 1981	10 100	
Issued share capital:		
Preference shares		100 000
Ordinary shares		150 000
Discount allowed	4 600	
Gross profit		109 800
Bank – current account	20 300	
Administration expenses	21 800	
12% Debentures issued 1 July 1981		50 000
Debtors	94 000	
Creditors		95 500
Freehold property at cost	220 000	
Furniture (cost £80 000)	60 000	
Bank interest		600
Bank – deposit account	50000	
Provision for bad debts		3 000
Balance of Profit and Loss Account at January 1981		20 000
	£536 000	£536 000

Notes:

(1) Rates amounting to £2200 for the half-year to 31 March 1982 had been paid.

(2) The provision for bad debts is to be increased to 5% of sundry debtors.

(3) Depreciation of furniture is to be provided for at 5% per annum on the written down value.

(4) The company declared a dividend of 10p per share on the preference share capital.

(5) Provide for a dividend of 20p per share on the ordinary share capital.

Required:

Prepare (i) A profit and loss account and an appropriation account for the year ended 31 December 1981.

(ii) A balance sheet as at 31 December 1981.

(30 marks)

2 Rice and Flower were partners in an old established business sharing profits and losses equally.

The Balance Sheet
as at 31 March 1980

Liabilities	£	£	*Assets*	£	£
Capital:			Fixed Assets:		
Rice	36000		Premises	35000	
Flower	36000		Machinery	20000	
		72000	Vehicles	4000	
Current accounts:			Fittings	6000	
Rice	2600				65000
Flower	1800		Current Assets:		
		4400	Stock	9800	
Current liabilities:			Debtors	12640	
Creditors	9850		Cash	60	
Overdraft	1250				22500
		11100			
		£87500			£87500

On 1 April 1980 the partners agreed to admit Peach as a partner under the following conditions:

(1) A goodwill account to be created at £16000 and to be written off over the first four years of the new partnership.

(2) Premises to be re-valued at £45000 and fittings at £8000.

(3) Peach is to introduce £20000 as Capital, part of which was used on 1 April 1980 to purchase a new lorry for £8000 and additional stock for £4000.

(4) Profit and losses are to be shared in proportion to the capital accounts.

(5) Interest on capital is to be allowed at 12% per annum and interest on drawings is to be charged at a flat rate of 15% on the total amount drawn by each partner.
(6) Peach is to receive a salary of £5000 per annum.

During the year ended 31 March 1981 the partners' drawings were:

Rice – £4200
Flower – £5000
Peach – £2800

The net trading profit (before writing off goodwill or allowing for the salary of Peach) for the year ended 31 March 1981 was £33 600.

The capital accounts remain unchanged from 1 April 1980 to 31 March 1981.

Required:
(i) Prepare the balance sheet of the new partnership as at 1 April 1980.
(ii) Prepare the appropriation account for the year ended 31 March 1981.

(25 marks)

3 E. James, a merchant, keeps a Sales Ledger which on 1 July 1981 showed the following debit balances:

	£
Jarvis & Co.	212
Smith Ltd	96
Berry & Berry	354
A. Diamond Ltd	187
Local Stores Ltd	465

His sales during the month of July were:

July 2	Berry & Berry	117
7	Jarvis & Co.	86
11	Local Stores Ltd	194
16	Adam & Son Ltd	116
20	Jarvis & Co.	62
24	A. Diamond Ltd	230
26	Local Stores Ltd	157
29	C. Border Ltd	78

The goods returned during the month were:

July 15	Local Stores Ltd	32
23	Berry & Berry	27

He received the following cash during the month:

July 9	Berry & Berry	354
11	Local Stores Ltd	450
	A. Diamond Ltd	187
12	Jarvis & Co.	212
15	Adam & Son Ltd	110

Discount of £15 was allowed to Local Stores Ltd and £6 to Adam & Son Ltd.
On 29 July James decided to:

(1) Write off the amount owing by Smith Ltd as a bad debt;
(2) Transfer a credit balance of £73 in the account of A. Diamond Ltd in the bought ledger to the account of A. Diamond Ltd in the sales ledger.

Required:

(i) Make the necessary entries in the personal accounts in the sales ledger and balance these accounts at 31 July.
(ii) Prepare a list of balances of the personal accounts.
(iii) Prepare the sales ledger control account as it should appear in the general ledger at 31 July.

(20 marks)

4 Smart Goods Ltd has a branch at Southness and for control purposes keeps the books of account at head office.

All goods are purchased by head office and invoiced to the branch at cost price plus 50%.

The branch transactions during the year ended 31 December 1981 were:

	£
Opening stock at invoice price	12000
Branch debtors at 1 January 1981	16600
Goods sent by head office at invoice price	147000
Credit Sales during the year	85600
Cash Sales during the year	56600
Goods returned to head office at invoice price	6300
Petty cash balance at 31 December 1981	30
Cash received from debtors and paid direct into head office Bank Account	83900
Branch expenses paid direct by head office	14500
Petty cash balance at 1 January 1981	20

On the first day of each week the head office sent £40 to the branch for petty cash payments.

The result of the physical stocktaking on 31 December 1981 agreed with the stock account.

Required:
Write up the following accounts for the year ended 31 December 1981 for the Southness branch:

(i) Stock account.
(ii) Branch adjustment account.
(iii) Debtors' account.
(iv) Petty cash account.
(v) Profit and loss account.

(25 marks)

Sample solutions

1

EREWHON TRADING CO. LTD

Profit and Loss Account

for the year ended 31 December 1981

	£	£
Gross profit, brought down		109800
Discounts received		7100
Bank interest received		600
		117500
Wages	48800	
Carriage outwards	3400	
Rates (2700 – 1100)	1600	
Bad debts written off	300	
Increase in provision for doubtful debts (5% of 94000 = 4700 – 3000)	1700	
Discount allowed	4600	
Administration expenses	21800	
Depreciation of furniture	3000	
Interest	3000	
		88200
Profit, carried to appropriation account		29300

Appropriation Account

for the year ended 31 December 1981

	£	£
Profit brought forward at 1 January 1981		20000
Profit for the year		29300
		49300
Preference dividend 10p per share of £1	10000	
Ordinary dividend 20p per share of £1	30000	
		40000
Profit carried forward at 31 December 1981		9300

Balance Sheet
at 31 December 1981

	£	£
Fixed Assets		
Freehold property at cost		220000
Furniture at cost	80000	
less acc. depreciation	23000	
		57000
		277000
Current assets		
Stock	10100	
Prepayment	1100	
Debtors *less* provision	89300	
Cash and bank balances	70300	
	170800	
Current Liabilities		
Creditors	98500	
Proposed dividends	40000	
	138500	
Net current assets		32300
		309300
Represented by:		
Authorised capital		
100000 10% Preference shares of £1 each		100000
200000 Ordinary shares of £1 each		200000
Issued share capital		
Preference shares		100000
Ordinary shares		150000
Revenue reserve		
Unappropriated profit		9300
Shareholders' interests		259300
12% Debenture		50000
		309300

(*Note:* It is assumed that Debenture interest has not been charged already. Accordingly, a charge has been made in the Profit & Loss Account for interest for the half year to 31 December 1981. 6% (half of 12% p.a.) on 50000 = £3000. This has reduced profit for the year and profit retained and increased creditors.)

2 (i)

RICE, FLOWER AND PEACH
Balance Sheet
at 1 April 1980

		£	£
Fixed Assets			
Premises, at valuation			45000
Machinery			20000
Vehicles (4000 + 8000)			12000
Fittings, at valuation			8000
			85000
Goodwill			16000
Current Assets			
Stock (9800 + 4000)		13800	
Debtors		12640	
Cash		60	
Bank		6750	
		33250	
less Current Liabilities			
Creditors		9850	
Overdraft		—	
		9850	
			23400
			£124400
Represented by:			
Capital Rice 50000			
Flower 50000			
Peach 20000			120000
Current account Rice	2600		
Flower	1800		
Peach	—		4400
			£124400

Notes

Revaluation:	Goodwill	+ 16000	
	Premises	+ 10000	
	Fittings	+ 2000	
		28000	14000 to Rice
			14000 to Flower

Overdraft £1250		
Introduced £20000 ∴	bank balance	£18750
Spent £8000 + 4000 =		£12000
	new balance	£6750

(ii)

RICE, FLOWER AND PEACH
Appropriation Account
for year ended 31 March 1981

		£			£
Goodwill written off		3200	Net trading profit		33600
Salary of Peach		5000	Interest on drawings		
Interest on Capital			(15%)		
(12%)			Rice	610	
Rice	6000		Flower	750	
Flower	6000		Peach	420	
Peach	2400				
					1780
		14400			
		22600			
Balance, profit divisible					
Rice	5325				
Flower	5325				
Peach	2130	12780*			
		35380			35380

* Calculate the total balance available to the partners and then divide it in the profit ratio Rice and Flower five-twelfths each; Peach two-twelfths (i.e. one-sixth).

3 (i)

ADAM & SON LTD

1981			1981		
July 16	Goods	116	July 15	Cash	110
			15	Discount	6

BERRY & BERRY

1981			1981		
July 1	Balance b/d	354	July 23	Returns	27
2	Goods	117	9	Cash	354
			31	Balance c/d	90
		471			471
Aug. 1	Balance b/d	90			

C. BORDER LTD

1981			1981		
July 29	Goods	78	July 31	Balance c/d	78
Aug. 1	Balance b/d	78			

A. DIAMOND LTD

1981			1981		
July 1	Balance b/d	187	July 11	Cash	187
24	Goods	230	29	Transfer	73
			31	Balance c/d	157
		417			417
Aug. 1	Balance b/d	157			

JARVIS & CO.

1981			1981		
July 1	Balance b/d	212	July 12	Cash	212
7	Goods	86			
20	Goods	62	31	Balance c/d	148
		360			360
Aug. 1	Balance b/d	148			

LOCAL STORES LTD

1981			1981		
July 1	Balance b/d	465	July 15	Returns	32
11	Goods	194	11	Cash	450
26	Goods	157	11	Discount	15
			31	Balance c/d	319
		816			816
Aug. 1	Balance b/d	319			

SMITH LTD

1981			1981		
July 1	Balance b/d	96	July 29	Bad Debt	96

(ii) List of balances of the personal accounts at 31 July 1981

	£
Adam & Son	—
Berry & Berry	90
C. Border	78
A. Diamond	157
Jarvis & Co.	148
Local Stores Ltd	319
Smith Ltd	—
	792

(iii) *Note:* Add the Opening balances 1314
Sales for month 1040
Returns for month 59
Cash received during the month 1313
Discount allowed 21

Control Account

1981				1981			
July 1	Sundry debtors		1314	31	Returns		59
				31	Cash received		1313
31	Sales for month		1040	July 31	Discount		21
				29	Bad debt		96
				29	Transfer from bought ledger		73
				31	Balance	c/d	792
			2354				2354
Aug. 1	Balance	b/d	792				

4

SOUTHNESS BRANCH STOCK ACCOUNT

		Fo.				Fo.	
1981				1981			
Jan. 1	Opening stock b/d		12000	Dec. 31	Goods returned		6300
Dec. 31	Goods from HO		147000	31	Credit sales		85600
				31	Cash sales		56600
				31	Closing stock c/d		10500
			159000				159000
	Opening stock b/d		10500				

SOUTHNESS BRANCH ADJUSTMENT ACCOUNT

1981			1981		
Dec. 31	Unrealised profit on goods returned	2100	Jan. 1	Unrealised profit on opening stock b/d	4000
31	Gross profit realised during year	47400	Dec. 31	Unrealised profit on goods transferred	49000
31	Unrealised profit in closing stock c/d	3500			
		53000			53000
				Unrealised profit b/d	3500

SOUTHNESS BRANCH DEBTORS ACCOUNT

1981			1981		
Jan. 1	Balances b/d	16600	Dec. 31	Cash received	83900
Dec. 31	Credit sales	85600	31	Balances c/d	18300
		102200			102200
	Balances b/d	18300			

SOUTHNESS PETTY CASH ACCOUNT

1981			1981		
Jan. 1	Balance b/d	20	Dec. 31	Sundry expenses	2070
Dec. 31	Cash from HO	2080	31	Balance c/d	30
		2100			2100
	Balance b/d	30			

SOUTHNESS BRANCH

Profit and Loss Account

year to 31 December 1981

Expenses paid by HO	14500	Gross profit	47400
Sundry petty cash expenses	2070		
Profit	30830		
	47400		47400

Acknowledgments

The author and publishers are grateful to the Royal Society of Arts Examinations Board and the London Chamber of Commerce and Industry for permission to reproduce the complete examination papers at the end of this book.

The source of the individual questions in the text has been lost through the passage of time, but the cooperation of the following examination bodies is gratefully acknowledged:

Birmingham Commercial College
College of Preceptors
East Midland Educational Union
Institute of Bankers
Institute of Book-keepers
London Chamber of Commerce
National Union of Teachers
Royal Society of Arts
Union of Educational Institutions
Union of Lancashire and Cheshire Institutes
University of Birmingham
University of Edinburgh
University of Manchester